Engaging Young Writers with Powerful Academic Texts:

Systemic Functional Grammar (SFG) based English Text Analysis

Bo-Ai Ko

Dept. of English Language Studies
Seoul Digital University, Korea

www.trafford.com
North America & international
toll-free: 1 888 232 4444 (USA & Canada)
fax: 812 355 4082

Abstract

In the era of globalization, growing numbers of children are living in situations where the language of their formal schooling is different from that of the everyday communication in their family. In such a bilingual context, this study documents biliteracy development of two Korean background children growing up in Australia. The children's written texts (both in English and Korean) were collected over the period of 5 years 8 months (from preschool through primary school) both in home and school contexts, and analyzed using the Systemic Functional Grammar as well as genre and register theory. Throughout the researcher's regular classroom observation and participation in their school's literacy activities as well as in the home context, a detailed documentation of the children's socio-linguistic environment is also provided as an important part of this longitudinal case study's data collection and analysis.

Over the period, the children's writing in both English and Korean developed quite significantly in terms of their control of the register in text. With the introduction of Genre-based Approach in their school, they had opportunities in learning to write a range of genres such as Narrative, Report, Explanation, Argument and Procedure in English to meet the expectations of the mainstream curriculum. The children's writing in Korean was mainly developing to satisfy their personal and interpersonal communication needs, largely through diary writing, E-mails and personal letters to extended family. Their developmental patterns of writing different genres as well as their control of written language have been examined largely through the analysis of the system of Transitivity, the use of nominal groups, Theme choice and Mood system. The similarity and difference in literacy practices between the two children (the brother and the sister) are also discussed.

As the key to the two ESL background children's successful biliteracy development throughout their primary schooling period, this case study emphasizes the importance of the supportive parents' role through mother tongue maintenance and an effective literacy program, such as Genre-based Approach, which provides practical guidance for developing written language through learning a range of genres with different social functions and purposes. The literacies in English and Korean have been found to be mutually supportive and thus it is argued that the whole biliteracy development in this case study has an enhancing effect on the children's academic achievement in their Australian schooling. Simultaneously, with their continuous biliteracy development, the children were able to enjoy being part of a caring Korean-speaking family and community. Moreover, this whole process of biliteracy development certainly provided the two ESL children with a positive self-concept and socio-cultural identity as a balanced proud bilingual. In this regard, it is argued that the successful outcome of this case study of the ESL children's bilieracy development can be identified as a case of an 'empowering' additive bilingualism.

Preface

The purpose of this book is to present the relevant and exclusive part of English text development from my PhD thesis on a longitudinal case study of the bilingual and biliterate development of two ESL Korean children.

The significance of this book is that it offers full guidance applicable to similar research efforts or instructional purpose for certain ESL or EFL home and primary school contexts. Along with the detailed documentation of the subject children's biliterate home and school contexts, this book focuses on the text analysis of English academic genres, including narrative, report, review, explanation, argument, and procedure, all powerful genres for the ESL children's further text development.

The text analysis was done in a systematic and comprehensible way applying SFG (Systemic Functional Grammar) and the genre-based approach, already proven effective by prominent scholars and educators studying discourse and text analysis. As a result, this book will be a good addition and useful reference source for detailed guidance of a range of text analysis using SFG on ESL primary children's writing samples. There have been quite a few of such research works, especially as a longitudinal case study (5 years and 8 months). The subject children's balanced development of narrative texts and factual texts provided a useful solution for the controlling process for appropriate schematic structures and linguistic choices, including for the range of process types, nominal groups, interpersonal modality choices, thematic choices, and cohesion devices. What kinds of complicated processes happened in their ESL English text development is documented thoroughly here with detailed explanation.

So who are the likely readers of this book entitled *Engaging Young Writers with Powerful Academic Texts*? First, the whole process of English text development during ESL Korean children's primary school is inclusive of the genre-based approach as it relates to instructional guidance and sample materials as well as detailed text analysis of each genre of writing. This analysis can provide ESL or EFL English teachers/instructors and researchers with approachable and concrete ideas and sources as well as greater insights into ESL/EFL children's English writing development. The explicit and visible pedagogy of the genre-based approach will be applicable to many other bilingual and biliterate writing development contexts. In addition, any ESL/EFL parents who are concerned about their children's English text development and greater scaffolding literacy roles will benefit, as the author addresses these topics enjoyably and successfully.

Recognizing that ESL children are the minority in an English speaking community, this book hopes to show that the key to prevent ESL children from lagging behind and help them successfully learn at the same time sequence of mainstream native English speakers is engagement with the full range of powerful literacy texts.

TABLE OF CONTENTS

Chapter 1. Introduction

1.0. Introduction

This chapter presents the research approach adopted in the thesis. First, in Section 1.1, the characteristics of the longitudinal case study method which is applied in the research is presented and similar case studies in the area of children's monolingual or bilingual language development are discussed. The method and process of data collection and data analysis for the present study are also documented in detail. The issues of validity and reliability in connection with the case study are addressed separately.

This present study is based on an exhaustive documentation of the writing of two bilingual children done in both English and Korean over their early and mid-primary years. Thus, the educational context of the children during the given period is presented in detail in Section 1.2.

In the next Chapter 2, a descriptive explanation of Systemic Functional Grammar (SFG) proposed by Halliday (1994) and Halliday and Matthiessen (2004) is given as this provides the main framework for the text analysis done as part of this research.

1.1. Developing a Longitudinal Case Study

In applied linguistics, research that uses the case study approach can centre on one or a few individuals. According to Brown (1995: 2), the case studies tend to be longitudinal, which means that an individual or individuals are observed over a relatively long period in order to trace some aspects of their language development. In line with the characteristics of case studies, the present study takes two Korean-English bilingual children in order to trace their biliterate development (particularly writing) over almost six years of the early and mid-primary periods.

According to Yin's more technical definition of 'case study', a case study is an empirical inquiry that "investigates a contemporary phenomenon within its real-life context; when the boundaries between phenomenon and context are not clearly evident; and in which multiple sources of evidence are used" (Yin, 1984: 23). This definition distinguishes the case study from other research strategies such as experiments and qualitative research. First of all, "an experiment deliberately divorces a phenomenon from its context, so that attention can be focused on a few variables, the context is controlled by the laboratory environment" (Yin, 1984: 23). Secondly, Yin's definition of case study extends the applicable methods in case study beyond the limits of qualitative research. That means a case study does not necessarily rely on qualitative research. The essence of qualitative research consists of two conditions: "the use of close-up, detailed observation of the natural world by the investigator" and "the attempt to avoid prior commitment to any theoretical model" (Van Mannen, Dabbs and Faulkner, 1982: 16). In this regard, the case study seems to be more flexible. It can rely partly or entirely on qualitative evidence, and it need not always include direct, detailed observations as a source of evidence. So, the case study's unique strength is its ability to deal with a wide variety of evidence such as documents, interviews, observations and even surveys.

Employing Yin's definition of case study, the present research is a case study which relies on qualitative research. The research data is the documentation of detailed observations in the natural contexts (in the classroom and at home environment). However, as an independent variable, one which "is selected and systematically manipulated by the researcher to determine whether, or the degree to which, it has any effect on the dependent variable", 'the Genre-based Approach' is additionally implemented and highlighted throughout the research (Brown, 1995: 11). Yet, it should be acknowledged that the Genre-based Approach in the children's writing development is not as in an experiment controlling other variables in the natural contexts, but has been added in the natural contexts as a new literacy teaching method in their school curriculum and as a powerful supporting tool by the researcher at home. This issue will be elaborated further in the section below about 'the dual role of mother-researcher' since the researcher in this study is as an active supporter of biliteracy development in the subject children's familial environment.

In applied linguistics, according to Nunan (1992: 78), the case study strategy has a long standing tradition. Even though each case study is unique in its combination of contexts, methods of data collection and analytical tools, the most prominent research using the case study strategy to study children's language development can be listed as follows: Halliday (1975), Painter (1984; 1993) and Oldenburg (1987) for monolingual children's language development; and, Ronjat (1913), Leopold (1939-1949), Aidman (1999) for bilingual children's language development. Another important area of research drawn upon in this study is that of genre writing in primary and junior secondary years in the mainstream Australian classroom, so that reference is made to writers such as Martin and Rothery (1984), Rothery (1989; 1990), Christie (1985; 1989), Derewianka (1995), Collerson (1983), Kamler (1990), Rothery and Christie (1995). The present research shares the research tradition of the two main areas given above. The longitudinal case study of children's language development is combined with research into genre writing based on functional grammar.

In particular, Aidman's research (1999) has been used as a model for this project. Her case study on biliteracy development through early and mid-primary years involved a longitudinal case study of bilingual writing (English and Russian combination) done by her own daughter. The object of the present case study is an attempt to replicate Aidman's research framework, using the same theoretical background, since it provided the researcher with inspiration and academic desire to pursue the similar work as a mother of two bilingual children. In the present case study, a very similar theoretical framework on biliteracy development to that used by Aidman has been adopted. The data collection process was similar and then the analytical method duplicated Aidman's analysis by using SFG (Halliday, 1994). However, it must also be acknowledged that there are some differences in contextual variables in the subject children's biliteracy environment both in the classroom and at home. Aidman's research was implemented in 1992-1996 in Victoria (Australia) when the Genre-based Approach to writing had not been fully introduced in the public primary schools. The present case study was performed later (1997-2002) when the Genre-based Approach had begun to be adopted and practised in this school sector. Another variable can be found in the role of researcher and the extent to which she participated in the explicit teaching and joint construction of the texts. In the present case study, the Genre-based Approach has been supplemented at home quite explicitly and on a regular basis. Therefore, in this respect, the present study cannot be categorized as a purely naturalistic case study which is similar to ethnography in its philosophy and methods. Aidman (1999: 82) indicates that her case study shares a number of characteristics of ethnographic research. She states that "the objective of this study was to observe the bilingual child's written language use in natural settings, that is, in situations where she would normally engage in writing" (1999: 82). However, the present study is not a completely naturalistic case study but a mixed model inclusive of experimental (but not deliberately divorcing the phenomenon being studied from its context) and qualitative research (except the condition that 'the attempt to avoid prior commitment to any theoretical model', since in the present study the prior commitment to Genre-based Approach to some extent is acknowledged). This issue is addressed further in the following section by considering in detail the methods of data collection and analysis used in this study.

1.1.1. Methods of Data Collection and Analysis in the Present Case Study

The main objective of this case study was to find out how the two bilingual children would develop their biliteracy, particularly in writing, in ESL (English as a Second Language) contexts in an English speaking country such as Australia. In addition, the case study sought to establish whether the Genre-based Approach applied in the given ESL contexts would be effective and beneficial to children

4

learning to write a range of texts in both languages. In order to achieve the main objectives of the present case study, the process of data collection was implemented as follows.

1.1.1.1. Data Collection

All the texts written by the children (both in English and in Korean) in the classroom and at home were collected, and special field notes were written to record the writing contexts. All the texts, including writing notes, worksheets, memos and presentation charts were kept in the original shapes and they were photocopied for sorting chronologically, and also by each genre (e.g. Narrative writing, Recount, Explanation, Argument and etc.). Since in a longitudinal case study this kind of data collection needed to continue over six years, adapting a thorough record keeping principle was a most important task for the researcher. Keeping the original notebooks, including a range of text types, seemed to be quite useful as a means of understanding the classroom curriculum and the sequence of writing activities as well as the more extended writing contexts and writing behavior of the subject children in the classroom.

To understand the classroom contexts of the writing activities the researcher made classroom observations on a regular basis during the research period (from 1997 through 2002). During the early period (1997-1998), mostly as a parent helper, the researcher participated in the reading sessions of the older child Jinha who went through Kindergarten and Year 1. In 1999 the Genre-based Approach was actively adopted in the subject children's school, and the researcher became involved in the second child's (Sunyoung's) Kindergarten and Year 1 classrooms as a teacher assistant, helping children in both reading and writing sessions. In Sunyoung's Year 1 classroom (in 2000, first and second term), the researcher assisted more intensively in leading reading and writing sessions every day of the week, Monday to Friday, from 9 a.m. to 1 p.m. for six months. During the classroom participation, the researcher was able to understand and recognize the efficiency of the classroom teacher's appreciation of the Genre-based Approach by noting the children's positive

5

attitude to the method and their resultant writing products. In the last one and half years (2001-2002/July) the researcher carried out classroom observations on a weekly basis. The energy, time and effort invested in the classroom observations and the participation as a teacher helper or assistant allowed the researcher to truly understand the classroom contexts and gain insights into the possible effects of Genre-based Approach on the children's writing. This kind of fieldwork would be a must for any researchers conducting similar case studies. Throughout the period of classroom observation and participation, the researcher performed several interviews with the class teachers, relating to the subject children's writing proficiency and behavior along with the issue of effective writing contexts. Also, during the writing sessions the researcher tried to take down field notes whenever practicable. The evidence from classroom observations and through multiple sources of evidence such as interviews, participation in the relevant writing sessions as a teacher assistant, field notes, interactions with other peer groups turned out to be a valuable asset for the researcher to implement a meaningful case study over the whole period. This kind of classroom experience as an ESL children's mother and researcher was an essential component of the case study, similar to field trips for the researchers doing ethnography.

The subject children's literacy related activities were also observed closely by the researcher in the home, and video tape recording (covering the whole research period) of the family home was also maintained to capture their bilingual social life in natural settings (in school community, family, friends, relatives) as well as some literacy related practices at home. All the texts (both in English and Korean) written in familial contexts were collected and kept with a brief note explaining the writing context. Since the texts written at home included some products which were jointly constructed with the researcher using the Genre Approach, the level of support provided by the researcher during the joint construction was noted. Also, the writing notes or homework sheets from the Korean ethnic school which the children attended on a weekly basis were also collected during the research period whenever these were available.

Informal interviews with the Korean school teachers were performed several times, in relation to the children's Korean writing proficiency (compared with their peers) and in relation to the writing program offered in the school. A later Section of 1.2 describes the educational environment (contexts) at home in further detail.

To sum up, as shown above, through the triangulation in data collection such as participant observation in classroom, video recording at home and written text products (followed by text analysis), the researcher attempted to reinforce the research evidence for this longitudinal case study over almost six years (5 years 8 months).

1.1.1.2. Data Analysis
As mentioned earlier, the subject children's writing products were sorted first chronologically, and again by genre. Then, some representative genres, both in English and Korean, were selected for further detailed analysis. Also, in order to find out how the subject children developed their biliterate writing in the various genres, SFG was used as a tool for text analysis. As Aidman (1999: 83) states, "SFG was used in relation to a particular social theory about the organization and construction of experience, and the role of language as a semiotic system used to make meaning of that experience". Following the genre theorists (Martin and Rothery, 1984; Christie 1985; 1989; Derewianka 1995), Aidman (1999) claimed that text analysis based on SFG is capable of offering a finer degree of delicacy, specificity and detail of analysis, compared to just descriptive and comprehensive accounts found in many other case studies in applied linguistics.

Aidman (1999: 83) also indicates that "the systemic analysis enabled the researcher to penetrate, discuss, and hopefully, explain how language is used to construct meaning in either of the child's written languages, and how the linguistic choices [the child] makes change developmentally over time." By using the SFG analysis, the specific linguistic features developed in each specific genre can be captured and reflected upon in the present study. The choice of an appropriate analysis tool for the range of genre writing was a key to the success of this research.

1.1.2. The Issues of Validity and Reliability

As Yin (1984: 14) points out, using the case study as a research tool specifically allows an investigator to obtain a holistic and meaningful understanding of real-life events such as the changes through an individual life cycle or the process of language acquisition. This can be the main advantage of the case study. Yet, we also have to consider the traditional criticism of the case study approach, questioning its lack of rigor, weaker documentation, subjectivity and the difficulty of developing generalizations from the results (Yin, 1984: 21). In general, research critics recommend that the following four categories be considered in order to perform high quality research work: construct validity, internal validity, external validity and reliability.

1.1.2.1. Construct Validity

Construct validity involves "establishing correct operational measures for the concepts being studied" (Yin, 1984: 36). It is accepted that the insufficient operational measures of case study research can result in the subjectivity of data collection. In order to increase the construct validity, Yin (1984: 37) suggests "the use of multiple sources of evidence" during data collection, in a manner encouraging convergent lines of inquiry. In the present study, specifically in regard to 'construct validity', the issue of mother-researcher has to be addressed.

The Issue of Mother-Researcher

As mentioned earlier, the present study was conducted by the mother of the two subject children. Thus, the issue of the dual role of mother-researcher might be one questioned when considering research validity. To date, almost all well-known case studies of language and literacy learning have been carried out by a parent (Halliday, 1975; Painter, 1984; 1993; Oldenberg, 1987; Bissex, 1980; Saunders, 1988; Aidman, 1999). Bissex (1980) highlights the possible strengths and weakness of a study conducted by a parent, noting there can be advantages and disadvantages in conducting a case study by parent-researcher. The level of

8

parent intervention in the process of writing and the subjectivity in data analysis and findings are recognized as disadvantages of a parent-researcher undertaking a case study. However, conducting a case study related to children's language development in both the natural contexts of classroom and home has been considered a special type of research which is quite challenging and perhaps too demanding for researchers other than parent-researchers (Saunders, 1988).

In the present study, the researcher performed the role of observer in both contexts – 'close-in observation' and 'participant observation' (Graves, 1983). According to Graves (1983: 290), the participant observation is based on questions that cannot be answered simply by observing. For example, the researcher may ask the child how he or she tackled certain problems in writing. In addition to being a participant observer, the researcher acted in the role of supporter, being the children's mother. Since natural contexts at home commonly have parents who support their children's language development in many ways, in the present study the mother's support can be considered similar to that offered by many other parents. Also, since the naturalistic case study was supplemented by genre-informed support of the children's biliteracy learning, the researcher had a more active role to play and was involved in explicit teaching, modeling and even joint-construction.[1]

1.1.2.2. Internal Validity
The second criterion essential to consider in research is

---

[1] In this respect, some critics argue the validity of the children's written products. Aidman (1999: 90-91), for example, points out this issue in her thesis stating "it may be argued that these texts may fail to provide very accurate information about what children in their biliterate development can do." Aidman (1990: 91) also claims that "while parental intervention may have assisted [the child], it could never cause her to do what she was actually incapable of doing. According to Vygotsky (1978), even when supported, the child can perform only within his or her ZPD (Zone of Proximal Development)." While admitting that the writing context at home was not completely naturalistic because it was supported by the mother-researcher, it must also be acknowledged that the level of support in the writing context was recorded so that the writing products can be evaluated with consideration of the support level. Moreover, the written products at school (both in English and Korean) were another source of evidence and thus helped provide a more objective picture of what the children could achieve in their writing with significantly less support, or completely unassisted.

internal validity, which concerns "establishing a causal relationship, whereby certain conditions are shown to lead to other conditions, as distinguished from spurious relationships" (Yin, 1984: 36). One significant problem of internal validity may be caused by making unreasonable inferences. In a case study an inference may occur every time an event cannot be directly observed. Thus, a researcher might infer that "a particular event resulted from some earlier occurrence, based on interview and documentary evidence collected as part of the case study" (Yin, 1984: 38). At this point, the researcher should consider the correctness of the inference by encompassing the counter-explanations and possibilities.

In the present study, to increase 'internal validity', the SFG framework was applied systematically in the analysis, following other prominent researchers in the area of children's writing development. Most inferences in the chapters of the data analysis have been based on the SFG and Genre-based Approach. In addition, for more effective data analysis the researcher designed a special format for organizing the texts (using an A3 sheet, the text copy was pasted in the centre and both side sections were allocated for analysis description). Using this, the researcher was able to write down and analyze the various ranges of linguistic features and analysis points in each genre without missing any important element. The analysis of the more complicated texts benefited most from using this format.

1.1.2.3. External Validity

The third criterion that must be considered for quality research is 'external validity' which is "establishing the domain to which a study's findings can be generalized" (Yin, 1984: 36). Deciding whether a case study's findings are generalizable has been a matter much criticized because a single case provides a poor basis for generalizing. However, as Yin (1984: 39) explains, such criticism arises because implicitly the case study is compared with survey research where a 'sample' readily generalizes to a larger universe. Instead, Yin (1984: 39) indicates that survey research relies on statistical generalization whereas case studies are based on analytical generalization. In Yin's view, "[i]n analytical generalization, the investigator is striving to generalize a particular set of results to some broader theory" (1984: 39). The generalization is not achieved immediately. A theory should be tested and proved through many replications of the findings. The present study's findings and results are carefully considered in the light of relevant theory and research, as are any generalizations made from the results of the study.

1.1.2.4. Reliability

The last principle to consider in performing good research is the issue of reliability. The researcher needs to demonstrate that "the operations of a study- such as the data collection procedures- can be repeated, with the same results" (Yin, 1984: 36). In the past, the reliability of case studies has been doubted by critics mainly because the procedures have been poorly documented. Thus, as specific tactics for case studies, Yin (1984: 40) says that "the use of a case study protocol" is needed to deal with the documentation problem in detail. Along with the protocol, "the development of a case study data base" is recommended (Yin, 1984: 40). In other words, it is advisable that the operational design of a case study ensures that the data collected is documented in as fine detail as possible.

To increase reliability, in the present case study the educational contexts of the subjects were documented in fine detail (followed up in Section 3.2) as was the process of data collection (inclusive of important tips for parent-researcher) so that other parent-researchers can replicate the study if they have similar contextual conditions (just like the present study was replicated without much difficulty by following Aidman (1999)'s case study).

1.2. The Subject Children's Educational Contexts in the Process of Bilingual and Biliterate Development

This section outlines the socio-cultural, psycho-linguistic academic contexts of the subject children's bilingual and biliterate development over the period of almost 6 years. These years saw one child, Jinha, go from Kindergarten (age

5) through Year 5 (age 10); and the other child, Sunyoung, go from Pre-school (age 3) through Year 3 (age 8). Even though the whole research period includes Sunyoung's two years (age 3-4) of pre-school, most written products come from the children's early to mid-primary years. The following sections document their educational history, both in English and Korean, with detailed description of bilingual programs or approaches that were applied to the children in an English speaking culture (so called ESL context), mainly combining family context and their classroom environments.

1.2.1. The Educational History of the Subject Children

The older subject, Jinha, was born in Korea in December, 1991 and arrived in Canberra, Australia for the first time at age two due to his father's PhD study. Before arriving in Australia he learnt his native language, Korean, relatively quickly from his parents and grandparents in an extended family environment. After he came to Australia, he spent most of his time with his mother (the researcher) in learning further Korean at home and also engaged in an English speaking play group with other Australian toddlers and their mothers twice a week (9-12am) for almost one year. The next year, in 1994, his family moved to Malaysia since his father had PhD field work there from 1994 to 1996. During this period, when Jinha was in the period of age three to five (pre-school period), his mother taught Jinha Korean literacy including reading and writing (alphabet, basic sentence writing) at home, while keeping him communicating in Korean. As far as his English language learning was concerned, he received private English tuition from an Indian English native speaker in order to obtain more native-like English pronunciation and speaking skills for one year. At age three, he started attending a Korean kindergarten in Malaysia in which the medium of instruction was Korean, for one year. After the one year period, for the purpose of preparing for the entry to an Australian mainstream primary school (in 1997), his parents transferred Jinha to an International Kindergarten where the medium of instruction was English for all subjects. At age 5, Jinha returned to Canberra in Australia with his family and directly entered an Australian mainstream public primary school. From 1997 to August, 2002 (Kindergarten to Year 5), Jinha attended Cook Primary school in Canberra, Australia, and also, from age 6 to 10, he attended the Korean school in Canberra at weekends.

The younger subject, Sunyoung, was born in January, 1994 in Canberra, Australia. Three months after her birth, her family left for Malaysia where they stayed for almost three years. While living in Malaysia, she spent most of her time at home with her mother (the researcher). Communication between mother and daughter occurred in Korean all the time. Sunyoung eagerly engaged in Korean language learning, even showing an interest in reading storybooks in Korean. Her older brother, Jinha, might have been of some influence here, encouraging her strong desire and motivation for learning to read Korean storybooks. When Sunyoung returned to Australia, she had just turned three. At that time she was not able to speak English at all. However, she had learnt the English alphabet and could read the letters. In preparation for entry to pre-school in Canberra, her parents enrolled her in a child care centre for 6 months from the age of three and a half. During that period, she regularly attended a public pre-school twice a week for three hours. This was by special arrangement for ESL children, even though she was one year younger than the other children in the pre-school. Reflecting on that period, it seems it was a very stressful and challenging time period for Sunyoung since she did not want to be with Australian children due to far limited communication problems. In those days, she was very confident in speaking Korean and had a strong desire to learn more reading and writing skills in Korean. With full engagement in her native language, she seemed to have more isolation in learning another language, English.

For the first term of this period, whenever the mother picked her up from the child care centre, she noticed that Sunyoung almost daily took home a pile of drawing which she drew by herself during her stay. Compared to other children in the centre, she must have been engaged much more in the activity of drawing due to her lack of confidence in speaking in English. She could not even go to the toilet because she could not express her need to the teachers at the right time. Until that time, Sunyoung had spoken in Korean only using it in the home, with both parents and her older brother. Given that her lack of English language skills made her socialization at the centre a very unhappy experience, the parents started to encourage her brother to speak English with his younger sister. So now Sunyoung would be spoken to in English by children and carers at the child centre, and by her 5-year-old brother in the home. The parents continued to talk with Sunyoung in Korean.

As time passed, she grew better in communicating with other children and following instructions. As her English grew so did her interest in English storybooks. When she was four, she was placed in a private pre-school (Wiradjuri in University of Canberra) where educators and caretakers were very enthusiastic about their educational programs and well equipped with educational resources. This one-year experience seemed to give her a lot of confidence in using English. All along, Korean was used in the home; her parents continued to speak Korean to their both children. At the end of the year (1998, age 4:11), she could read a simple storybook both in English and Korean.

When Sunyoung entered the Australian public primary school at age 5 where her older brother attended, she was able to follow perfectly all her kindergarten teacher's instructions and curriculum contents in English. Her literacy skills were far more advanced than most other kindergarten children. Sunyoung was one of the two children in her Kindergarten class who could read the presenter's notes reporting what happened in each class (K-Y6) during the week. As a result, Sunyoung had valuable opportunity to read out the presenter's notes in front of the whole school in the school assembly whenever the kindergarten class had to lead the assembly. Her confidence in participating in school life was growing more and more along with her outstanding literacy skills and understanding of the new school environment. From age 4, her parents also organized for her to attend an informal Korean school supported by a Christian Korean church that was held once a week (for 3 hours) in order to maintain her Korean language. Until

August in 2002 (Year 3), she attended Cook Primary school along with the Korean school at weekends. The following section will present more details about the subject children's school context.

1.2.2. The School Context

1.2.2.1. Attending an English Mainstream School in Canberra, Australia

The school environment where the two subject children, Jinha and Sunyoung, attended might be the one of main influences in their bilingual and biliterate development during their early and mid-primary years.[2]

In general, the Australian mainstream primary school where the subject children attended pursued policies of being multicultural and promoting multiple intelligences. To the researcher's eyes, at the beginning of the subject children's schooling, it seemed that the school was not oriented to literacy learning (skill-based learning) but more encouraging to participation in oral activities. In each grade there were between 25 and 28 students on average, and about 3-4 children in a class were from an ESL background. The small number of students allowed teachers to get involved in oral interactions in their classrooms. Apart from a few naughty children who teased the subject children with race-related comments (such as 'you are yellowish'), the subject children did not seem to have any other bad experiences by the reasons of their different appearance and country of origin.

As Cummins (1986) suggests in the theoretical framework of empowering minority language children, the school supported the idea that incorporation of home language and culture in the school would be beneficial to non-English-speaking background children (ESL children). Even though the school could not provide instruction through ESL

---

[2] Both started their formal schooling in Australia so they did not feel any difference coming from Korean schooling, which other ESL Korean children who had been studying in Korea might have when they came to Australia to continue their studies. They did not suffer from having to adapt themselves from a different school environment.

children's native languages during their transition period, it certainly encouraged the ESL children to share their cultural experiences and languages through news time, oral presentations or special cultural events. The school and class teachers made efforts to help the ESL children feel proud of their cultures and for the other children to be aware of cultural differences and varieties. When Jinha was in Year 1, the class teacher asked the researcher (Jinha's mother) if she could demonstrate how to cook Korean food in front of the class. The researcher is convinced that her son gained more confidence in himself as a Korean as a result of doing this. Another chance to present the brief features of Korea (language, map, culture) to the class came when Jinha was in Year 2 through a suggestion of the class teacher. The researcher willingly took the suggestion since she anticipated positive effects on her children. The children's traditional Korean dress was highlighted and photographed by teachers during some cultural events.

With specific regard to the writing approach, the children used to do journal writing that was free from a teacher's correction on forms such as spelling errors, punctuation errors and grammatical errors.[3] Some teachers tended to

---

[3] Regarding the school's literacy approach, it was running a 'Whole Language Approach' along with 'theme-based integrated teaching'. According to Cameron (2001: 181), in this setting, "different areas of the curriculum can be taught in an integrated way, without being separated into subject areas that have to be taught as specific times by separate teachers." In this approach, the umbrella-like theme is connected to the content of a lesson, and the children take part in a range of activities (e.g. sorting, measuring and playing games) on the theme (Cameron, 2001: 182). However some areas, such as mathematics and English spelling, were taught as a separate unit as well as an integrated unit (theme) so that children would be able to enhance their learning with more focused and subsequent content. It appeared that the balanced 'theme-based teaching' with skill-based approach would make for more organic learning for the children. It is often thought that the theme-based teaching might create classroom chaos and big individual gaps for children's learning since the classroom teacher has much more difficulty having to cater to different individual needs in classroom management and assessment. Also, if the classroom teacher is not capable of playing the important roles of resource person and language teacher, the positive effect from the theme-based approach will be diminished. However, here the children developed their awareness and sense of research skills and problem-solving strategies in dealing with different tasks and themes. They seemed able to link their knowledge with other previous knowledge in a variety of subject areas.

The researcher's big concern was that the children's basic skills, such as spelling and punctuation, were not developing at an impressive speed. Compared with children in Korean primary schools, generally their accuracy rate for spelling and other grammar related areas seemed to be much lower. Also it should be noted that there can be a risk of developing some big gaps between advanced groups and

give their feedback to the children's journal writing by making some comments mainly on meaning. During the first child's lower grades (Kindergarten, Year 1 and Year 2), he mostly wrote such journal writings in his classrooms under Whole Language Approach. His Year 2 teacher tried to combine a 'Process Writing' approach in which children practise their writing through multiple drafting. Since the children were so young the class teacher used two-step drafting (first copy and good copy). During the first draft, the children were to write focusing on meaning and to complete within a reasonable time. After finishing the first draft they had some time to edit their writing assisted by the class teacher and to make a good copy based on the checked copy. At that time, Jinha was exposed to a great amount of story reading and factual book reading through the class teachers' curriculum as well as home readers (homework) and library borrowing. He had chances to write Narrative writing and Recount writing but to the researcher's eyes, his writings for those text types seemed to need more structured helping or assistance. In particular, the researcher noticed that regular practice through journal writing at home could not give him some essential practical guidance on how to write. His writings were filled out with frequently used expressions, habitual mistakes and clumsy organization. While the researcher was disappointed by the limited outcome of the first child's writing proficiency, the researcher noticed that the school later adopted more guided and explicit teaching on different text types such as Narrative, Report, Explanation, Procedure and Argument. During 6 months' intensive volunteer work in the second child's classroom and other ESL groups in the school, the researcher became convinced that the school's changed or combined approach with Genre-based Approach, Children's Literature based Literacy and Whole Language Approach along with Process Writing improved the children's writing development in many ways. As a parent of ESL children, the researcher found that she could support the children's writing practice more effectively and clearly, particularly by

others in the general basic skills of reading and writing. The subject children, therefore, were supported by the researcher assisting with the basic skills at home. The methods the researcher applied with children at home will be elaborated in the later sections.

explaining the purpose of writing, organizational structures according to different text types, connection words, describing words and other language features both in Korean and in English. It was a great help for the researcher to have very useful reference books about Genre-based writing.

1.2.2.2. Attending a Korean School Sponsored by a Korean Church and Korean Community in Canberra, Australia

From 1998 the subject children attended a Korean school which was a small and informal organization in Canberra, Australia. The Korean school was sponsored by a Korean church and the registered number of Korean students was about 25 to 30 for primary school groups. The materials the voluntary Korean-parent teachers used were the Korean textbook (one or two levels lower than age appropriate group or peer group in Korea) and some other worksheets. Teachers generally asked students to write a diary in Korean or to copy one or two paragraphs from their textbook. The Korean literacy level among the participant students ranged from – very competent (those who had recently come to Australia from Korea) through average (those who had spent some years in Australia but were preparing to return to Korean schooling) to marginal (mostly Korean immigrants' family members born in Australia). The subject children's Korean proficiency level was generally higher than that of other children in the Korean school in Canberra since they had been supported consistently at home by the researcher's scaffolding literacy program. Even though the Korean school was not quite organized in terms of a consistent curriculum, teachers' qualifications and the amount of study time (only 2 hours per week), the researcher encouraged her children to attend the Korean school in order for them to make Korean friends and meet other adults in the Korean community.

1.2.3. Bilingual Education – Viewing

In regard to children's bilingual education in the home environment, the use of various media such as TV, video, movie, computer, CD and the internet seems to have been significant because it allowed experience of two different

18

cultures (Australia and Korea) not only through contact with their family members but also through seeing many other people's way of talking, thinking and acting in soap dramas, comedy or movies. Typically, ESL children are often exposed to a relatively limited English language experience in comparison to native speaking children's wide range of community contact in English. ESL children's limited experience both in their native countries and the English speaking countries where they are living and studying often leads to gaps in their cultural understanding. The importance of viewing program to increase the range of cultural contexts and enhance ESL children's balanced and integrated bilingual education should be emphasized here again.[4]

For instance, in order to help the children's understanding of Korean history (especially ancient times), the historic drama 'Wang Gun' was selected and watched from the beginning to the end (about 200 sessions) with parents. In the early sessions, the parents tried to explain the basic introduction about the drama setting and characters along with the meaning of difficult words and expressions. Assisted with this scaffolding strategy, the children became interested in watching different types of drama in Korean. As time passed, watching the video tapes of the historic drama regularly supported the children's understanding of Korean history, ancient aspects of culture such as old Korean architecture, old costumes (royal family members and ordinary people), and the different style of olden day

---

[4] The following principles were guidelines for the subject children's viewing programs (especially for TV and video) in the home context while living in Australia (Jinha aged 5-10, Sunyoung aged 3-8):

1. TV programs or videotapes were selected according to some criteria and were watched through a planned viewing time schedule.
2. Parents would watch some TV programs or videotapes together with their children and after watching them, discussion sessions followed.
3. If possible, the programs selected (e.g. a series of drama, documentary) were watched to the end so that children could develop a critical view (film review, program review).
4. The TV programs or videos included a wide range of different types (genres) such as drama, documentary, news, show programs and educational children's programs.
5. In selecting TV programs or video tapes, parents asked the children for their opinion so that the children could have a better sense of participation in the viewing process.

spoken language. They often asked questions for understanding or clarification of meaning. The drama selected was of a high quality, combining both accurately presented historical facts and entertainment, making it really enjoyable for the children and parents to watch. Joint watching and discussion of the historical drama was a regular event in family life.

The important point is that, through this viewing, a range of literacy activities involving speaking (discussion, questioning), reading (newspaper article, review), listening and writing (film review writing) were integrated and linked authentically in the home environment. The parents were able to help the children shape their critical thinking processes and develop a sense of evaluation through program selection, questioning, discussion and reflection.

1.2.4. Bilingual Education - Speaking

When the subject children returned to Australia (from Malaysia), Jinha was 5 years old and Sunyoung was 3 years old. At this time they were competent and age-appropriate Korean speakers. After Jinha started schooling at Kindergarten in Canberra, Australia, his spoken English became stronger and stronger as time passed. Compared with the first child's rapid English learning development, particularly in speaking, Sunyoung did not seem to make so much progress. She seemed to be enjoying a sense of achievement in mastering the Korean language at home and was keen to try out what she learned there. During almost one year (from age 3 to 4), she might have had a silent period, listening through the process of familiarization of English phonetic properties and intonation. However, the children's successive bilingualism (firstly acquiring their native language and later the second language) seemed to have some positive effects especially in relation to cognitive development (Cummins, 1976; 1978). Since they could already learn new concepts in their native language, it seemed they were able to learn and understand more quickly in the second language. Learning the second language (in case of successive bilingualism) in an ESL context appeared to enhance the children's learning (chance to learn again).

20

More practically, for the children's bilingual development, especially in speaking, the researcher kept speaking in Korean at home from the time they arrived in Australia in 1997. Their father was also very strict in applying the ground rules for the children's bilingual education which meant that parent-child communication was through Korean at home and the children's English development had been through their schooling.[5]

For the subject children's maintenance and development of their Korean language during their six years in Australia, especially in speaking, the researcher applied the 'Home-Community Approach'. It was quite demanding to explain why they needed to keep using Korean at home.[6] As the

---

[5] The approach chosen to support the subject children's bilingual development was the 'Home-Community' approach in which they acquire one language in the home and a different language outside the home (Baker, 2006:102). This was decided because, during the primary years, if the ESL context provides only a small amount of Korean input to the ESL children who will live for an extended period in an English speaking country, their parents had better apply the strict ground rules of the 'Home-Community Approach'. If an ESL context can provide more Korean input through the presence of a strong Korean community (as living in Sydney would), the Home-Community approach might be adaptable depending on each case. However, if the children are living in an ESL context where the Korean language input outside the family is quite limited (as in Canberra), the influence of English will be stronger and stronger as time passes. Without strong support for their native language at home, competency in the first language will diminish eventually so the children can only use it to function in limited contexts.
[6] School appeared to be the major environment for the children's exposure to the English language. At the start, the children's English was not sufficient for them to study different subject areas at school which means there could be some temptation for any capable parents who can speak English to assist with English to some degree. They want their ESL children to improve their English much faster and effectively. Also, sometimes the ESL children's parents themselves need to practice their English more comfortably with their children who are getting to be more native-like speakers. For these reasons, some ESL children's parents become to use English for communication with their own children at home. Once the children know that their parents can communicate with them in English at home, their use of the native language becomes diminished more and more. As a result, after one or two years their native language proficiency level in speaking is lowered. By the time the parents recognize the reality of unbalanced bilingualism (by sacrificing the first language for more competent second language acquisition) and try again to use more Korean at home, the children might well have a very low motivation to follow their parents' changed policy in using their native language at home. The children's strong language is English and their native language might be very weak one. When their parents try to explain some demanding concepts or have conversation at deeper levels (apart from everyday routine) with their children, they need to borrow a great number of English words or expressions and often they end up with incomplete and ineffective discourse. So, the parents will not be able to effectively provide some of their valuable assets such as their background knowledge, philosophy, deeper understanding on some demanding concepts, values and identity to their own children in their cognitive development which is crucially important for their life. This could be subtractive bilingualism. According to the researcher's observation during her six-years of

children became more fluent in English, they would speak English in the home. Whenever they arrived home from school, they would talk in English to each other and to their mother. They were ready to pour their experience at school in English to their mother. It was hard to stop them speaking in English so excitingly and enthusiastically. However, the researcher would consistently talk to them in Korean. She would also prompt the children whenever they attempted to use Korean. This often resulted in the children switching over to talking in Korean. Sometimes, however, they seemed to lose enthusiasm for sharing what had happened at school and they discontinued the conversation.

However, as they grew older, the children seemed to understand that being bilingual is something to be proud of and something valuable. Their sense of identity and cultural awareness grew as well. Also their necessity to communicate with Korean relatives regularly encouraged them to use Korean at home. Apart from a lot of encouragement and praise by the researcher and a strict rule by their father that forced them to speak Korean to their parents, there were other necessary strategies for successful 'Home-Community Approach'. This included a Korean literacy program such as reading and writing as well as some viewing programs. Without the integrated program for language development the children's bilingualism would have been unbalanced.

The researcher consciously ensured that the parents only spoke in Korean with the children but she fully let the children choose the language of communication between them. When Sunyoung began to catch up in English speaking proficiency, they communicated in English in most instances. At the beginning of their stay in Australia, the children frequently resorted to code mixing (borrowing another language's words to fill in where they are unsure). For example, since they were more familiar with everyday routine words in Korean (eat rice, brush your teeth, wash your hands and etc.), they often mixed codes from sentence

---

living in Australia, this typically happened to in many immigrant Korean children whose parents were able to speak English.

22

to sentence or used English syntax while borrowing some lexical items such as one or two Korean nouns or verbs. Another reason why the researcher wanted the children to use English in conversation between themselves was that she considered that this would support children's English conversational competency as well as habit (or English code making between them) which could then be maintained on their return to Korea.

It should be noted that, in spite of their excellent English speaking proficiency in general, the children's speaking in English seemed to lack cultural appropriateness in certain contexts. Since they could not get parents' everyday conversation in English, particularly in the home environment, or conversation from some other extended English community, their English speaking did not have the flexibility that allowed them to adapt themselves to varied situations. For instance, the researcher noticed that, in some cases, the children were not able to use proper English expressions in phone conversations even though they had been living in Australia for a long time. Compared with Korean family culture, the Australian English speaking parents seemed to be making more efforts in oral discussion with their children. So, even little children in Australia seemed better able to express themselves in different ways. In the case of the subject children, even though they achieved outstanding academic records in every area from the beginning year, their speaking proficiency, apart from academic contexts, appeared to be less developed than their reading and writing competency.

To support the children's oral English development the researcher encouraged them to do oral presentations at school as often as possible. Also, for one year, there were very good opportunities for oral discussion with people attending the Catholic Church. Through other extra-curriculum activities they were able to meet other adult English native speakers during their lessons. Having friends also gave the subject children regular opportunities to visit Australian families. At home, additionally, the researcher tried to point out or explain some important situations and the proper English speaking with manners by watching TV programs (viewing program) together – particularly home drama.

1.2.5. Bilingual Education - Reading

1.2.5.1. English Reading in an ESL Context

From their earliest exposure to English in Australia, the children were positive about reading in the new language. They happily engaged in English reading and reading related activities at home, in school and in community libraries. After the children went through letter recognition (alphabet) with a phonetic approach and awareness of the print concept, they got gradually involved in the pleasant process of story book reading – mostly picture books. The school they attended provided a series of very useful methods for beginning readers (Kindergarteners and Year 1 students) such as a 'Home Readers' program, shared reading and guided reading. Particularly, for the 'Home Readers' program, some parents were involved as parent helpers in order to help the class teachers in lower grades manage the reading program more effectively.[7] The researcher was also

---

[7] With this program, parent helpers help children choose a suitable book for their reading level from level-based 'basal reading' books. The books are designed to learn the skill of reading through repetition of frequent words and simple rhymes from the easiest level (e.g. one word or two words) to more advanced level (one sentence to two or three sentences to a text level). In each level, there is a range of books on different themes but there are two main groups such as short story books (fiction) and factual books (non-fiction). The children are encouraged to select and read from each type of books in a balanced manner. The procedure is that after the parent helper helps the children choose a new book at their reading level, they read the chosen book together (usually in one corner of the corridor, outside the classroom where tables and chairs were set up for such a reading session). Before the first reading, the parent helper might do a brief book orientation by asking the child about the book (e.g. a relevant experience with the book, what can be in the story?). After the first reading (while a child reads, a parent helper assists the reading.), a parent helper usually gives the child another chance to read the book independently. The parent helpers had been instructed to encourage the child to finger point when reading, and to give the child time for trying out unknown words.

This intensive basal reading program for lower graders seems to be very helpful for them to improve their reading skills step by step. Even for ESL children's parents this program seems to open a road to help their children read English books at home. If it gets routine (everyday reading by returning a read book and borrowing a new book) and the parents can monitor the children's progress through leveling up their 'home reader books' at appropriate time, the children will be able to improve their reading much faster. Admittedly, basal readers have been criticized on the grounds that they fail to use 'authentic' language, using artificially constructed texts instead. If the basal reading program is over-emphasized during the beginning period of young readers, it might get the readers focus on grapho-phonics at the expense of reading for meaning (over-relying on

involved several times in the program: when the first child was in Kindergarten and Year 1; and then later, when the second child was in Kindergarten and in Year 1.

In addition to the 'Home Reader' Program, the researcher took advantage of the community library program, so the children would have a strong motivation for reading from the beginning stage. The community library provided excellent reading programs for young readers by encouraging them to borrow books regularly and rewarding the good readers. Some librarians offered a check or feedback session by asking simple questions (e.g. What was the book story about? Can you tell me the exciting parts? Did you like it? Why?) when the readers (who joined the library as club members) returned their books. From the large collection of children's books in the community library, the children chose books with much pleasure and developed a taste for different book types. Also, particularly at the early stage of their learning to read in English, the researcher used computer CDs (reading series programs – e.g. Arther series, Jumpstart series and Reader's Rabbit series) and books with audiotapes. As a result, both children's reading improved so fast that the class teachers always placed them at the highest level in the reading program at school.

When the subject children moved into a more advanced level of reading, from picture books to story (sometimes without picture or illustration) and chapter books, they responded differently to the change. The first child (Jinha) had a quite smooth transition from picture book to chapter book without illustration, but the second one (Sunyoung) did not want to move onto chapter books even though she appeared quite a capable reader at that time. Also, she insisted on always reading aloud rather than reading silently. During his period of transition from picture books to chapter books, Jinha enjoyed reading Paul Jennings' books. Based on this experience, the researcher suggested Jenning's books to

---

phonetic cues). However, the researcher's view on this issue is that the basal reading program can be effectively combined with other reading approaches such as children's literature based reading, guided reading and shared reading in which a strong emphasis on meaning is maintained.

Sunyoung. However, she did not like this book series. The researcher discussed this matter with the class teacher, who suggested 'Matilda' by Roald Dahl. It was a great success. Sunyoung seemed to become magically engaged in reading to a great degree. After finishing the book, the researcher had a discussion with her about the book; she also congratulated Sunyoung on such an impressive achievement. After that, the researcher bought some books from local book shops and this made Sunyoung keep reading her favorite books continually. The two children were truly developing their own tastes in their reading. Often they chose different authors and types of books, but sometimes they enjoyed the same ones. When Jinha was in Year 3, he was able to read the famous 'Harry Potter' series (J. K. Rowling) successfully and with great enthusiasm. The book series was also very successful for the second child when she started reading them in Year 2.

1.2.5.2. Reading Korean Books in an ESL Context

While the children's English reading skills were developing at a fast speed, their engagement with Korean reading decreased. The researcher faced a dilemma as to how the children could develop a balanced bilingual competency. Even though the researcher knew that keeping up literacy skills in both languages was important, there was a limited time for the children to get involved in literacy learning at home. Their reading in Korean was getting slower and slower (low fluency) with low comprehension. Particularly during the school terms, the children's involvement in Korean literacy events decreased.

Through trial and error, the researcher decided to modify the approach to learning in the home environment. For Korean reading and writing, the children could learn them more intensively during the school break. If they were to enter the Korean education system some years later, they would be expected to have kept up with the Korean textbooks, according to the Korean mainstream primary school's curriculum. So, during every school holidays from 1999 to 2002, the children were involved in Korean literacy learning through Korean textbooks and other workbooks their grandparents sent to them from Korea. For a smooth start to the question-based workbooks in Korean, the researcher needed to use 'scaffolding literacy' strategy (see Section 2.2.4) providing detailed explanations and word-meaning support so that they could catch up with concepts which they were already familiar with in English. When they started learning Korean literacy through the Korean textbooks in different subject areas, the children seemed to expand their Korean vocabulary related to academic concepts and learning areas. Through this kind of learning and teaching in Korean, the researcher was able to support the bilingual development of the children by explaining more knowledge and academic concepts in Korean at a deeper level and by linking concepts known in English with learning in Korean.

1.2.6. Bilingual Education - Listening

The area of listening in the ESL context was mostly integrated through viewing such as TV programs, video, computer CD (educational software) and audio tapes of story books and songs. Also, in order to expand the children's listening ability in various social contexts, the researcher organized a range of opportunities which would expose them to spoken English. The children were encouraged to participate in such out of school activities as music and sports lessons, religion discussion groups, traveling around Australia, visiting Australian friends' houses, inviting friends, joining a swimming club, excursions (e.g. museums, art gallery, parliament house) and guided tours.

It should be noted that the listening skills cannot be improved only through the process of sound and intonation awareness and familiarization; the whole integrated process of lexical, syntactical and text level coordination is needed. In addition to these, the background knowledge of various aspects of socio-cultural contexts must be acquired. For this purpose, the researcher told the children about the importance of attentive listening and flexible listening. The children were also encouraged to adapt their listening methods depending on different text types such as news, drama, documentary or story telling or teacher talks. Also, whenever they traveled by car, the researcher had audio tapes of different story books prepared for listening. The children always seemed to be very attentive and comfortable listening to audio tapes.

1.2.7. Bilingual Education – Writing

1.2.7.1. English Writing Development in an ESL Context
Since the area of writing both in English and Korean has been a focal interest for the researcher from the start of the children's schooling, all possible curriculum and writing approaches / sessions from the children's school were closely examined through class observation and interviews with teachers. Overall, from the observation the researcher became convinced that writing could be a particularly demanding area for young writers in comparison to other areas of language learning such as reading or speaking. The literacy program in the children's school encompassed a range of approaches including 'Whole Language Approach', 'Process Writing' as well as 'Genre Approach'. Throughout the research period the subject children's writing samples were collected by the researcher, with their notebooks; there were mainly two different notebooks used in school – Journal notebooks and Theme notebooks. During the lower grades (Kindergarten, Year 1 and Year 2), the classroom teachers encouraged children to write a diary entry (a type of free writing) in the Journal notebooks almost every day. Also the children were expected to keep a 'Theme notebook' with each term having a different theme (e.g. space, media, water and fire). For instance, if they were studying about space for a term, all the related writing products were attached to the 'Theme notebook' that had the title 'Space'.

At home the children were engaged in writing English on a regular basis. The researcher introduced the following routines. During the lower grades (Kindergarten, Year 1, Year 2), a child's writing practice focused more on journal writing including Recount writing, diary and Narrative or letter/card writing. Whenever they had a special event, excursion or traveling, they were expected to write a Recount. The discussion session (5 to 10 mins) prior to the writing activity always allowed them to engage more meaningful writing.

The other skill which the researcher encouraged them to learn from Year 2 was to use of the computer keyboard (this was introduced after the children had mastered the cursive handwriting). As ESL children, in order to quickly access information on the internet in English, this skill seems to be beneficial even to the young writers. Through familiarizing them with computer skills and fast and proper typing in English, they were able to satisfy their need to construct a presentation, access information for a school project or search for resource material from the Internet. They also used the computer to send e-mails and write a diary.

Another important matter to note in relation to their English writing development in the home environment is that the children were involved in the researcher's case study, over a seven-month period, for an MA TESOL dissertation titled 'The Effective Error-Correction/Feedback in ESL Children's Written Work in terms of Fluency and Accuracy'. Jinha was in Year 2 and Sunyoung was in Kindergarten at the time. The children were expected to compose a piece of Recount writing twice a week on a regular basis. Over the seven month period the children read 30 different storybooks and had pre-discussion sessions about each book. After this regular writing practice for the particular text type of Recount, the children improved their writing skills significantly, in terms of fluency and accuracy in comparison to pre-test compositions undertaken prior to the case study. The researcher is convinced that the children's sense of good writing, ownership of writing and clarifying the purpose of writing, in fact the whole process of writing, developed very positively through the period of the case study. Also, both children seemed to integrate their reading activities with writing activities and their awareness of some characteristics of written languages gained from reading books appeared to be reflected in their writing compositions in many ways. For example, the children's use of more formal expressions increased. The expressions also became more lexically dense.

For Jinha's first two years in an Australian school (in Kindergarten, Year 1), the literacy program was largely

Whole Language and Process Writing oriented. When Jinha started in Year 2 (Sunyoung in Kindergarten), the Genre Approach was introduced, and there was with more explicit teaching about how to organize different text types such as Recount, Argument, Explanation or Procedure. Until the time that the Genre Approach was introduced, Jinha appeared to be mostly writing journals (similar to diary entry – what I did today or what I learnt today) or some Narratives during the writing sessions at school. Overall, during the first two years, Jinha's writing proficiency did not seem to increase significantly in terms of word level, sentence level or text level. However, after the Genre Approach was introduced to their school, Jinha and Sunyoung had more opportunities to write a range of text types. The classroom teacher modeled and jointly constructed the texts and, as a result, the children looked more confident and showed more interest in their school writing than they had in the previous period.

Also, the researcher noticed that there was a big difference between the first child and the second child in their writing motivation, approach and outcomes (preference to certain type of text). The first child was more interested in reading factual, informative books and he seemed to have engaged more easily in Report writing or Explanation, whereas the second child loved to write Narratives among other writing activities. When she was in Year 3 (age 8;04), Sunyoung wrote a chapter novel (2000 words) by herself through strong self-motivation (a novel entitled Face to Face Santa), which appeared to be an advanced writing example for an 8 year-old child.

The children's experience of writing began to expand, including different text types introduced in the school curriculum, and by the researcher at home. On the introduction of the Genre Approach at school, the children were now learning to organize their texts depending on the text type; they were also learning to make genre-appropriate lexical choices. The teachers commented on both children's outstanding writing achievement in their academic reports. The children also showed excellent results in a NSW English Composition tests.

1.2.7.2. Korean Writing Development in an ESL Context

According to the researcher's observations through the entire period of the subject children's bilingual development (early and mid-primary years) in Australia, the most difficult and demanding area was the writing development in both English and Korean. While their English writing improved gradually with the support of the school curriculum and regular practices at home and school, their Korean writing seemed to stay at the beginning level. Both children mastered the Korean alphabet (HanGul), and were able to write a sentence in Korean. However, when Jinha was in Year 3 (aged 8), he still used a lot of unconventional spelling, and inappropriate lexical choices in his Korean writing.

At the Korean school in Canberra (2 hours per week), the teachers used Korean textbooks for their reading materials, sentence pattern practices (syntactical pattern) and word usages. During the class the Korean ESL children could hardly have Korean composition lesson in an explicit manner, but often the class teachers gave them homework to write a diary entry (twice per week) or write letters to relatives or Korean friends in the same class. Younger children (age 4-6) were expected to copy some paragraphs from the text book as part of their homework. However, the subject children did not seem to benefit much from attending the Korean school for their writing development, most likely due to the limited amount of school time and the inconsistent teaching approach and curriculum.

Given the seeming ineffectiveness of the Korean Saturday school, the researcher tried to organize for the children to have a period of an intensive Korean writing practice during school holiday time. As mentioned earlier, the main problem was the children's limitation of working time during the school time. When children got home after a day at the English-medium school they were reluctant to engage in Korean writing. It seemed to be a big burden physically and psychologically. They did not appear to be self-motivated. However, the children did not mind reading in either English or Korean on the same day. The situation was clearly

31

different with writing. This could be so because writing requires further discipline and effort. The following routines were introduced for the children by the researcher. During school holiday times, the children were to practice Korean writing more, focusing on one or two text types such as the diary (journal writing) and Recount (story retelling) with the researcher's scaffolding. Through accumulated practice with the text types, along with demonstration of them, prompting and modeled writing, they started to develop their Korean writing up to text level length without much effort.

Another remarkable thing in their Korean writing development in the ESL context was that they could use e-mail with their relatives in Korea. To make this happen, the researcher taught the children how to type Korean on the computer using a typing software program when Sunyoung was in Year 1 and Jinha in Year 3. As a result they were able to type in Korean with speed and they could manage to write a simple e-mail to their grandparents, who enthusiastically replied to them. This writing activity was a real success, perhaps due to the authenticity of the context and the purpose for writing.

Although the children made significant progress in their learning to write in Korean at home over the school holiday period, their Korean writing remained less developed than their English writing while they resided in Australia.

So far, in the Section 1.2., the subject children's bilingual and biliterate contexts have been reported. In the next Chapter 2, a descriptive explanation of the SFG is provided, this being the main framework for the text analysis that is applied in this research.

Chapter 2. Systemic Functional Grammar and Genre-based Approach

2.1. Systemic Functional Grammar

2.1.1. A Functional Grammar of English

Compared with the traditional structural linguistics which emphasizes the forms of a language (syntax) rather than its meanings, in a functional grammar language is interpreted "as a system of meanings, accompanied by forms through which the meanings can be realized" (Halliday, 1994: xiv). In other words, a functional grammar takes the notion of 'natural grammar' in which languages have been evolved by the natural need of human beings to express meanings by certain symbolic code systems. In this respect, grammar is not arbitrary but reflects how to use language as a meaning-making resource. With the basic perspective of functional grammar, Halliday (1994: xiii) conceptualizes three fundamental components of meaning in language as follows:

> All languages are organized around two main kinds of meaning, the 'ideational' or reflective, and the 'interpersonal' or active. These components, called 'metafunctions' in the terminology of the present theory, are the manifestations in the linguistic system of the two very general purposes which underlie all uses of language: (i) to understand the environment (ideational), and (ii) to act on the others in it (interpersonal). Combined with these is a third metafunctional component, the 'textual', which breathes relevance into the other two.

The three types of metafunctions (ideational[8], interpersonal, textual) construe a range of different texts, or 'Register', depending on variables from each component's linguistic features, variables such as 'Field', 'Mode' and 'Tenor'. The language metafunctions and register variables are also said to be influenced by the context of language functioning (the context of culture and the context of situation). As for the

---

[8] At the same time, in interpreting group structure, we have to split the ideational component into two: Experiential and Logical (Halliday, 1994: 179).

downward links, the three types of meaning are realized through relevant lexicon-grammatical patterns of 'Transitivity', 'Theme' and 'Mood'. The relationships between the language metafunctions and the register of the text are detailed as follows:

> The **field** of a text can be associated with the realization of **experiential** meaning: these experiential meanings are realized through the **Transitivity** patterns in the grammar. The **mode** of a text can be associated with the realization of **textual** meanings; these textual meanings are realized through the **Theme** patterns of the grammar. The **tenor** of the text can be associated with the realization of **interpersonal** meanings; these interpersonal meanings are realized through the **Mood** patterns of the grammar. (Eggins, 1996: 78, quoted in Aidman, 1999: 104, Bold in original)

Figure 2-1. represents the relationships between the register components, the language metafunctions and their realization in the lexico-grammar.

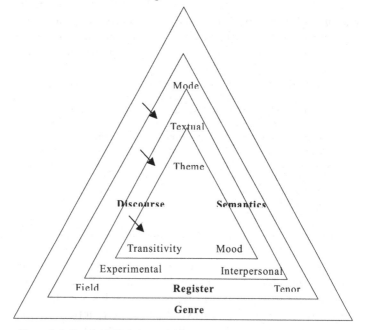

Figure 2-1. Context in Relation to Discourse Semantics and Lexico-Grammar
(Source: Eggins, 1996: 79)

The present study explores the children's control of a range of different registers (genres) in written mode and is shown the choices they made in regard to Transitivity as building experiential meanings, Theme as realizing the textual metafunction, and Mood and Modality system as constructing the interpersonal dimension of the children's texts. A more elaborate explanation of the three metafunctions with lexicon-grammar follows in the next sections.

2.1.1.1. Experiential Meanings: Transitivity

This section is concerned with the clause in its experiential function as a way of representing patterns of experience. The experiential meaning includes making sense of what is going on around us not only in our outer world but also inside our minds. According to Halliday, "the clause plays a central role, because it embodies a general principle for modeling experience – namely, the principle that reality is made up of PROCESSES" (1994: 106). In other words, the wide range of the world of experiences (including happening, doing, sensing, meaning and being and becoming) can be represented as "a manageable set of PROCESS TYPES" with the relevant grammatical systems called 'Transitivity' (Halliday, 1994: 106). In principle, basically, a process is composed of three core components as follows (Halliday, 1994: 107):

1. the process itself;
2. participants in the process;
3. circumstances associated with the process.

Table 2-1. Basic Components of Process

The postman	delivered	the parcel	with care.
Participant 1	Process	Participant 2	Circumstance

As shown in Table 2-1, in the English grammatical system the process is typically realized by a verbal group whereas the element of participant is constructed as nominal groups. As for the circumstance part, an adverbial group or prepositional phrase performs the grammatical and semantic role. This realization of experiential meaning is through a transitivity system in which a range of different process types have their typical grammatical and semantic patterns. This is what makes the SFG distinctly different from the traditional structural grammar which is much more focused on morphological form. That is, to understand the structure of a clause the focal emphasis is placed on the functional relationships between the components, such as 'participant' and 'process', on the basis of semantic interpretation. This kind of functional grammar approach goes beyond the traditional structural concept of 'verb', in which the verb category is mainly differentiated into transitive or intransitive based on whether it has an object or not. Rather, it is based more on semantic and functional views of the English language so that the transitivity system as the grammar of experience includes the following six types of process (along with relevant participants) which can then be used to interpret more meaningfully our experiential world:

Figure 2-2. English Transitivity System

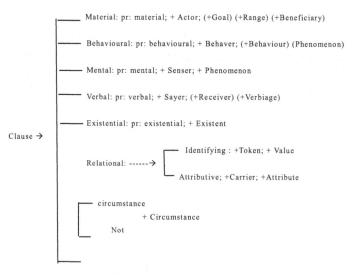

(Source: Eggins, 1996: 228)

In the English transitivity system, among the above six process types, the material process of the outer experience of the external world, the mental process of inner experience (the process of consciousness) and the relational process of classifying and identifying are the three main ones (Halliday, 1994: 109-138).

The first, material processes, are processes of 'doing' which express the notion that some entity 'does' something. They are not necessarily concrete, physical events but also maybe abstract doings and happenings as follows:

e.g.) She played the violin. (Actor + Material process + Goal)

    The captain selected the right solution. (Material process as abstract doing)

The mental processes represent the areas of perception (seeing, hearing), affection (liking, fearing) and cognition (thinking, knowing, understanding) with the participants of 'senser' and 'phenomenon' (which is sensed, felt, thought or seen):

e.g.) That question puzzled me. (phenomenon + mental process + senser)

    I believe you. (senser + mental process + phenomenon)

The third important process type to construe experiential meaning is that of relational process. As the name implies, relational processes relate one fragment of experience to another. The relational processes broadly include attributive and identifying processes. "In the attributive mode, an entity has some quality ascribed or attributed to it" (Halliday, 1994: 120). Thus, the participants are called 'carrier' and 'attribute'. In the identifying mode, something has an identity assigned to it. The relationship between the participants can be said to be as 'token' and 'value', which tend to dominate in certain highly valued registers such as scientific, commercial, political and bureaucratic discourse:

e.g.) Today's weather is going to be warm and sunny. (carrier + intensive

    attributive process + attribute)

    Today's meeting represents the valuable story summary. (identifier – token +

    identifying process + value)

"On the borderline between material and mental are the BEHAVIOURAL processes: those that represent outer manifestations of inner workings, the acting out of processes of consciousness and physiological states" such as breathing, coughing, smiling and staring (Halliday, 1994: 107). The participant in this process is displaying 'behavior' typically as a conscious being:

e.g.) He <u>yawned</u> in the middle of the class.

    Jane <u>was grumbling</u>.

On the borderline between mental and relational is the category of verbal processes which have rather distinctive patterns of their own (Halliday, 1994: 107). The verbal processes of saying and meaning are inclusive of both conscious and unconscious participants (e.g. the clock says-, the sign said-) as 'sayer' and also can include the other elements of participant such as 'receiver', 'verbiage' and 'target'. They often have projected clauses in two ways-directly quoted or indirectly reported:

e.g.) Michael <u>said</u>, 'I need to go to school.' (sayer + verbal process + directly

    quoted clause)

    Michael <u>said</u> that he needed to go to school. (sayer + verbal process +

    indirectly reported clause)

The last category is existential process on the borderline between the relational and the material ones (Halliday, 1994: 107). The existential processes commonly represent something as existing or happening mostly by typical verb-be along with the meaningless starter 'there'. The participant is called 'Existent':

e.g.) There <u>isn't</u> enough time.

    There <u>seems to be</u> a problem.

These six categories of processes along with relevant participants make up the main syntactic and semantic field of experiential function. In addition to the participant-process structure, it is necessary to introduce another element of transitivity structure, the so called 'circumstance'. Most circumstances in English are constructed in prepositional phrases and adverbial groups. In building experiential fields in clauses, the element of circumstance serves as an expansion of something else through various aspects of meaning (see Table 3-2).

Table 2-2. Types of Circumstantial Element

Type	Specific categories (subtypes)
Extent	distance, duration e.g.) The visitor had to stay <u>for two weeks</u>.
Location	place, time e.g.) I enjoy cooking <u>in the kitchen</u>.
Manner	Means, quality, comparison e.g.) The young girl got involved in the work <u>with great enthusiasm</u>
Cause	Reason, purpose, behalf e.g.) He studied hard <u>for his bright future</u>.
Contingency	condition, concession, default e.g.) <u>Despite his illness</u> he continued his study.
Accompaniment	comitation, addition I will be going to Europe <u>with my parents</u>.
Role	guise, product I participated in the conference <u>as a presenter</u>.
Matter	<u>Regarding the science theory</u>, there will be a hot discussion.
Angle	e.g.) <u>According to his statement</u>, he was not happy at that time.

(Modified from Halliday, 1994: 151).

2.1.1.2. Nominal Groups and Logical Metafunction: Relationships Below Clauses and Above Clauses

Along with the main elements of the transitivity system such as process and circumstance, we shall now consider the structure of the nominal group which is another resource for construing experiential information as 'participants'. The following example demonstrates the basic modification structure of a nominal group:

Those two splendid old electric trains with pantographs

Deictic	Numerative	Epithet		Classifier	Thing	Qualifier
		Attitude	Quality		(Head)	

(Modified from Halliday, 1994: 191, Fig. 6-4).

The element following the Head (thing) is also a modifying element which is called the 'postmodifier'. As shown above, the postmodifier can be attached to the prepositional phrase as in 'with pantograph' and also it can be composed of a relative clause (embedded one) as in 'those electric trains <u>that are resting at the platform</u>'. This kind of nominal group

39

construction to pack more detailed information relating to the field of discourse is significant in the present study as it is the key to demonstrating the children's growth in written language development. One of the characteristics of written language, compared with the spoken mode, is known to be the higher level of lexical density that is involved, and this is related to how to pack or include more lexical items in nominal groups.

In connection with the modifying structure in English clauses (below the clause), we need to extend our concern up to the complex sentences (between the clauses, or above the clauses). Since the children's text development is closely related to the logical organization of ideas realized in language, here we shall briefly introduce the logical metafunction in text construction. According to Halliday (1994: 218), the relationship between clauses needs to be considered along two separate dimensions: 1) the type of interdependency or taxis; and 2) the logico-semantic relation.

Based on the type of interdependency, all 'logical' structures in language can be classified into two groups of 'paratactic' and 'hypotactic'. "Hypotaxis is the relation between a dependent element and its dominant, the element on which it is dependent. Contrasting with this is PARATAXIS, which is the relation between two like elements of equal status, one initiating and the other continuing" (Halliday 1994: 218). Also, in the logico-semantic relations, clauses are connected in the manner of expansion or projection. The expansion of clauses can be achieved in one of the following three ways (Halliday, 1994: 220):

1. elaborating where "one clause expands another by elaborating on it (or some portion of it): restating in other words, specifying in greater detail, commenting, or exemplifying";
2. extending where "one clause expands another by extending beyond it: adding some new element, giving an exception to it, or offering an alternative";
3. enhancing where "one clause expands another by embellishing around it: qualifying it with some circumstantial feature of time, place, cause or condition".

One other kind of hypotactic relationships is projection, which is involved in reporting sayings (locutions) or in reporting thoughts (ideas).

The following Table 2-3 shows the examples of clause complex by the divisions:

Table 2-3. Basic Types of Clause Complex

	i) paratactic	ii) hypotactic
1) Expansion		
a) elaboration	John didn't wait; he ran away.	John ran away, which surprised everyone.
b) extension	John ran away, and Fred stayed behind.	John ran away, whereas Fred stayed behind.
c) enhancement	John was scared, so he ran away.	John ran away, because he was scared.
2) Projection		
a) locution	John said: "I'm running away."	John said he was running away.
b) idea	John thought to himself: 'I'll run away.'	John thought he would ran away.

(Modified from Halliday, 1994: 220, Table 7(2)).

2.1.1.3. Textual Metafunction: Theme
In constructing or understanding the meaning of clauses, 'thematic structures' contribute to distinction between the message of one part of a clause from other structural elements. Thus, for overall development of a text, the writer's choices of thematic structures could be crucial in realizing the textual metafunction. In this section we shall examine the grammatical structure of Theme in English as the first part of clause message by defining and categorizing it into a range of types. Since this awareness and control of the Theme system is significant in children's written language development, the subject children's English texts (narrative and factual writing) and Korean texts (diary writing) are analyzed in terms of the Theme choices.

First the definitions of the relevant terminology are introduced. As Halliday (1994: 37) explains, "the Theme is the element which serves as the point of departure of the message; it is that with which the clause is concerned. The remainder of the message, the part in which the Theme is developed, is called in Prague School terminology the

41

Rheme." As a message structure in English, a clause consists of a Theme accompanied by a Rheme; and the Theme is foregrounded in the clause. The following Table 2-4 illustrates the basic structure of Theme and Rheme:

Table 2-4. Basic Structure of Theme and Rheme

a) My friend	gave me a piece of pleasant advice.
b) With pride and satisfaction,	he announced his future plan to the audience.
Theme	Rheme

As shown above, the Theme is one element (rather than one word put in the very beginning of the clause) in a particular structural configuration which, taken as a whole, organizes one clause as a message. In the English structure Themes can be a structural element of the nominal group (mainly subject or complement), circumstantial elements (adverbial or the prepositional phrases), conjunctions and even predicates. As in b) given above, the prepositional phrase of two groups forming a single structural element also can be Theme.

Now, it is important to consider the varied range of Theme types in English which includes such distinctive choices as marked/unmarked, obligatory/optional, single/multiple, predicated theme and thematic equative. Firstly, according to the sentence type, (more exactly called Mood system – refer to the next section (see, Table 2-5)), Theme can be sorted further as to whether it is marked or unmarked as follows:

Table 2-5. Theme Choices as Related to Mood Type

Mood type		Unmarked Theme	Marked Theme
Interrogative	Yes/No type	Finite verbal operator	Other Theme (prepositional phrase, adverbial group)
	WH-element	WH element (how, where, who, what...)	Other Theme (e.g. prepositional phase, adverbial group)

42

		A Theme something other than the subject (e.g. Adverbial group – 'today', 'suddenly'; Prepositional phrase – 'in the corner', 'without much help'; Complement – the most marked Theme)
Declarative	Subject	
Imperative	Verbal group, let's, don't let	Other Theme (adverbial group, prepositional phrase, subject)

(Modified from Halliday, 1994: 44-48).

As shown in Table 2-5, in the English Theme system, each clause type (declarative, interrogative and imperative) naturally tends to present its key element as Theme in the intrinsic structural order. For example, in most declarative clauses, subject is expected to be put first as Theme if there is no special intention of the writer to emphasize another element (e.g. adverbial group or complement) as a message starter in a clause. If the element of complement is foregrounded, the clause will have the most prominent so called 'marked' Theme in a declarative clause:

e.g.) Much more unexpected things they had to buy in their shopping yesterday.

     Complement   Subject

       |

     as a marked Theme

Halliday indicates that the interrogative clauses of English "embody the thematic principle in their structural make-up" (1994: 46). He argues that "[i]t is characteristic of an interrogative clause in English that one particular element comes first; and the reason for this is that that element, owing to the very nature of a question, has the status of a Theme" (Halliday, 1994: 46). Thus, considering the English word order of interrogative clauses, the Theme choices as default, unmarked ones (the WH element or the finite verbal operator) seem to be properly matched with the characteristic of the Theme system in which the message starter that has prominence is put first. The WH element (where, who, what, which) used to seek the missing piece of information and the finite verbal operator used to signal the seeking of the yes or no polarity are thus considered to be unmarked Themes in usual interrogative clauses:

e.g.) <u>Where</u> have you been so long? (WH element as unmarked Theme)

<u>Are</u> you saying the truth without adding any facts? (Finite verbal operator as unmarked Theme)

Again, there can be infrequent cases of interrogative clauses with a marked Theme if necessary:

e.g.) <u>Without any bag and money</u>, where have you been so long? (prepositional phrase as marked Theme in interrogative clause)

In the imperative clauses of English, 'the basic verb form', 'don't' and 'let's' are unmarked Themes signaling the imperative mood. They also seem to reflect the characteristic of the English Theme system since the application of a predicator Theme does have significance in constructing meanings (like 'I want you to do something') as message in such an imperative mood:

e.g.) <u>Hit</u> the ball!   <u>Don't say</u> the harsh words!

However, in some infrequent cases imperative clauses with marked Themes occur as follows:

e.g.) <u>First</u> do your homework!   <u>You</u> keep silent!

So far we have introduced the definition of Theme, the basic structure of the English Theme system (Theme-Rheme structure) and the default unmarked Theme and marked applications according to the mood type of clauses (interrogative, declarative, imperative). Next, the other aspect of the English Theme system, whether it is single or multiple Themes, will be addressed by presenting the relevant Theme components of each metafunction (textual, interpersonal, experiential).

According to Halliday, "the Theme extends from the beginning of the clauses up to (and including) the first element that has a function in transitivity. This element is called the 'topical Theme'; so we can say that the Theme of the clause consists of the topical Theme together with anything else that comes before it" (1994: 53). With this compulsory topical Theme as the only one experiential element (among the three experiential elements participant, circumstance and process), some clauses may have further structural elements preceding the topical Theme which are textual and/or interpersonal in function. In these cases, the other elements before the topical Theme are also part of the Theme, and are referred to as the 'multiple Theme'. The typical Theme sequence would be textual ^ interpersonal ^ experiential:

e.g.) On the other hand, maybe on a weekday it would be less crowded.

        textual   interpersonal   experiential

Table 2-6 represents the specific components of a multiple Theme. The new structural terms are defined and exemplified based on Halliday's (1994: 48-54) explanation.

Table 2-6. Specific Components of a Multiple Theme

Metafunction	Component of Theme
textual	Continuative (one of a small set of discourse signalers – e.g. yes, no, well, oh, now)
	Structural conjunction (items which relate the clause to a preceding clause in the same sentence not only semantically but also grammatically; obligatorily thematic – e.g. co-ordinator; and, or, nor, either, neither, but, yet, so, then subordinator; when, while, before, after, until, because, if, although, unless, since, that, whether, (in order) to, even if, in case, supposing (that), assuming (that), seeing (that), given that, provided (that), in spite of, the fact that, in the event that, so that)
	WH-relative (obligatorily thematic; e.g. definite; which, who, that, whose, when, where, why, how indefinite; whatever, whichever, whoever, whosever, whenever, wherever, however)
	Conjunctive Adjunct (those which relate the clause to the preceding text only semantically e.g. in other words, in any case, in conclusion, in face, also, however, meanwhile, next, finally, likewise, in the same way, otherwise, despite that and etc*
Interpersonal	Vocative (any item, typically (but not necessarily) a personal name, used to address)
	Modal Adjunct (those which express the speaker's judgment regarding the relevance of the message; e.g. probably,

	possibly, maybe, always, generally, obviously, personally, frankly, no doubt, fortunately, regrettably, mistakenly, surprisingly** Finite Operator WH (interrogative)
experiential	Topical (participant, circumstance, process)

(Modified from Halliday, 1994: 54, Table 3(7)).

Note: *For the full range of Conjunctive Adjuncts, see Halliday, 1994: 49, Table 3(2).

    **For the full range of Modal Adjuncts, see Halliday, 1994: 49, Table 3(3).

Choosing further Themes (see Table 2-6) before the compulsory topical one, more textual or interpersonal meanings can be emphasized along with the topical theme. That means the thematic power or effect can be still extended to, or embody, the different layer of metafunctional elements (textual, interpersonal, experiential) in order to effectively realize the complexity of the starting point of the message.

Finally, the following two example clauses will demonstrate the additional special features of the English Theme system, the so called 'predicated Theme' and 'thematic equative':

a) It is my daughter's smile (that makes me always happy). (Predicated Theme: 'it + be + ...')
      Theme   Rheme

b) What I like is the strawberry ice-cream. (Thematic Equative: Theme = Rheme structure)
   Theme   Rheme

The predicated Theme is used to put more emphasis on the Theme by presenting the explicit formulation of contrast (Halliday, 1994: 58-60). Especially in written language, this kind of predicated theme is frequently used as a marked Theme. Thematic equative is composed of any nominalized phrase or clause along with Rheme. As in 'what I like', the thematic nominalization in English "enables the message to be structured in whatever way the speaker or writer wants" (Halliday, 1994: 42). The identifying structure of Theme and Rheme expresses the semantic area of exclusiveness (nothing else but the Theme). These two important features of the English Theme system will be further elaborated in the text analysis chapters of this thesis.

46

2.1.1.4. Interpersonal Meanings: Mood and Modality

In this section, we turn to the aspect of clauses as the exchange in a transaction between speaker and listener. In the clauses that are organized as an interactive event including speaker, writer or audience, interpersonal meanings are likely to be more highlighted than are other previous metafunctions of experiential representation or textual messages. The principal grammatical system to realize these kinds of linguistic features is Mood. According to Halliday's explanation, the speech functions of exchange can be mainly differentiated into the two categories of giving and demanding (1) goods and services, and (2) information. The semantic function of a clause in the exchange of information is a proposition which relates to the forms of statement and question; the semantic function of a clause in the exchange of goods and services is defined as a 'proposal' which is represented by the forms of offer and command. (Halliday, 1994: 71)

Halliday (1994: 74) identifies the indicative mood as the grammatical category that is characteristically used to exchange information which can then be further differentiated into the declarative used to express a statement, and the interrogative used when posing a question. The interrogative category further comprises choices for yes/no interrogative for polar question, and WH-interrogative for 'content' questions.

To realize the meaning of proposal, the imperative mood choice is selected:

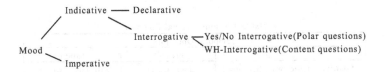

The above range of clause types has the key elements of mood structure such as subject and finite operator. These elements are closely linked together, and combine to form one constituent called the Mood in the English language. The other elements in a clause such as predicator, complement and adjunct are called Residue (See Table 3-7).

Table 2-7. Mood Elements in English

A little gargoyle	was	watching	the city	below him.
Subject	Finite	Predicator	Complement	Adjunct
Mood		Residue		

In English, the basic word order for the declarative mood is subject followed by the finite element as shown in (a) of Table 3-8 below; whereas the interrogative clauses have mostly the preceding finite element followed by the subject as (b) of Table 3-8.

Table 2-8. Basic Word Order for the Declarative and Yes/No Interrogative Clauses

a) declarative

The child	has	finished his homework right away.
Subject	Finite	Residue
Mood		

b) Yes/No interrogative

Has	the child	finished his homework right away?
Finite	Subject	Residue
Mood		

In the mood structure the finite element has special significance by circumscribing the proposition (that is, making it finite as the name implies). Basically, the finite element specifies the clause in terms of three references: the time of speaking (primary tense), the judgment of the speaker (modality) and the choice between positive and negative (polarity). The following Table 3-9 provides the possible patterns of finite verbal operators sorted by the three aspects of temporality, modality and polarity.

Table 2-9. Finite Verbal Operator

Temporal Operators			
	past	present	future
Positive	did, was, had, used to	does, is, has	will, shall, would, should
Negative	didn't, wasn't, hadn't, didn't + used to	doesn't, isn't hasn't	won't, shan't, wouldn't, shouldn't
Modal Operators			
	low	median	high
Positive	can, may, could,	will, would,	must ,ought to,

	might (dare)	should, is/was to	need, has/had to
Negative	needn't, doesn't/didn't +need to, have to	won't, wouldn't, shouldn't, (isn't/wasn't to)	mustn't, oughtn't to, can't, couldn't, (mayn't, mightn't, hasn't/hadn't to)

Source: Halliday, 1994: 76

In addition to the basic structure of subject and the range of finite elements (Table 3-9), we need to know the important role of 'mood adjuncts' that are most closely associated with the meanings constructed in the mood system including those of polarity, modality, temporality and mood:

e.g.) He is <u>probably</u> in the safe area.

The captain will <u>definitely</u> do the right thing.

These tend to occur in a clause near the finite verbal operator and contribute to building the range of delicate variation of modality meanings. The principal items functioning as mood adjunct include the following.

Table 2-10. Mood Adjuncts

Adjuncts of Polarity and Modality	
a) polarity	not, yes, no, so
b) probability	probably, possibly, certainly, perhaps, maybe
c) usuality	usually, sometimes, always, never, ever, seldom, rarely
d) readiness	willingly, readily, gladly, certainly, easily
e) obligation	definitely, absolutely, possibly, at all costs, by all means
Adjuncts of Temporality	
f) time	yet, still, already, once, soon, just
g) typicality	occasionally, generally, regularly, mainly, for the most part,
Adjuncts of Mood	
h) obviousness	of course, surely, obviously, clearly
i) intensity	just, simply, merely, only, even, actually, really, in fact
k) degree	quite, almost, nearly, scarcely, hardly, absolutely, totally, utterly, entirely, completely

Source: Modified from Halliday, 1994: 82-83.

As shown above, the mood elements of subject and finite operators, along with the above listed mood adjuncts, circumscribe the clauses of exchange whether they are declarative statements, interrogative or imperative. At the same time, the mood elements, including the mood adjunct, provide listeners with the speaker's judgment based on different aspects (polarity, probability, usuality, readiness, obligation, typicality, obviousness, intensity and other degrees) by choosing the appropriate level (low, medium, high) of finite operators or by selecting the right modal adjunct from the range of intermediacy given above. Most young children's speaking and writing tends to be more direct (abrupt) and definite because they are not capable of using the range of finite operators and modal adjuncts in the necessary areas. As a result, some remarks or writing texts might reveal an oversimplification or directness of facts or statements and, in some cases, the politeness requirements are not appropriately met because of the lack of mood elements or their misapplication. The development of awareness and control of mood elements can be considered very significant in the growth in control of sociolinguistic features that are closely related to the area of interpersonal metafunction. The following Table 3-11 illustrates the overall picture of the English mood and modality system.

Table 2-11. English Mood and Modality System

commodity exchanged	speech function		type of intermediacy	typical realization	example
information	proposition	modalization	probability (possible /probable /certain)	- finite modal operator - modal adjunct (both the above)	- They must have known - they certainly knew - they certainly must have known
	statement, question		usuality (sometimes /usually /always)	- finite modal operator - modal adjunct (both the above)	- it must happen - it always happens - it must always happen

50

goods and services	proposal	command	modulation	obligation (allowed /supposed /required)	- finite modal operator - passive verb predicator	- you must be patient! - You're required to be patient!
		offer		inclination (willing /keen /determined)	- finite modal operator - Adjective predicator	- I must win! - I'm determined to win!

Source: Modified from Halliday, 1994: 91, Table 4(5).

2.2. Genre-based Approach

2.2.1. The Origin of Genre-based Approach and the Definition of 'Genre'

Knapp and Watkins (2005) state that Genre-based Approaches to writing emerged in Australia in the late 1980s, and now underpin primary English syllabus documents in Australia, New Zealand, Singapore, Malaysia and Hong Kong. This pedagogy has been mainly linked to the Australian Systemic Functional Linguistics development with substantial influence from M.A.K. Halliday's (1978; 1985) social aspects of literacy and the subsequent linguistic research in genre theory undertaken by J. R. Martin (1986; 1987; 1992) and Joan Rothery (1986). In other words, the Australian approaches to genre have been centered within a larger theory of language known as Systemic Functional Linguistics which emphasizes the relationship between language and its functions in social settings (Hyland, 2004: 24-27). While the Australian Genre Approach has been introduced in Australian schools as a result of cooperation between school, teachers and educators, other genre theories that are different in their contexts and implications, have also been evolving around the same period.[9]

---

[9] For more reference on the origins and influences (both applied and non-applied

According to Hyon (1996), there have been three different scholarly traditions of Genre theories, including the above Australian Genre Approach.[10] These are: 1) English for Specific Purposes (ESP), 2) North American New Rhetoric Studies, and 3) Australian Systemic Functional Linguistics (The Australian Genre Approach). Briefly, as its name implies, ESP tends to regard genre as a tool for analyzing and teaching spoken and written language; its target group has been mostly nonnative speakers in academic and professional settings (Hyon, 1996: 695). The New Rhetoric Studies include a body of North American scholarship from a variety of disciplines concerned with L1 teaching, such as rhetoric, composition studies and professional writing (Hyon, 1996: 696).

In comparison with ESP and the New Rhetoric Studies, the Australian Genre Approach has been interested in helping both L1 students with literacy learning difficulties and L2 learners (ESL students) in classroom settings. To elaborate again, the first important difference among the three Genre theories is that while ESP scholars have been targeting mostly non-native speakers of English in different academic professions (or tertiary education) by helping them master the functions and linguistic conventions of texts, the Australian Genre Approach has been applied in primary and secondary schools, and has more recently extended to areas of adult migrant English education (e.g. AMEP – Adult Migrant English Program) and workplace training programs (Hyland, 2004: 28). In contrast, the New Rhetoric Studies have their target group mostly in L1 professional writing.

---

fields) of the Genre-based Approach, see the Section 1.3 of 'Genre Analysis' written by J. M. Swales (1990).

[10] Paltridge (2001: 2) also indicates the different references of 'genre' according to the three approaches:

> In ESP genre work, the term *genre* refers to a class of communicative events, such as for example, a seminar presentation, a university lecture, or an academic essay. In "systemic" genre work, a genre is more often referred to as a kind of text, such as description, procedure, or exposition. In new rhetoric work, genres are often described as events or social actions that help people interpret and create particular texts. (italics in original)

In addition, Hyon (1996: 693) points out another significant difference between the three genre theories:

> ...ESP and Australian genre research provides ESL instructors with insights into the linguistic features of written texts as well as useful guidelines for presenting these features in classrooms. New Rhetoric scholarship, on the other hand, offers language teachers fuller perspectives on the institutional contexts around academic and professional genres and the functions genres serve within these settings.

As indicated above, both the ESP and the Australian Genre Approach have placed their emphasis on the linguistic features and forms in order to give practical and explicit guidance to learners. Particularly the Australian Genre Approach has also attempted to link the form and function of language with its influential social contexts. In contrast, the New Rhetoric Studies have placed greater emphasis on the social purposes or actions that the genres fulfill within these situations and have been against providing direct instruction on the forms of language.

Lastly, based on Hyon's explanation (1996: 700-709), quite evidently the three Genre theories differ in their instructional frameworks, even though all three seem to share as their primary goal 'helping students succeed in their writing'. Hyon indicates that while the New Rhetoric studies have rarely focused on classroom methodology, the Australian Genre Approach has developed several instructional frameworks to be applied in classroom contexts.

In particular, the Australian Genre researchers founded the Literacy and Education Research Network (LERN) in the late 1980s and developed a teaching-learning cycle for implementing a Genre-based Pedagogy in the classroom context. Detailed lesson plans were developed for mastering a variety of school genres such as narratives, report, procedure and argument (Hammond et al, 1992). Using Hallidayan schemes of linguistic analysis inclusive of both global text structure and sentence level register features associated with field, tenor, and mode, the Australian genre researchers criticized the Process Writing Approach which had been popular in Australia immediately before the emergence of the Genre Approach. It de-emphasized direct instruction about text form and teacher intervention in the writing process. The Australian genre researchers argue that if students are left to work out for themselves how language works and especially if the writing process is involved, a number of students are likely to struggle and fail (Hammond, 1987: 176). In other words, they believe that the Process Writing approach definitely is not an effective solution to learning writing, especially for those from minority and other non-mainstream groups with less exposure to "the powerful school genres", such as report or exposition, than mainstream students have (Hyon, 1996: 701).

The Australian Genre theorists, particularly Martin and his systemic colleagues, have defined genres as "staged, goal-oriented social processes" (Martin, 1992: 505). It can be elaborated more as follows:

> Genres are referred to as social processes because members of a culture interact with each other to achieve them; as goal oriented because they have evolved to get things done; and staged because it usually takes more than one step for the participants to achieve their goal. (Martin, Christie and Rothery 1987: 59)

Thus, from now on, we adopt the definition of 'Genre' from the Australian Genre theories since it is appropriate in this case study when considering the whole teaching-learning contexts, target group and the instructional methodology. In this case study, the process of a range of genres will be claimed as a sequenced social process with the clear purpose of becoming a competent member of society.

2.2.2. The Instructional Framework of the Genre-based Approach: Moving from the Whole Language Approach and Process Writing

In terms of the instructional framework used in literacy education, the Genre-based Approach is based on the value of providing language learners with practical tools and guidance for their preparation to be competent members of society. To fulfill a range of social purposes, the language learners are expected to use language appropriately (in socially acknowledged and approved conventions) to perform the following social functions: describing, explaining, instructing, arguing, narrating (Knapp and Watkins, 2005: 27). In line with this, the Genre-based Approach has the goal of making accessible to the learners language choices to effectively perform important social functions (in the academic and work-related areas). To control the range of genres in a variety of social contexts the Genre-based Approach advocates learning the social purposes of the various text types along with their typical language features, as well as developing language to analyze/reflect upon such language choices (developing metalanguage). The Genre theorists believe the successful development of students' literacy does not happen naturally, that is without teachers' intervention and scaffolding. Christie (2005: 145) explains the importance of metalanguage:

> Text types or genres are said to be ways of making meaning in a culture. In schools students need to learn a range of text types, all relevant for mastering the areas of school knowledge. Text types or genres are as they are, because they are used to organize information, knowledge and ideas in socially important ways.... The more confident people are in using genres the more they will adapt and play with them. Learning a metalanguage for talking about the various text types is part of developing important knowledge about language. Developing such a metalanguage is part of developing the critical skills needed to be active users and interpreters of written texts.

As stated above, the Genre-based Pedagogy emphasizes the importance of explicit teaching about language through active scaffolding and intervention such as modeling, shared reading and joint written text construction. This can be opposed to the so-called 'natural' approach to literacy education such as 'Whole Language' and 'Process Writing' in which the individual's learning process (self-construction with originality and creativity) is significantly appreciated rather than social interactions and guidance by more competent others. In order to compare these literacy approaches with the Genre- based Approach, we need to know more about the Whole Language Approach and

Process Writing which prevailed in Australia in the 1980s and early 1990s.

First, the Whole Language Approach, commonly referred to as the Natural Approach, emphasizes the assumption that young children acquire written language as naturally as they learn to walk and talk when they engage in self-motivating activities that are stimulating, interesting, social, meaning-based, purposeful, interactive and most of all enjoyable (Goodman, Goodman and Hood, 1989). 'Whole Language' theorists argue that traditional education has complicated the learning of language by fragmenting it into smaller sub-sets and sub-units (Cambourne, 1988: 206). So, for example, writing was broken up into grammar, spelling and punctuation, all taught as discrete units divorced from their natural contexts. Such teaching was based on the belief that in order to understand a 'big bit' like writing, one first had to understand or get control of the 'little bits' like spelling (Brown and Mathie, 1990). However, the Whole Language advocates believe that fragmentation unnecessarily complicates language and literacy learning. Literacy learning takes place within the context of reading and writing natural, authentic and whole texts, rather than through dividing language into bits or sub-skills and practicing these sub-skills beforehand.

Hudelson (1989) claims that Whole Language educators emphasize a content-based program from the start, instead of a literacy skill focused education such as reading and writing. She points out that "as learners explore topics of interest to them, they naturally engage in reading and writing about these topics by carrying out meaningful reading and writing activities" (1989: 47). According to Enright and McCloskey (1988), the Whole Language program can be an integrated curriculum organized and constructed around central themes or big ideas selected to obtain certain desired outcomes. The term 'integrated' is used to distinguish this curriculum from the type which is set up in divisions by subjects (Peregoy and Boyle, 1993: 38). Teachers using the integrated curriculum must be available as consultants and resource persons for work on topics or themes, ready to help children as they proceed.

Process Writing was introduced in Australia in the early 1980s. It arrived under the strong influence of the persuasive arguments of Graves (1983) which include the point that writing should not be seen as something artificial to be produced once a week in composition class but, rather, as a process of composing meaning with real readers. This approach to school writing was successfully integrated with literacy learning and the Whole Language Approach, with a great deal of encouragement and support from Cambourne (1988). Walshe (1981) emphasizes the importance of Process Writing, pointing out that children have to master the disciplines of writing by themselves. According to Walshe (1981: 11), "since writing is expected to be polished, each child must discover his or her own "process" of moving from rather messy drafting ("first thoughts") through revision to the polished form." He claims that writing is a "craft" (1981: 16). The cycle of writing is basically defined as pre-writing, draft writing, revising/editing, product/publication and reader's response (1981: 21). The publication can vary in form, but mostly in-school publication.

Both the Whole Language Approach and Process Writing are categorized as progressivist views in the sense that language learning is considered to be an entirely natural and individual matter. However, both approaches have come under criticism on the grounds that only a limited number of learners can discover the underlying rules and language features by themselves through their own learning process. Many other students need more practical help through explicit teaching from teachers (Christie, 1992; Macken-Horarik, 2002). According to Knapp and Watkins (2005: 22), "[t]he genre, text and grammar model of language proposed here recognized that while language is produced by individuals, the shape and structure of the language is to a large degree socially determined". It should be noted that, so far, there has been a longstanding debate between the 'process-oriented' and 'product-oriented' approaches (Hyland, 2004: 20). However, Christie (2005: 145) and Knapp and Watkins (2005) claim that, to some extent, the Genre-based Approach shares some features with the original 'process' approaches since "process and product are part of the same pedagogical phenomenon". Christie (2005: 145) adds that "[i]n a genre-based pedagogy considerable attention is devoted to fostering processes that scaffold learning, and to teaching a metalanguage for dealing with the genres". In the following section, we will examine more closely the four major stages of the Genre Approach, pointing out important features.

2.2.3. A Model of Genre Pedagogy and Its Important Features

The Genre-based model of writing pedagogy suggests there are four major stages involved in implementing its principles (Hammond et al. 1992). They are: 1. Building Knowledge of Field, 2. Modeling of Text, 3. Joint Construction of Text, and 4. Independent Construction of Text. The model emphasizes that in the process of writing, students can get practical guidance through the various stages rather than vague encouragement on writing itself.

In the stage of 'Building Knowledge of Field', students get a preparatory orientation for the target text by discussing the purpose of the text and its social context, and learning the relevant vocabulary and grammatical patterns. In the next stage of 'Modeling of Texts', students are exposed to a sample text by shared reading and a teacher demonstrating the schematic structures and linguistic features. The next stage of 'Joint Construction of Text' offers students the opportunities to practise writing under teacher guidance, which is intended to make them feel a sense of involvement in and awareness toward the process of writing the target text. This can be important for students because the most difficult part in writing any text type seems to be writing the first draft, even though the students may be equipped with the theory on how to write. At this stage, students can implement their ideas in construction of the initial target text by adding words, phrases, clauses or sentences, and teachers can then prompt or suggest specific ways of expression, and advise on sentence construction. The last stage of the Genre model is 'Independent Construction of

Text' at which let students have an opportunity to write their own text independently, applying all they have learnt through the previous stages. This process can be repeated either in part or in its entirety if necessary.

The Genre-based model of writing pedagogy proposes the importance of explicit (overt) teaching and active assistance from teachers in the process of students' learning socially significant ways of making meaning. Their teaching is, however, not prescriptive and does not involve rules which student writers have to follow in all cases. Rather, the teachers provide the suggestive guidelines which students can apply within the socially acceptable framework. The primary goal of this model is to help large numbers of students (not only the small limited number of privileged students) learn a range of genres which are significant in their social purposes and functions. Christie (1992: 228) also points out the primary goal for the Genre-based model as follows:

> The linguistic patterns in which people build the discourses
> of the various school subjects are thus made explicit in this
> model, and much opportunity given to rehearse and use these.

Since the Genre model was adopted in Australia in the early 1980s, important principles for implementing a Genre-based pedagogy have been developed by genre theorists and educators based on research in classrooms (Derewianka, 1990; Christie, 1992; Rothery, 1996; Martin, 1999).

Particularly, Macken-Horarik (2005) elaborated the Genre-based educational application to two ESL students (Year 5 and Year 10) through the case study of classroom context. More notably, in her research, the category of register such as 'field', 'tenor' and 'mode' is combined to the best known 'genre' or 'text types' of the functional metalanguage as a set of tools for promoting the ESL learners' literacy development. By taking a specific case of Hoa (in Year 10), she exemplified to cater for the areas of the field and mode (for example – background knowledge on topic, sentence level grammar) rather than concentrating only on the text structure on genre. Emphasizing the four dimensions of text in context – genre, field, tenor and mode in the real field of TESOL literacy teaching, Macken-Horarik (2005) carefully visualized the important connectivity of the Halliday's tripartite model of register focusing on context and meaning with the category of genre

Even though the Genre-based Approach to learning writing proposes practical and accessible alternative ways to address the problematic areas of the 'natural' approach discussed earlier, there has been some criticism of its marked features of explicit teaching and what was misleadingly seen as 'prescriptive' grammar. Thus, lastly, the next section addresses such criticism, particularly arguing the importance of explicit teaching of writing for ESL background children.

2.2.4. Some Controversial Issues on the Genre-based Approach

2.2.4.1. The Issue of Explicit Teaching

First, the explicit teaching as the one of marked features of Genre approach has been criticized by some scholars (Freedman, 1993; Perl, 1979; Krashen, 1981). Perl's study (1979) suggests that explicit teaching can be harmful by documenting evidence of overuse or misuse of conscious learning in the writing process. Freedman (1993) particularly questions the usefulness of explicit teaching with respect to genres. She raises some issues such as whether explicit teaching helps novice writers master a new genre of writing or not, and if so, to what degree, what kinds of formal features or underlying rules can be usefully explicated and how many rules can be learned at a time and in what order. She also seems to have concerns about the teacher's expertise in the Genre-based Approach that includes explicit teaching. As the theoretical base for Freedman, Krashen's view (1981), which distinguishes conscious learning from unconscious inference of rules in second language acquisition also implies negativity toward explicit teaching. In other words, Krashen's view is based on a model of learning in which there are two distinct processes: 'learning' which involves the conscious learning of rules such that they can be formulated explicitly by the learner; and 'acquisition' which entails the unconscious inference of rules on the basis of exposure to the target language. Krashen's essential notion is that conscious learning can never become acquisition and that the two are separate processes resulting in different kinds of knowledge. The knowledge is stored separately with no interface between the two possible (Freedman, 1993: 233). More recently Krashen (1991) has extended this argument to the acquisition of written discourse. He argues that writing competence does not come from the study of form directly but can be acquired subconsciously mainly through learners' experience when reading for pleasure.[11]

With respect to the doubts and skepticism about explicit teaching within the Genre approach (Freedman, 1993; Williams and Colomb, 1993; Fahnestock, 1993), the following L2 research has demonstrated that such claims are not based on clear evidence. Firstly, a body of research on L2 reading points out that L2 reading comprehension can be significantly improved by explicit teaching about rhetorical structure (Carrel, 1985; Davis, Lange and Samuels, 1988). In particular, Hewings and Henderson (1987) and Hyon (1995) indicate that students can be positively influenced by genre instruction in learning the text structure and thus increase their reading effectiveness. In addition to the area of L2 reading, L2 writing (Swales, 1990; Aidman, 1999; Macken-Horarik, 2005) has also been reported to benefit from Genre-based scaffolding and instruction. Of course, further research in ESL is needed, including controlled teaching experiments on the effects of Genre-based

---

[11] Compared with Krashen, however, Ellis (1990) does allow for certain limited conditions under which explicit teaching may enhance learning. He distinguishes two kinds of instruction: form-focused instruction and meaning-focused instruction. The form-focused instruction leads to explicit knowledge while meaning-focused instruction (reading and writing for meaning) leads to implicit knowledge. In addition, his central argument is that even the form-focused instruction can lead to implicit knowledge in certain restricted cases: firstly, if the student is at the appropriate stage of development and has an appropriate style; and, secondly, if the student is engaged in an authentic task that calls on the use of this structure. In this regard, the Genre-based approach is definitely meaning based because it has as its primary goal to teach how to use the language in real social contexts. Also its inclusion of scaffolding takes care of a particular learner's ability and learning style in setting the appropriate supporting level (see Vygotsky's Zone of Proximal Development – Vygotsky, 1978).

approach on nonnative students' reading and writing abilities along with case studies tracking individual students' progress through Genre-based courses. The current case study contributes to research evidence that suggests the effectiveness of the Genre-based approach to ESL children's instruction in reading and writing.

As a counter to Perl's (1979) claims regarding overuse or misuse of conscious learning in the writing process, it can be argued that any language learning, including first language acquisition, involves similar processes of 'over-generalization' or 'misuse' of language rules by trial and error. Therefore, it would seem desirable to provide some room for student creativity in any language teaching. However, it is not true that explicit teaching means almighty rules, or, that there is only one way to write in a particular genre. Hyland (2003; 2004) clarifies the issue of explicit teaching within the Genre-based Approach as follows:

> This explicitness gives teachers and learners something to shoot for, a "visible pedagogy" that makes clear what is to be learned rather than relying on hit-or-miss inductive methods whereby learners are expected to acquire the genres they need from the growing experience of repetition or the teacher's notes in the margins of their essays. (Quoted in Hyland, 2004: 11)

Another point supporting explicit teaching is closely connected to the set criteria, or assessment schemes used to assess academic writing. Most language tests or assessments are constructed with an expectation of products which can be achieved /facilitated through explicit teaching. In other words, language assessment, especially writing tests, commonly have overall text organization and language features included in assessment criteria. Assessment itself does not expect creative writing which allows for more flexible writing styles. In particular, second language learners would have much more benefit in their school exams or more standardized writing tests (e.g. IELTS, TOEFL) if they were aware of the structural organization and language features of particular genres. We cannot disregard traditional and still existing assessment tools used in language education, including writing tests, which have been part of the formal channel or route of achieving our social and academic goals. Hyland (2004: 20) sums up these arguments that explicit Genre teaching leads to lack in creativity:

> The key point is that genre *do* have a constraining power that restricts creativity and places limits on the originality of individual writers. Once we accept that our social and rhetorical goals are best achieved by, say, writing a postcard, a lab report, or a five-paragraph essay, then our writing will occur within certain expected patterns. The genre does not dictate that we write in a certain way or determine what we write; it enables choices to be made and facilitates expression, but our choices are made in a context of powerful incentives where choices have communicative and social consequences. Genre pedagogies make both constraints and choices more apparent to students, giving them the opportunities to recognize and make choices, and for many learners, this awareness of regularity and structure is not only facilitating but also reassuring. (italics in original)

2.2.4.2. The Issue of Critical Literacy

Within the circle of Australian Genre-based pedagogy, some scholars (Cope and Kalantzis, 1993: 15) have been concerned that the LERN teaching-learning cycle, with its focus on modeling and subsequent construction of mainstream texts, represents "transmission pedagogy" that presents texts such as Report and Exposition uncritically and excludes other, non-mainstream genres that might be culturally important in students' lives. Cope and Kalantzis, two of the original LERN members, advocate a more critical approach to genre teaching, one that leads students to challenge the principles found in some mainstream texts. Cope and Kalantzis have proposed the need to make the learning of different genres not a matter of duplication of a standard form, but mastery of a tool which encourages development and change (even disruption) rather than simply reproduction (Cope et al., 1993: 245). Using a more inclusive definition of 'critical literacy', Lee (1997) and Luke (1993; 1996) have also argued that genre teaching might serve to reinforce the existing power structure in our society.

However, most Australian Genre theorists and educators'

concern for teaching has been associated with attempts to teach 'powerful' school genres such as Report and Exposition to students from minority language backgrounds and other non-mainstream groups who have had less exposure to such texts than mainstream students have. AMEP (Adult Migrant English Program) as well as other workplace training programs involve students who are also from limited educational and non-English-speaking backgrounds. By teaching writing, genre educators may be accommodating such disadvantaged learners to the powerful dominant discourses in our society. Nevertheless, it is noteworthy that most other pedagogies fail to provide students with better access to powerful genres (Hasan, 1996). In this regard, Hyland (2004: 18-19) views access to dominant discourse as a foundation on which to build students' critical literacy skills:

> In fact, learning about genres that have accumulated cultural capital in particular professional, academic, and occupational communities does not rule out critical analysis but provides an essential foundation for their critical evaluation.

Kress (1993) argues that genre work in Australia has been both a pedagogical and political (ideological) project. Christie (1991: 83) also proposes that teaching students about genres and language in general is an ideological matter of social justice, insisting that "as long as we leave matters of language available to some and not to others, then we maintain a society which permits and perpetuates injustice of many kinds" (quoted in Hyon, 1996: 701). Therefore, they suggest a different notion of 'critical literacy' in which students can read and write any text more critically with logical thinking and as a result, they will be able to read the society and world in which they live. Hammond and Macken-Horarik (1999: 529) regard "the ability to read *resistantly* and write *critically* as central aspects of critical literacy, particularly within the context of school education." By introducing a case study of ESL students' science program in which critical literacy was implemented systematically over a sequence of lessons, they successfully exemplify and demonstrate ways of practical implementation of 'critical literacy' in the classroom. It can thus be claimed that the Genre-base Approach with critical literacy can empower ESL learners to become competent members of society. That might be the primary and final goal of the Genre-based Approach.

In specific regard to the broader view of critical pedagogy, Lingard (2006) reports on a large Australian commissioned research study which mapped classroom pedagogies called 'productive pedagogies'. The research was conducted by a large research team including Pam Christie, Debra Hayes and Allan Luke who worked across the critical pedagogies literature and also empirical studies of classrooms. The statistical analysis of approximately 1000 classroom lessons observed in this research indicated that "there were four dimensions of productive pedagogies, notably, intellectual demand, connectedness, supportiveness and working with and valuing of difference" (Lingard, 2006: 1). More fundamentally these four dimensions of productive pedagogies have a theoretical root advocating "political/social justice project of equality and difference, for a more equal distribution of capitals through schooling" (2006: 24). In today's globalizing society, guiding students to accept the socio-cultural diversity and differences and helping them develop a sense of connectedness from local to larger communities along with much higher order intellectual thinking ability should be an important role for current classroom teachers. In this umbrella-like critical pedagogy, the Genre-approach can be a real propelling power that weaves a difference into many literacy classroom contexts, beyond racial, ethnic, gender, sexual and religious boundaries.

2.2.4.3. Explicit Teaching + Process Writing + Critical Writing

So far the advantages of and issues around the Genre-based approach have been considered. Based on the discussion, the following summary of the balanced view on children's writing can be drawn: it would appear to be productive to try to achieve the teaching goal which helps children develop competency in writing effectively through a balanced way of teaching by combining all these writing approaches: Genre-based Approach, Process Writing and Critical literacy.

For example, Badger and White (2000) propose a process-genre model of writing in which the multi-draft writing in Process Writing and the contextual elements such as field, tenor and mode in Genre-approach have been considered and combined. Also, Johns (1997: 17) suggests an integration of different literacy views and pedagogies, warning not to ignore each child's different individual and social factors.[12] While teaching construction of different written text types, teachers should allow for children's different writing styles and views and get them try to reflect on their own writing, hopefully, using critical thinking. Also, teachers should be very careful in sequencing their writing curriculum according to their children's developmental stages and learning styles. With regard to the sequence, especially for children, they need to be exposed more to different text types in a systematic and repetitive pattern and learn the basic text structures and linguistic features through modeling and joint construction. After that, or during the process, explicit teaching might need to be combined with the Process Writing approach, emphasizing more creativity and independent ownership as well as the multi-stages of writing process. And of course, the final goal for writing education should be critical independent writing in which children are able to express their ideas and thoughts clearly, logically and creatively.

---

[12] For more reference, see also the Figure 1 - Integration of literacy theories (Johns, 1997: 18).

Chapter 3. Narrative Writing in English

3.0. Introduction

From this chapter onwards we will explore Jinha's and Sunyoung's biliterate development through systematic text analysis (using SFG) of both their English and Korean writing products. There is also a description of the writing contexts. In this chapter the Narrative texts are analyzed with a focus on the children's growth in control of written English.[13]

It is well known that "[t]he purpose of narratives is to tell or narrate a sequence of events involving the problems and conflicts faced by certain characters in specific times and places" (Wing Jan, 2001: 129). The overall pattern of stages of genre is Orientation, Complication, Evaluation and Resolution (Rothery, 1990: 190-210):[14]

- Orientation: context creation primarily in respect of settings, participants and their behavioural situation;
- Complication: introducing problem(s) and cumulating in a crisis with a sequence of events;

---

[13] Among many other kinds of text that the children wrote in English, their Narrative writing has been chosen for detailed text analysis for the following reasons:
  (1) Narrative is a common text type in the English-speaking culture.
  (2) Narrative is one of the most commonly used text types in the Australian primary school curriculum.
  (3) Narrative writing is a common assessment task in national literacy assessment, in Years 3 to 6 in the primary school as well as further at the secondary level.
  (4) Narrative was the text type which the children were engaged in writing from early on in their schooling in Australia, and which they continued over a 4-5 year period. The examples of their Narratives collected over that period make it possible to see their developing control of the structure and features of the English Narrative, as well as English written language more generally.
  (5) In addition, Narrative was the genre that both children, Jinha and his younger sister Sunyoung, wrote when living in Australia, which allows for some comparative analysis between the brother's and sister's Narrative writing.
[14] Even though there are some other views on the generic structure of Narrative text (e.g. whether it should include minor elements such as abstract and coda, whether the element of Evaluation should be optional), in this study, it is claimed that the Evaluation element should also be identified as a main element in Narrative text.

- Evaluation: pointing up the significance of what happens in the Narrative (for other characters and/or readers);
- Resolution: the Resolution of the crisis developed in Complication, changing the course of events from 'unusuality' to 'usuality'.

The four main elements of Narrative text are considered in this chapter for the purpose of examining each child's growing control of the English Narrative genre (structure and language choices within the stages). We shall start with Jinha's Narrative texts (Section 3.1) and then follow with a discussion of Sunyoung's (Section 3.2). Particularly for Sunyoung's Narrative writing, which includes a large volume of novel-like narratives, further detailed text analysis based on SFG is provided separately in Sections 3-3 and 3-4. This part of the analysis focuses on several aspects of Theme choices, Mood system, Transitivity and the use of Nominal groups. [15] After presenting the two children's Narrative text analysis, further comment is made on the similarities and differences between the two children's development of Narrative writing (Section 3.5).

3.1. Jinha's Narrative Writing Development

3.1.1. The Brief Overview of Jinha's Narrative Writing: The Classroom and Home Contexts

The Classroom Context of Jinha's Narrative Writing
Jinha's Narrative writing during his early and mid-primary years (Year 1- Year 5) developed mainly through his school curriculum and reading experiences at home and school. Before his first attempt at Narrative writing he had been exposed to the experience of story reading (both shared

---

[15] It is acknowledged that further detailed text analysis only for Sunyoung's Narratives (in Sections 3-3 and 3-4) might break a balance of the comparative text analysis of two children's writing. However, since Sunyoung's Narrative texts demonstrate her special strength in this particular genre along with far more amount of Narrative texts than Jinha's, this has to be done selectively. Another thing is noted that for readers' smooth understanding, the first part (Jinha's Narrative text analysis, Section 3.1.) in this chapter mainly includes the detailed explanation of each stage in Narrative's schematic structure and the next Section 3.2 (along with Sections 3-3 and 3-4), Sunyoung's Narrative text analysis, introduces more about the relevant SFG terms while analyzing further detailed text analysis, focusing on Theme, Transitivity, Mood and Nominal groups.

reading and independent reading) in Korean first (regularly, from age 3 to age 5) and subsequently in English (from age 5) with the supportive guidance of the researcher in the home environment. The experience of reading and discussing storybooks with the parent always seemed to be enjoyable to him, and he had shown strong enthusiasm in the whole process of story reading and oral discussion. Although Jinha enjoyed reading and discussing stories he did not show interest in Narrative writing. Thus, during his first two years in school (Kindergarten and Year 1), Jinha would only attempt Narrative writing if instructed to do so by the teacher. During that period Jinha's writing at school was restricted mostly to Journal writing (diary entry) without the teacher's active involvement. However, with the introduction of the Genre Approach at his school from his Year 2 period Jinha's Narrative writing was more guided in terms of structure as there was explicit teaching on the schematic structure of Narrative writing through the use of worksheets, shared reading sessions and writing modeled by the teacher on the whiteboard.[16]

The Home Context of Jinha's Narrative Writing
Jinha's Narrative writing was mostly conducted in school classrooms, particularly in the lower grades (Year 1- Year 3). However later on, in Years 4 and 5, the teachers would sometimes ask the children to finish off their Narratives (which were started at school) as homework mainly due to

---

[16] Typical lessons for Narrative writing which occurred at Jinha's classrooms were as follows. The class teachers handed out a range of worksheets outlining the Narrative plan prior to the students writing. The worksheets were mainly designed for students to fill in some notes in the divided sections such as Title, Orientation, Initiating Event, Complication, Resolution and Coda/Moral/Concluding Statement. Sometimes the class teachers constructed the opening sentence in a Narrative and students were required to continue the text. There were some opportunities for students to write different ending parts after an independent reading session. Also several opportunities to become familiar with the Narrative structure were provided for the students as they filled in the worksheet called 'story structure' which was composed of the sections such as Title, Characters, Events, Settings and Favorite Parts. The use of all these classroom materials meant that, to certain degree, Jinha was explicitly helped in constructing his awareness of the schematic structure of Narrative. Even though the class teachers did not seem to teach the students in detail about such linguistic features as process types, or usage of conjunctions in Narrative, the students were provided with Narrative sampling (during shared reading sessions), some model writing and lessons on the Narrative schematic structure. One of Jinha's 'Learning Journal' entries (Year 4, age 9) also reveals that the class teacher provided Jinha with some chances to learn about the schematic structure of Narrative writing in an explicit way.

time constraints. In the process of doing homework Jinha would initiate discussions with the researcher mostly about the storyline of the Narrative, and whenever the researcher showed interest in his work he seemed more confident and motivated to continue his writing. When he successfully finished his Narrative texts the researcher praised him as much as she could. This kind of encouragement provided a sense of achievement that seems to have helped Jinha keep up an interest in this genre. It appeared as though he really needed enthusiastic readers with whom he could share his stories. In regard to this matter it can be said that parents can play a valuable role in the home context as, in most cases, class teachers are not able to cater to such individual children's needs as, for instance, responding to the Narrative writing process in a timely manner in the way a parent working with a child one-on-one can.

Another important factor in Jinha's learning about Narrative was storybook reading to which he had been exposed from an early age in his home environment. As mentioned before, his experience of reading storybooks started with reading in the mother tongue of Korean at age 3. From age 5, when he could read storybooks in English as well, the researcher started taking the child to the Community library on a regular basis in order to engage him in a range of storybook reading, as well as for following up the school reading curriculum. As he grew older Jinha was able to read longer stories, and he increased the number of books he read and the number of pages per day. He was still happy, however, to have the researcher help him select books; he liked discussing book choice before he read and he was eager to talk about the chosen texts as he was reading them. The researcher would at times encourage Jinha to complete the book he had started to read. The mother showing interest seemed to motivate the child to continue reading the book. The researcher (mother) would also organize for a comfortable reading environment and make sure that he had time for reading.

From Year 3 Jinha's reading storybooks (mostly chapter books) entered a new phase of more challenging texts. From this period he started reading the Harry Potter series and series of other favorite authors such as those by Paul Jennings, Emily Rodda and Eoin Colfer. It seems that Jinha's Narrative writing (particularly in Year 4 and 5) was heavily influenced by one particular author, Paul Jennings, given his writing style (brief, comic and witty, plenty of imagination, the story being told from the first person perspective) and the themes of his stories.

The Brief Overview of Jinha's Narrative Writing

The influence of the school teaching on Narrative, along with Jinha's independent reading of a wide range of story books in the home context, helped Jinha develop this genre of writing. Overall, Jinha's Narrative writing has a variety of story themes ranging from science, fantasy, adventure, school life and so on. Throughout the five-year period (Year 1 through to 5) Jinha constructed 11 Narrative texts in English, which is a relatively small number. This could be explained by noting his preference to write factual rather than fictional texts. In terms of his attitude toward Narrative writing, Jinha, particularly during the earlier periods (Year 1 to Year 3), did not show much interest in Narrative writing at home. However, he started to get more motivated and interested in this genre from Year 4. In Year 5 he showed his pleasure and sense of achievement after writing several Narrative texts which were recognized as successful by the teacher and the researcher. Starting from embryonic Narrative texts in Year 1, mostly done in the school context, the overall length of Jinha's Narrative texts increased year after year. There was particularly remarkable growth in length in Year 4 and in Year 5. Even though Jinha's earlier Narrative texts (Year 1 to 3) appear less developed in many aspects including length, his later texts (Year 4 to 5) show his increased control of the Narrative genre in such important features as schematic structure (there is a more distinctive Complication and Resolution), the use of Evaluation elements, Transitivity system (a range of process types including mental processes), Mood system (using dialogic exchange), an increased range of thematic choices and elaborate nominal groups and circumstantial phrases to describe participants and setting.

Now we shall see how Jinha has developed his control of

Narrative writing in these important aspects by examining each stage in more detail.

3.1.2. Orientation

In this section we shall examine Jinha's Narrative texts chronologically (from Year 1 to Year 5) by focusing on 'Orientation' as the first element of generic structure in Narrative.[17] As stated earlier, in the stage of 'Orientation' the characters, setting and time of the story are established. Usually the answers to who, when and where are provided in this part of the Narrative. According to Rothery (1990) the primary function of Orientation in the schematic structure of Narrative is context creation in respect of settings, participants and their behavioural situation. Overall, Jinha's Narratives, written over five years, demonstrate his growing understanding of the schematic structure as well as something of the semantic property of Orientation in Narrative. He learns to build up setting (when and where) and to introduce characters (who). Also, very significantly, he learns to construct 'Foreshadowing' of the problem (to be discussed in detail later in this section). His Narratives also show an increased repertoire of ways of constructing Orientation.

Jinha started his English Narrative writing at school in Year 1 with the help of teachers; at first the Orientation part was written by the teacher and students were expected to construct the rest of the text. Therefore, the only text produced in Year 1 can be regarded as one that is an embryonic Narrative constructed jointly with the teacher. His first Narrative writing written independently at school shows his awareness of the primary function of Orientation in the schematic structure of Narrative. Thus, he creates some context in respect of setting, participants and their

---

[17] The reason why the text analysis of Narrative has been done by separating each element of the generic structure (not by handling the whole text of each Narrative product at a time) is that the researcher aimed to trace out the children's Narrative genre development, focusing on each stage's specific characteristics and features (Orientation, Complication, Evaluation and Resolution), which appear to be more distinctive in this than in other genres. All the whole Narrative text samples (typed by the researcher) are in Appendix 3-1 (Jinha's) and in Appendix 3-2 (Sunyoung's) for further reference.

behavioural situation even though it includes a typical indefinite space setting 'once upon a time' and indefinite temporal setting 'one day' with the simple introduction of characters by their names.

Table 3-1: Jinha's Orientation of Text B-1[18]

(Year 2, Age 7:4)
Once upon a time <u>there lived</u> two children. One <u>named</u> Jack and one <u>named</u> Jessy. One day Jessy and Jack <u>went</u> for a walk. They <u>sat</u> a bench and they <u>were getting ready</u> for lunch.

Note: no title was given by Jinha for this narrative.

A year later (in Year 3, age 8) Jinha tries to create a different style of Orientation by establishing a behavioural situation. Rothery (1990: 213) distinguishes two main types of Orientation, one which constructs an existential context and another which creates a behavioural situation. Compared with the Orientation in the first independently written Narrative (Text B-1) which is represented by existential and relational processes (*there lived; one (was) named Jack and one (was) named Jessy*), Text B-2 attempts to achieve Orientation mainly through material processes (*started, moved, go*), and the mental processes of perception and cognition (*saw, wonder*):

Table 3-2: Jinha's Orientation of Text B-2

Title: The Problem of the Flushing Toilet!	(Year 3, Age 8:3)
It <u>started</u> at school. I <u>saw</u> a person <u>go</u> into the toilet. I <u>wonder</u> why... Just then I <u>saw</u> the toilet <u>had moved</u> out of place ("like a G string").	

While the Orientation of Text B-1 does not include any conjunctive links between clauses, Text B-2 shows the typical temporal conjunctive '*Just then*' to connect the clauses.

Another example written in Year 3 (Text B-5) demonstrates that Jinha has learned to introduce the participants in the Orientation more effectively by using relational processes. Thus, he clarifies the relationship between the participants

---

[18] In the children's English text samples and excerpts, only their misspelled words (not grammatical errors) are corrected for readers' understanding. In Appendix 3-1 (Jinha's) and 3-2 (Sunyoung's), their whole Narrative texts are presented with their original spellings.

73

through relational processes as in '*in addition, they are all friends so they were used to each other*'. Also, by using more detailed circumstantial phrases (location and extent) than in the previous texts, he unfolds the space and time setting – *one million years ago, one fine day, in their patch, out of the ground* (refer to the boxed phrases in Table 3-3 below).

Table 3-3: Jinha's Orientation of Text B-5

Title: Run Away Vegetables!	(Year 3, Age 8:6)
One million years ago there lived some vegetables. Surprisingly they were alive. One fine day they were resting in their patch when tug! Someone pulled carrot, potato ad celery out of the ground. In addition, they are all friends so they were used to each other	

In Text B-6 (Table 3-4) written in Year 4, the usage of circumstances can be highlighted in Jinha's construction of Orientation in Narrative. The range of experiential meanings constructed in the circumstance becomes an important means of building field in the text. A demonstration of Jinha's developing control of fields by his use of expanding repertories of circumstance choices follows.

Table 3-4: Jinha's Orientation of Text B-6

Title: Fantasy Story	(Year 4, Age 9:4)
One dark stormy night, the people in the street including me stopped dead still in the middle of the road because we saw a quick flash and there, we could see just there hovering in the sky a balloony figure. It was not just an ordinary balloon, It had teeth. Some people thought it was a UFO but others thought it was some sort of a alien from mars. Some people thought it was a friendly alien but not for long.	

Compared with the Orientations in Jinha's earlier texts, the Orientation of Text B-6 appears to be more successfully constructed, especially in terms of introducing temporal and space setting and also participants. By using prepositional phrases and adverbial groups (refer to the underlined phrases above - *one dark stormy night, in the middle of the road, but not for long*) as well as non-finite dependent clauses (*hovering in the sky, including me*), Jinha adds a detailed description to create the overall mood in this Orientation. This semantic expansion and use of multiple circumstantial choices is an indicator of his developing control of written language. The experiential meanings are established mainly through mental processes (refer to the boxed words above - *could see, saw, thought*) and relational processes as in '*It was not just an ordinary balloon*' (along with emphasizing the negative effect) and '*It had teeth*' (by using a relational process of possession).

One way to create a successful Orientation is by introducing characters and foreshadowing the problem through a dialogue between the main participants (Rothery, 1996). The next Orientation, composed in Year 4, again shows a good example of Narrative writing development this time through the use of dialogue from the stage of Orientation. The title of the Narrative is 'The Mystery of the Haunted House'. The story begins like this:

Table 3-5: Jinha's Orientation of Text B-7

Title: The Mystery of the Haunted House   (Year 4, Age 9:6)
I was at school talking to my friends, Tom and Michael. "Have you heard about the haunted house? They say that people go in and never come out!" said Tom. "Cool! Let's go explore it!" exclaimed Michael. "Wouldn't our parents get worried?" I said. "I don't really care if they get worried or not." Said Michael. "Okay, then. We'll meet each other at the playground." Tom and I said.

First, the shift towards the start of the verbal activity is signaled by use of the behavioural process '*talking*' in the opening sentence of this Orientation. The dialogic exchange between the participants primarily functions to give information as in '*Have you heard about the haunted house? They say that people go in and never come out*' and to offer and accept something as in '*Let's go explore it*' and '*Okay, then...*'. Also, throughout the dialogic exchange the participants' (Tom, Michael and I) personalities come to be revealed, at least to a certain extent. When Tom talks about 'the haunted house', Michael's response is straightforward, without any hesitation, as in '*Cool! Let's go explore it!*' On the other hand, the writer's reference to parents potentially getting worried reveals a character who cares for other people.

Another significant semantic property of the Orientation in Narrative which distinguishes it from other story genres is 'Foreshadowing'. 'Foreshadowing' points to potential problems without, however, providing sufficient information to see what these are likely to be. It is thus the first step in creating suspense. Rothery (1990: 199) explains 'Foreshadowing' as follows:

> Foreshadowing suggests or hints at problems but at the same time withholds information so that mystery and suspense are created.

In Text B-7 the things that the boys discuss all work together to build Foreshadowing of the problem. The first word *'haunted'* triggers the reader's sense of apprehension, which gets further intensified in the next clause through the use of usuality adjunct *'never'* (Halliday, 1994: 82). Along with the verbal processes such as *'said'* and *'exclaimed'*, the mood elements (modality) as in *'Wouldn't our parents get worried?'* and *'Have you heard about the haunted house?'* also seem to build up the sense of uncertainty at the beginning of the story. Finally, the reference to the parents potentially getting worried further builds the sense that things might go wrong later on, when the boys go to visit the above mentioned house.

The next Orientation of Text B-8, in a sense, also reveals the element of 'Foreshadowing' by introducing the participants' habitual things through contrast and, also, by using identifying relational process to convey the relationship between the participants as in *'They were all friends except the white blood cell'*. The readers may be able to sense that the story will be developing through the conflict between the participants.

Table 3-6: Jinha's Orientation of Text B-8

Title: Blood Plague	(Year 4, Age 9:11)
Once upon a time there lived a heart, a white blood cell and a red blood cell. They were all friends except the white blood cell. Every day the red blood cell would bring oxygen to the heart and the white blood cell would watch television all day long.	

Jinha wrote the following entry in his school (learning) journal in relation to Narrative writing:

Table 3-7: Jinha's Journal Entry in Relation to Narrative Writing

(Year 4, Age 9:8)
Today I wrote a Narrative for my homework and I knew a Narrative had an Orientation, Complication and a Resolution. The Orientation includes the thing who, when, where and why. The Complication includes the problem and your Resolution tells you how they fixed the problem. Today I learned that the Orientation could include a thing called Foreshadowing which means to give clues that bad things are going to happen to make the reader more exciting than just tell what the Complication is. I also learned that there can be more than one Complication like there could be a minor problem and a major problem. And the more describing words (adjectives) and more adverbs words that describe verbs there are the interesting our story is. I found that rather than one short Resolution fixes all the problem, it is better to have lots of minor problems solving the whole story. I think I have learnt a lot towards Narrative writing through the experience of actually writing it. I think next time I will try some of these things I have experienced.

The journal entry reflects Jinha's developing awareness of the schematic structure of Narrative and of the semantic properties of its stages. The underlined part of this learning journal on Narrative writing particularly, demonstrates quite clearly his awareness of the element of 'Foreshadowing' in Jinha's own words.

Jinha's later Narratives, written at age 10 (Year 5), demonstrate his exploration of the first person perspective. For example, particularly the following Orientation of Text B-10 shows Jinha's quite successful exploration of this new style, a more mature Narrative writing from the first person perspective.

Table 3-8: Jinha's Orientation of Text B-10

Title: Remote Control	(Year 5, Age 10:3)
Hi, I'm called Michael and I'm 10 years old. I love flicking the channels with our remote control. One day, when I was watching T.V and clicking from channel to channel ('cause there was nothing to watch), I was about to turn the tele off., my dad came in with a shoebox. Inside was a brand new remote control. Dad said that it could control not only a T.V but also everything else. Just then mum came in and started a lecture about how I watched too much television and how I didn't do any homework. For a little joke, I pointed the remote at mum and pressed the mute button. Magically and most surprisingly she started the lecture silently. So I pressed mute button again and her voice returned.	

In this Orientation the main participant 'I' is first introduced very briefly by name and age, and his favorite thing to do is introduced through use of the mental process of affection *'love'*. This rather abrupt style (using the first person perspective) of constructing the Orientation could be influenced by the writing of Paul Jennings, as mentioned earlier. Mostly material processes (underlined) contribute to creating the initiating event that will be linked to the main event in the stage of Complication. Particularly in the expression of 'started a lecture', Jinha uses material process metaphorically in the meaning of a verbal process.

Another significant area of growth in Jinha's writing is in his control of the nominal group structure. There is evidence of lexical expansion in the nominal groups constructing the participants in the Orientation. Addressing the issue of the difference of spoken and written mode, one of the linguistic differences between spoken and written modes of language lies in the lexical density which can be realized through the way information is packaged in a nominal group. A nominal group can be explained as a group of words organized around a noun which forms the head of the group and serves in participant roles (Halliday and Matthiessen, 2004: 310). The analysis of Jinha's Narrative writing reveals that Jinha increasingly uses this grammatical resource to construct the Orientation stage in his Narrative texts - particularly in introducing characters (participants – served both in the positions of Subject and Complement). Specific examples of the developmental change in the nominal group will now be examined.

Jinha's early Narrative texts, the Orientation of Text B-1 (Year 2, age 7) and Text B-2 (Year 3, age 8) show that he uses mostly a one word nominal group, two words composing Deictic and Thing (Head) or, Numerative plus Thing as in *'I'*, *'It'*, *'Jack'*, *'Jessy'*, *'One'*, *'two children'* or *'the toilet'*. However, the Orientation of Text B-3 (age 8) is notably different in its use of nominal groups because it provides additional details of the participant (introducing his name and his action description) as in *'a dog called Ragbag'* and *'Ragbag chewing on my uncle's shoe'*. The full sentence of the projected clause is *'Also in the corner of the room I saw Ragbag chewing on my uncle's shoe'*. If changed to a more spoken-like mode, it could be reconstructed in two clauses as follows: 'And I saw Ragbag in the corner of the room. He was chewing on my uncle's shoe.' Thus, Jinha's use of a more complex clause structure in this sentence is significant in the sense that he successfully applies the linguistic function of post-modifier using non-finite clause which is one of the typical features of the written mode. More remarkably, the Orientation of Text B-8 (Year 5, age 10) involves a complex nominal group which is modified by two embedded clauses as in '*a lecture about how I watched too much television and how I didn't do any homework*':

> a <u>lecture</u> [[about [[how I watched too much <u>television</u>]] and [[how I didn't do any <u>homework</u>]]]]
> (Note: [[ ]] is used to mark an embedded clause.)

As shown above, 'a lecture' as Head in the structure of nominal group has an elaborate Qualifier of two clauses linked by the preposition 'about'. That is, the two clauses in this nominal group function as post-modifier. Inside the nominal group there are other smaller noun groups such as 'television' and 'homework' which are composed of the indefinite Numerative 'too much' and non-specific Deictic 'any', respectively.

To sum up, over his Years 2 through 5 in school the composition of the nominal groups in the Orientation stage of Jinha's Narrative texts has become more complex. Longer nominal groups have appeared in order to enable the written texts to compress information and convey more content within the clause. The nominal group structure has expanded from the early 'Deictic + Thing' to 'Deictic + Epithet + Thing' structure to the more elaborate 'Modifier + Head + Qualifier' structure. This expansion of the nominal group signals growing control of the written mode. More specifically, this reveals his growing control of the process of constructing the Orientation stage in Narrative writing.

3.1.3. Complication

The presence of the Complication stage in the schematic structure of the text distinguishes Narrative from other story genres, particularly from the Recount genre commonly written by children in their early years in school. Jinha's learning to construct a more effective Complication over the period from Year 1 through to Year 5 demonstrates his growing control over Narrative writing. Rothery (1990: 215) states that "[a] crucial aspect of Complication is the change in expectations regarding the events associated with the field." This change from usuality to create the effect of suspense or sense of crisis in the story is the semantic property of Complication. Also, experiential meaning in the stage of Complication is largely constructed by material and behavioural processes (Rothery 1990: 215).

In addition, in terms of the schematic structure of Complication, an important feature of more mature Narrative writing is that it includes the function of 'Evaluation'. Rothery (1990: 209) argues that whereas an unpredictable change in the sequence of events commonly associated with a given field is a critical feature of Complication, there needs to be an "interpersonal thrust" as well. According to Rothery (1990: 203), Evaluation is a stage where the events of a Narrative are given significance so that they are perceived as Complication and Resolution. Following Rothery, Aidman (1999: 187) explains that the Evaluation stage in fact highlights the sense of disruption of the expected course of events.

Jinha's Narrative texts show his growing control of the genre in the way he constructs the Complication stage. The following analysis shows Jinha's developing control over the main semantic properties of Complication. His texts construct the unexpected change of events as signaled through the use of material and behavioural processes, as well as through the choice of conjunctive relationships. Also, and very importantly, Jinha's Narrative texts show his growing control of the Evaluation element in the Complication, which is critical for realizing its interpersonal 'thrust' and for intensifying the sense of build up to a crisis, as well as for making predictions about ways of resolving the problem. In Evaluation the action of the Narrative gets suspended, and the events get evaluated. In the Transitivity system this is signaled through a switch from material to mental and verbal processes. Where material processes are used, they would be projected by mental and verbal ones (Rothery, 1990: 222). There are also changes in mood and modality and in the polarity systems. Now we shall see how Jinha's Complication texts have developed in constructing the relevant semantic properties.

Text B-1 starts the stage of Complication with the participant (Jack) facing a problem, which is that he didn't like vegetables.

Table 3-9: Jinha's Complication of Text B-1

	(Year 2, Age 7:4)
Jack had vegetable and he didn't like it. When he had dinner, he had a sandwich. He thought it was yum. Mum said it has vegetable.	

Note: no title was given by Jinha.

In the Complication of Text B-1, the shift of process type from a material one (*had= ate*) to a mental one with negative polarity (*didn't like*) helps the readers anticipate that the participant as a 'Senser' shows a potential conflict toward a 'Phenomenon' (*vegetable*). The following subsequent events building up the Complication use a range of process types such as material, mental, relational and verbal processes. The participant's internal conflict toward the phenomenon was tossed to the next clause very naturally, without giving the reader much surprise. In other words, there is no element of unusuality, and the participant's conflict has reached the Resolution stage without any conscious effort or difficulties.

Another early Complication in Text B-2 below, compared to the Complication in Text B-1, seems to be more successful in inviting the reader to feel a sense of crisis by the choice of the first person perspective and the thematic structure.

Table 3-10: Jinha's Complication of Text B-2

Title: The Problem of the Flushing Toilet!	(Year 3, Age 8:3)
But when I turned around I heard something crack. When I turned around I saw that the toilet had moved again! So I went in and flush!	

In terms of the thematic structure, the Complication in Text B-2 is signaled through a marked textual Theme '*But*'. In this way the field of 'a strange situation in a toilet' appears to be turning into another problematic event. And the next event seems to be back to normal. When the subsequent movement by the participant was introduced (*So I went in and flush!*), the sense of suspense seems to have been built to some degree. This Complication seems to be more successful than that of Text B-1 in the sense that the Complication in Text B-2 invites the readers to get involved in the strange situation by using the first person 'I' as the main participant, the Senser, and having more direct effect. We seem to have a greater feeling of crisis through the eyes and ears of the first person participant (I heard... I saw...). According to Halliday's definition, "[t]he Senser is the conscious being that is feeling, thinking or seeing. The Phenomenon is that which is 'sensed'- felt, thought or seen" (1994: 117). In this Complication, the two participants 'I' and 'the toilet' can be presented as Senser and Phenomenon respectively in connection with the mental processes 'saw' and 'heard'.

In the next Complication, that is in Text B-3, a more elaborate Evaluative element,[19] one of the most important features of successful Complication, is found. It occurs as follows.

Table 3-11: Jinha's Complication of Text B-3

Title: A Scruffy Dog called Ragbag (Year 3, Age 8:4)
So my mum got very angry and she said that I had to clean all of it up. <u>I tried to explain to mum but the words seem to be stuck</u>. So I had to clean the mess up. And I sent my dog Ragbag out of the house.

In the Complication that appears in Text B-3 the Evaluation element (underlined above) is constructed through the use of the contrastive conjunction '*but*' signaling the upset of expectation. Also, '*seem to be stuck*' creating one verbal phrase that realizes a material process here implies 'I was unable to speak'. These language choices help construct the protagonist's mental state of frustration and desperation.

To elaborate further, the problem between the protagonist 'I' and the dog called Ragbag, which has been foregrounded in

---

[19] Since the elements of Evaluation have been elaborated in a range of ways in Jinha's Complication texts, we shall see more examples focusing on this issue in the following Section 3.1.4. separately.

the Orientation stage, seems to be going on in the stage of Complication by extending to a new participant, 'mum'. And, the above underlined clauses contribute to highlighting the significance of the conflict between the participants 'I' and 'mum'. The effect of the crisis is intensified by the relational attributive process 'got angry' and the verbal process of projecting the mother's strict order (*'So my mum got very angry and she said that I had to clean all of it up'*). Most logical relations are constructed to reflect the temporal and logical consequence (*so, and, but, so, and*). However, the usage of these connectives as marked thematic choices seems to implicitly build up a certain degree of internal tension, which means that the participant's limited solution to the conflict (why 'I' had to choose the next action or decision in the given situation) has been represented in a sense.

The following Complication in Text B-4 illustrates Jinha's more developed sense of using a range of different process types:

Table 3-12: Jinha's Complication of Text B-4

Title: The UFO	(Year 3, Age 8:5)
The fight began. Well the UFO had great powers and so we could not escape the UFO and the UFO had set a bomb in the forest, and soon the wildlife will be doomed! But when I was thinking, the UFO had trapped us in a ring of fire. Just then Michael saw a red button. It said in clear black words "WARNING,"	

In establishing the field of escaping from a dangerous situation, the Complication of Text B-4 engages a range of process types such as a possessive relational one as in '*the UFO had great powers*' in order to describe the UFO's reality, material processes as in '*UFO had set a bomb in the forest, the UFO had trapped us in a ring of fire*', mental processes as in '*But when I was thinking* (cognition), *Michael saw* (perception) *a red button*' and a verbal process as in '*It said in clear black words*'. According to Halliday (1994: 140), unlike mental processes, verbal processes do not require a conscious participant and for this reason verbal processes might more appropriately be called 'symbolic' processes. In this Complication Jinha used the symbolic verbal process as in '*it said in clear black words*'. 'It' as 'sayer' refers to a red button which is not a conscious participant. This kind of usage is a good sign in terms of the emergence of metaphorical expression being one of the important features in written language development. Also significant is the use of relational process *'will be'* introducing the attribute *'doomed'*, of which the lexical meaning is critical in construction of a sense of a problem.

The following Complication of Text B-5 also creates a mood of emergency through engaging marked topical Themes realized in a clause and in a prepositional phrase (boxed below) as well as a shift in process choices between material and mental ones (underlined):

Table 3-13: Jinha's Complication of Text B-5

Title: Run Away Vegetables! (Year 3, Age 8:6)
Oh, Oh, the human was making vegetable soup! Just as the knife went down, the fruits ran away! They ran as fast as they could and just as they thought they were safe a dark shadowy figure in front of them. It was that human. Carrot couldn't stand it. In a blink of an eye, he poked the human!

First of all, in specific regard to Theme choice, the above Complication of Text B-5 starts with *'Oh Oh'*, the exclamatory words indicating that something unexpected and unusual has happened. Subsequently, on the whole text level, the thematic structure is realized as a marked clause Theme (special thematic prominence) as in *'just as the knife went down'*, *'just as they thought...'* and a marked prepositional phrase as in *'in a blink of an eye'*. All these marked Themes contribute to creating the mood of emergency in an urgent situation by representing the time related conjunctives and phrases.

In terms of Transitivity, there are mainly material processes such as *'was making'*, *'went down'*, *'ran away'* and *'poked'* to construct the participants' actions. Also, in the middle of the text, there are some mental processes interspersed to express the participants' (as Senser) mental states such as *'they thought they were safe'*. Thus, the Complication of Text B-5 shows Jinha's awareness of the necessity to construct the participants' external world (actions) in a series of events as well as their internal world (mental states such as conflict, hesitation and patience) which the participants have to go through within the Complication.

The nominal groups that construct participants have become more elaborate. For example, in '*a dark shadowy figure in front of them*', the Head, 'figure', is modified by the pre-modifier 'a dark shadowy' and the post-modifier 'in front of them' which is a prepositional phrase. The semantic property of an unknown figure conveys the mood of suspense in this Complication. The use of Epithets such as '*dark*' and '*shadowy*' in the description of the appearance of the unknown figure further intensifies the sense of suspense.

Text B-6 written in Year 4 shows a more mature Complication element, compared with the previous examples by attempting a multi-Complication text, combining an increased number of Evaluative elements and engaging temporal marked Themes.

Table 3-14: Jinha's Complication of Text B-6

Title: Fantasy Story	(Year 4, Age 9:4)
In a blink of an eye, it started launching missiles at us. We quickly hid in a safe place and some police started shooting at it with their guns. Luckily the creature escaped and no people died. We heard on the news people in Africa and Asia have reported about the same creature. It had known to be called 'mega snap'. There was one major question. Was it evil...? The next day a plane saw the creature and that Mega snap bit that plane's wing off! Now this was getting deadly serious. That same night the people switch on the spotlights to look for the Mega snap. We didn't know where it was but this meant one thing, war! The next day the general of the army sent an interplanetary spy to look and destroy the creature. Now it was pretty obvious that this creature was evil.	

In terms of the schematic structure, for the first time Jinha attempts to compose a chain of Complications (more than one Complication), also engaging an increased number of Evaluation elements in the Complication of Text B-6. In the process of identifying the unknown creature, there is an initial attack resulting in no harm to anybody and there is a subsequent event introduced by the phrase '*The next day*'. The above underlined clauses construct the elements of Evaluation which produce the effects of building up cumulative tension in the process of identifying what the unknown creature is. Most clauses are composed by relational processes and existential processes, which marks a difference from the earlier written texts. By these Evaluative clauses interspersed within the Complication, the writer creates suspense and builds up a sense of tension. There is an alteration in the material events and the mental plane of activity as well. The physical activity gets suspended, and the reader is invited to engage with the participants' reaction towards the events. This is a significant sign of maturity in Narrative writing (Toolan, 1988; Bruner, 1986).

In terms of thematic structure in the Complication of Text B-6, the Themes as the starting point for messages are mostly related to the temporal locations (largely to do with temporal sequencing) such as '*in a blink of an eye*', '*the next day*', '*that same night*' and again '*the next day*'. They appear to play an important role in signaling the beginning of the next move or event that may bring about a change in the stage of Complication. Another Theme choice is '*luckily*' which is a circumstantial adverb as a marked topical Theme (written originally as 'luckylily'; *Luckylily the creature escaped and no people died*). 'Luckily' successfully signals that the initial attack (Complication 1) is solved without any trouble. So the Complication Text B-6, as a whole text level, allows the readers to make predictions with regard to further developments by engaging temporal marked Themes along with Evaluative elements interspersed between the events.

The following Complication in Text B-8 shows Jinha's growing control of constructing the semantic property of Complication through use of dialogic exchange. Through this Complication text we will see how successfully Jinha has used the Mood system as well as Transitivity systems in building up the sense of conflict and urgency.

Table 3-15: Jinha's Complication of Text B-8

Title: Blood Plague	(Year 4, Age 9:11)
One day, on December the 19th, a disease got into the heart. "White blood cell, come and help fight the	
disease." pleaded the red blood cell. "Oh, shut up, will you? I'm trying to watch this cartoon!" said the	
White blood cell. In his dream, one day he heard a man's voice. 'White blood cell, if you don't help fight the disease, the heart will die. So therefore you	

86

> will die as well. It is your choice.' White blood cell woke up startled. "I have
> a mission to complete" With that, the While blood cell raced over to the heart
> and mumbled a few words and all of a sudden, "pop!" and he was inside the
> heart. He had a sword in his hand. He marched over the disease fearlessly and
> said, "Disease, you shall be destroyed!" "Ha! You can't destroy me! Prepare
> to die!" "Clang, clang! Clang! Arrrrrrrrrrrrrrrr!" The White blood cell with a
> lot of stabbed the disease in the chest. As if by magic, the disease started to
> disappear.

At a text level Text B-8 successfully uses the dialogic
exchange to build up the field of the protagonist's heroic
battle (the White Blood Cell's battle with the Disease in the
heart). In the beginning of the Complication there is
discordance between the protagonists, the White Blood Cell
and the Red Blood Cell as they help to fight the villain as in
'the disease in the heart'. The sense of conflict between the
participants is vividly demonstrated by the conversation,
particularly as in 'Oh, shut up! Will you?'. The protagonist's
reaction to the Red Blood Cell's appeal is a strong rejection
which is constructed through the use of the imperative mood
(Shut up!) followed by an interrogative mood clause in 'Will
you?' which is typically used as an interrogative clause (that
of asking a question), but which functions here to modify or
slightly soften the command to shut up.

After that a mysterious man appears in the protagonist's
dream and makes a sort of warning. The events are all
constructed in declarative mood clauses. At this point the
readers would predict that the mysterious man might play an
important role in changing the state of the protagonist's
stubbornness about the issue in question. In other words,
through the dialogic expression, we can follow how the
protagonist has changed his mind before getting into another
series of physical actions. The mysterious experience is
followed by the protagonist's definite declaration 'I have a
mission to complete'. This is an interior monologue which
reveals that the protagonist's inner conflict has finally been
resolved. The remainder of the Complication in Text B-8 is
also composed of another conversation between the
protagonist and the villain. The protagonist's other
declaration, 'You shall be destroyed!', is a declarative clause
using modality; 'shall' whereas classified as a 'temporal'
(future) finite verbal operator in the Mood system (Halliday,

1994: 76) here seems to be used as a modal operator (see 'will' – 'median' modal operator). As a whole, in Text B-8 Jinha explores the interpersonal dimension of Narrative. The dialogic exchanges between the participants quite strongly relate the conflict and power struggle between the two. The tension in the dialogue, which intensifies the crisis, is constructed through the choices in the Mood and Modality system, in addition to the choice in Transitivity (as noted in relation to his earlier texts).

At the clause level, Text B-8 is composed of material processes representing the participants' action movements such as *'help, shut up, fight, die, woke up, raced, destroy, marched, stabbed and disappear'* as well as verbal processes projecting the participants' internal states such as *'pleaded, said and mumbled'*. What seems significant is that the child uses a range of material processes that helps construct the field of fight (e.g. *fight, die, destroy, stabbed*). Lexical choice is important here. To construct the sense of movement different material processes are used (e.g. *raced, marched, disappeared*). According to Rothery (1990: 224), in Complication the role of 'Actor' is mostly realized by material processes and, in this regard, a range of material processes related to participants' action in Complication can be a sign of mature writing. In the meantime, in this Complication different meanings are constructed through the use of relational processes: there are three examples of relational processes representing the participants' current status as in '*I have a mission to complete* (intention), *He was inside the heart* (location: space), *he had a sword in his hand* (possession)'.

The last example of Complication in Text B-10 demonstrates Jinha's increased a control of writing Complication in his ability to orchestrate important elements such as the use of the Theme system, more elaborate Evaluation, the Transitivity system, the use of embedded nominal groups and, lastly, the flexible positioning of adverbial as modal adjunct.

Table 3-16: Jinha's Complication of Text B-10

Title: Remote Control	(Year 5, Age 10:3)

At first I thought having a remote control that could control even humans was very fascinating and so I brought it along to school. That's when matters started to get out of hand. Firstly, I got it confiscated for fiddling with it in class. And then a boy made a smart remark about me having to bring a remote control. In class and then everybody started cracking up. When I finally got it back I slipped into the canteen to get something to eat. I purposely froze the canteen manager and unfroze her again. Then just for fun I froze another kid and nicked off with his food. After class, at lunchtime, I decided to beat up the bullies in the whole school. They were called Jack, Sharky and Jake. They were all one year older than me and they had bashed me up tones of times and I am paying back. So I called them out to the soccer field. They came and I bravely said, "come on fight me!" and they charged at me as if they were mad bulls. In the blink of an eye I whipped out my remote and pressed the pause button at them. But it didn't work! Just then I saw that the batteries had run out. Sweat was tickling down my face. Just as they were about to charge into me....

In this Complication (Text B-10), Jinha seems to have driven the story event to the problematic corner by developing the field of 'trying out the power of the mysterious remote control'. In a sense, Jinha has attempted to construct a major problem along with minor ones (as emerging multi-Complications and Resolutions) in this text. Before facing the main problem of the school bullies, the protagonist goes through the trial-out of the strange remote control on another participant, the canteen manager. In escalating the troublesome mood Jinha uses many temporal adverbial groups throughout the text as marked topical Themes such as 'at first', 'firstly', 'then', 'after class', 'in the blink of an eye' and 'just then'. The sense of crisis gets increased with the change in conjunctive relations – from temporal (both explicit and implicit) to contrastive ('but') as well as the use of the negative polarity in the Mood system ('*But it didn't work!*'), which highlights the disparity between what would have been expected and what actually is. At this point, the sense of crisis rises to its flood mark and tension has been built up.

Another significant feature of the Complication in Text B-10 at text level is that it contains a good example of an Evaluation element as in '*At first I thought having a remote control that could control even humans was very fascinating and so I brought it along to school.*' The protagonist's dangerous thought about the remote control is clearly revealed in these underlined clauses that are located at the very beginning of the Complication stage. This Evaluation element of the Complication stage works to help the readers to build up the initial expectation for the forthcoming events.

In Transitivity, this Complication is mostly composed of material processes (*brought, got it confiscated, started cracking up, slipped, froze, unfroze, nicked off, charged, whipped out, bashed up, pressed, run out and tickling down*), interspersed with mental processes (*thought, decided, saw*) and relational processes as in '*was very fascinating*' and '*as if they were mad bulls*' (to identify the bullies and the protagonist's judgment of these). The interspersed mental processes highlight the significance of the forthcoming events by revealing the protagonist's inner state. The relational processes also serve to confine the protagonist's plotting and the bullies' reaction so that the readers can predict the forthcoming event or can be engaged in the climax of the Complication with the sense of urgency.

In addition, the Complication in Text B-10 is significant as it uses the resource of the nominal group structure to build the field. This Complication uses nominal groups which include rank-shifted (embedded) clauses as Qualifiers following after the Things in the nominal group structure (experiential structure of the nominal group, the Thing underlined in the examples below).

(a) a   remote control   [[that could control even human]]
    Deictic + Thing +   Qualifier
                                Material Process + Goal

(b) a   smart   remark   [about me]   [[having to bring a remote control in class]]
    Deictic + Epithet + Thing + Qualifier 1 (phrase) + Qualifier 2 (clause)
                                Range   Material process + Goal + Range

(c) the   bullies   [in the whole school]
    Deictic + Thing +   Qualifier (phrase)

Note that [[ ]] signifies an embedded clause, finite or non-finite; [ ] signifies an embedded phrase (or group).

Another sign of the child's written language development

demonstrated in this text is the use of adverbs in the clause. Commonly, young writers locate the circumstantial adverbs in the beginning of the clause as a marked topical Theme. According to Perera (1984: 223), the location of this circumstantial adverb between the Subject and Predicate, thus functioning as a modal Adjunct in the Mood system, is considered to be a sign of more mature writers.[20] Thus in '*When I finally got it back*' and '*I purposely froze the canteen manager*' and '*I bravely said*', Jinha uses the circumstantial adverbs between the Subjects and Predicates to reveal the protagonist's intention (purposely) and attitude (bravely) as well as signaling the turning point of the move within the context (finally).

Overall, the Complication of Text B-10 can be considered as an example of more mature writing. Thus, Jinha successfully uses an interweaving of adverbial marked Themes throughout the whole text in order to create the temporal sequence with the sense of urgency. As to the schematic structure, there emerge multi-Complications and Evaluative elements to emphasize the significance of the main Complication. Secondly, at the clause level, the use of mental and relational process types along with a majority of material process effectively represents the inner and outer world of the protagonist and identifies the villain's status. The mental processes particularly, allow the readers to interpret the forthcoming Complication by following the protagonist's thought and decision. Lastly, below the clause level, this text shows use of complicated nominal groups, which is a sign of more mature writing. Further evidence of the child's growth in control of writing is found in use of adverbs as the Modal Adjunct in the Mood system.

---

[20] More accurately, Perera (1984: 223) cited Yerrill's (1977) report that "older children show more flexibility in the positioning of adverbials and will sometimes insert one between subject and verb." That means if children begin to attempting more flexibility in positioning adverbials, (not always foregrounding them), it will be a sign of mature writing. Perera's book called 'Children's Writing and Reading; Analyzing Classroom Language' includes valuable chapters for study on children's writing development – particularly, Chapter 4 (Some Differences between Speech and Writing) and Chapter 5 (Children's Writing) are very informative for language teaching.

3.1.4. Evaluation

The element of Evaluation in the Complication stage has been considered as evidence of the children's growing control of Narrative writing in terms of its schematic organization.[21]

---

[21] To use Rothery's definition, Evaluation is the obligatory stage where the events being related "are evaluated and thus given significance so that they are perceived as Complication and Resolution" (Rothery, 1990: 203). That means, without the Evaluative elements, the Narrative events can fall flat like a boring sequence of story events. Also Rothery (1990) points out that Evaluation can be a discrete element of the generic structure, or it can be interspersed with Complication. Even though, among scholars, there hasn't been any consensus on ultimately distinctive or prescriptive boundary what elements can be Evaluative ones, there exist several guidelines or general concepts for the criteria of Evaluation elements among many scholars. At first, Rothery (1990: 203) provides us with the following semantic properties of Evaluation which can be condensed as the functions of highlighting unusuality and making predictions:

- the expression of attitudes or opinions denoting the events as remarkable and unusual;
- the expression of incredulity, disbelief, apprehension about the events on the part of the narrator or a character of the Narrative, including highlighting the predicament of characters;
- comparisons between usual and unusual sequences of events in which participants in the Narrative are involved;
- predictions about possible courses of action to handle a crisis or about the outcome of the events.

As shown above, Rothery's semantic properties of Evaluative elements are very consonant with the interpersonal meanings which are constructed through revealing characters' attitudes (i.e. anxiety, confusion and fear) and reactions to the unusual or unexpected events. In other words, the semantic properties of Evaluative elements can be realized by foregrounding interpersonal meanings "so that the experiential meanings of the Complication and Resolution stages are seen to be significant and memorable" (Rothery, 1990: 203). As to the concrete methods of realization of such Evaluative elements, we also need to consider Bruner's "Dual perspectives" and "the effect of Subjectivising" in connection with the usage of mental process mostly reflecting participants' states of consciousness (1986). He defines the "Subjectification" as the depiction of reality not through an omniscient eye that views a timeless reality, but through the filter of the consciousness of protagonist's in the story (Bruner, 1986: 25). That is, the writer's description of the participants' inner world using metal processes engages the readers' empathy more effectively than in the case of Complication composed of mainly material aspects. Moreover, this "Dual perspectives" in which the readers can experience the Complication events through the protagonist's eyes and thoughts as well as the reader's special position which can involve an awareness of some important information which is not available to the protagonist, will heightens the sense of suspense and the degree of the reader's empathy.

With regard to the usage of mental processes which can contribute to creating the effect of subjectification, Jinha's Complication texts demonstrate that from the early grades (Years 2-3), he quite successfully attempts to include Evaluative elements using mental processes as in 'he thought it was yam' (Text B-1), 'I heard something crack' (Text B-2), 'I saw that the toilet had moved again!' (Text B-2), 'But when I was thinking (Text B-4)' and 'Just then Michael saw a red button' (Text B-4).

Another semantic property of Evaluation, that of "presupposition", emerges in Jinha's Narrative. Along with the unusuality, this can be realized by the usage of

Jinha's later Narratives (Years 4-5, age 9-10) demonstrate development of the Evaluation element. There emerge clauses using relational and existential processes as in '*there was one major question. Was it evil...?*', '*Now this was getting deadly serious.*', '*We didn't know where it was but this meant one thing, war!*', and '*Now it was pretty obvious that this creature was evil*". In the process of describing the unknown creature Jinha experiments with another way to realize the Evaluative element this time she uses attributive and existential processes rather than mental processes, and successfully builds up the cumulative tension, thus maintaining the readers' curiosity. Jinha's later Narrative writing also begins to feature dialogic exchange used in the Complication stage, in order to highlight the sense of unusuality and urgency. To construct Evaluation, Jinha uses a range of interpersonal choices, in the Mood system, such as imperative and interrogative mood choices and modal operators as in '*Oh, shut up, will you?*', '*Disease, you shall be destroyed!*' and '*Prepare to die!*'

Finally, the Evaluation in the child's Narratives comes to mark the crisis point of a Narrative through semantic properties which refer either to the preceding events in the text, those of the Complication stage, or to the events that are likely to follow, those of the Resolution (Rothery, 1990: 203), as is demonstrated in Text B-10:

Table 3-17: Extract from Complication of Text B-10

At first, I thought having a remote control that could control even humans was very fascinating and so I brought it along to school.

From the above Evaluative comment the readers can predict that the protagonist's dangerous thought might be realized in some ways soon. At the same time the readers can guess that the protagonist will realize the wrongness of his idea and that he might reconsider it later on. That means this

---

mental processes. Thus in 'and soon the wildlife will be doomed!' (Text B-4), 'just as they thought they were safe' and 'Carrot couldn't stand it' (Text B-5), the writer makes the readers predict what will be happening in the next stage as well as building up the sense of urgency and crisis. These examples, in a sense, can be explained as an embryonic attempt at a "Dual perspectives" in which the writer allows the readers to know some facts regarding the forthcoming crisis that are not available to the participants, while at the same time the readers can get involved in the events through the eyes of the protagonists.

Evaluative element in the Complication stage can be referred to the Resolution stage in terms of the semantic property of 'presupposition'. With respect to the 'presupposition' which can be one of the crucial features of the Evaluation element, it is noticed that more mature writers are able to build up the semantic property of 'presupposition' in rather implicit ways so that the readers are allowed to enjoy the uncertainty of a range of possible presuppositions. In Jinha's Narrative texts these presuppositions as Evaluative elements are realized explicitly so that the readers will be able to predict the forthcoming events with certainty. The ability to construct an Evaluative element which would have the property of 'presupposition' appears to be a sign of a mature Narrative writer.

3.1.5. Resolution

According to Rothery (1990: 210), the semantic property of Resolution is defined as "the Resolution of the crisis developed in Complication, changing the course of events from 'unusality' to 'usuality'". In other words, the problem part of Complication must find some way of being resolved in the final stage of Narrative so that it does not make the readers feel frustrated or angry at the end. Also, for a more satisfying and mature Resolution, as Rothery (1990) argues, it is important that the Resolution of a crisis is achieved through the active intervention of the protagonist, not through just by chance. Jinha's Narrative texts demonstrate his growing awareness of this necessity for the protagonist to be active in resolving the problem. We will consider Jinha's construction of the Resolution in Narrative over Years 2 through 5 (age 7-11), to see how this has developed over time.

Jinha's Resolution of Text B-1 shows that the protagonist's problem (he didn't like vegetables) is solved without any purposeful efforts or any deliberate action on his part. The problem gets resolved just by coincidence which happens naturally in the situation.

TABLE OF CONTENTS

Table 3-18: Jinha's Resolution of Text B-1

	(Year 2, Age 7:4)
From then on he liked vegetables.	

Even though the marked Theme as in 'From then on' foregrounds the turning point of the protagonist's changing the eating habit, the whole Resolution does not seem to be effectively appealing to the readers. The use of mental process of affect does not provide for a satisfying Resolution.[22] A more distinctive Complication-Resolution pattern can be found in the next Resolution.

Table 3-20: Jinha's Resolution of Text B-4

Title: The UFO	(Year 4, Age 8:4)
So Michael got a stick and threw it to the button. It hit and boom! The lights turned off and the five elements shot out and hit the spaceship and the bomb amazingly disappeared! And at the end we saved the wildlife!	

In the Resolution of Text B-4 the crisis gets resolved by the protagonist's (Michael) active efforts (acts of bravery). The effect of Resolution is maximized because the crisis itself had been developed effectively in the stage of Complication. The marked Theme as in '*And at the end*' signals that all the problems have been resolved and signals return to usuality. As is the expectation of the Resolution stage, material processes (*got, threw, hit, boom, turned off, shot out and disappeared*) are dominant in expressing the end of the battle with the spaceship.

A similar pattern of grammar use occurs in Resolution of

---

[22] The following Resolution of Text B-3 (Year 3, age 8) can also be considered as Jinha's initial attempt at the stage of Resolution in the sense that it also does not include the element of a more satisfying Resolution achieved by the protagonist's deliberate action or efforts:

Table 3-19: Jinha's Resolution of Text B-3

Title: A Scruffy Dog called Ragbag	(Year 3, Age 8:3)
But when I came 1 hour later, I saw he was digging in the garden. What a naughty dog!	

The Resolution element itself is likely to be linked with Orientation in which Ragbag (the dog's name) is introduced as a troublesome dog making a lot of mess, and, in a sense, the readers can attain a feeling that in the stage of Resolution, the crisis for the dog who has been sent out of the house is back to normal (usuality). But, as in 'What a naughty dog!', the exclamatory clause reflects a strong feeling of the protagonist 'I' that is to accept the hopeless naughty dog without any other choice.

Text B-5, where the protagonists (vegetables) realize their bravery against 'the human' by determination and subsequent active actions:

Table 3-21: Jinha's Resolution of Text B-5

Title: Run Away Vegetable!	(Year 3, Age 8:6)
In a blink of an eye, he poked the human! The human ran off in pain and anger and never came back again.	

As in '*In a blink of an eye*', the marked Theme choice signals that something unexpected will be occurring in an urgent manner and that event can be a turning point in resolving the problem in the Complication. The use of a sequence of material processes in the system of Transitivity constructs an active action of the protagonist, and the resulting defeat and retreat of the 'baddies'. The use of marked topical Themes in the Resolution stage is important for construction of a satisfying Resolution of a problem. Jinha's later Narrative texts demonstrate his beginning to take up this thematic choice. Thus he begins to put in thematic position circumstantial phrases as well as other temporal conjunctives introducing temporal clauses (underlined below).

Table 3-22: Jinha's Resolution of Text B-6

Title: Fantasy Story	(Year 4, Age 9:4)
When the spy had found Mega snap, they fought and fought. At the end the trees were all ashes there was fire everywhere and the spy had died but the good news was that Mega snap had	

The above Resolution in Text B-6 is incomplete, but it reveals the child's attempt to write up the Resolution as restoration of 'usuality' in this Narrative. The underlined thematic choices, including a hypotactic temporal choice as in '*When the spy had found*', seem to contribute in building up the mood of settling down the Complication.

Further control of thematic choices in the Resolution stage is revealed in Text B-8 which otherwise involves a typical conventional happy ending of 'lived happily ever after'. Particularly in this text, the underlined clause as thematic equative should be considered as an evidence of Jinha's growing control of thematic choices.

Table 3-23: Jinha's Resolution of Text B-8

Title: Blood Plague	(Year 4, Age 9:11)
And the next thing the white blood cell knew was he was standing next to the heart. The red blood cell came over and said, "Thanks! Without you we couldn't survive." So they became good friends and live happily ever after.	

Halliday (1994: 41) explains the concept of "thematic equative" as follows:

> In a thematic equative, all the elements of the clause are organized into two constitutes; these two are then linked by a relationship of identity, a kind of 'equals sign', expressed by some form of the verb be.

In '*The next thing the white blood cell knew was he was standing next to the heart*', the Theme is 'the next thing the white blood cell knew' and the remainder 'was he was standing next to the heart' is the Rheme. A form such as 'the next thing the white blood cell knew' is an example known as "nominalization", whereby an element or group of elements is made to function as a nominal group in the clause (Halliday, 1994: 41). In this case, the nominalization serves a thematic purpose as the prominent element in the clause. Successful usage of nominalization as thematic equative can be claimed as a sign of more mature writing since it makes the readers concentrate their attention on the message more clearly and strongly due to the distinctive structure of Theme-Rheme division. By using the thematic equative structure, writers can adjust the emphasis as thematic message. That young writers have started to use such a thematic equative structure in their writing is a remarkable sign as it allows them greater control in emphasizing a specific point as a prominent message.

Another example of the thematic equative is found in the Resolution of Text B-10: '*that's when I realized I had fallen asleep on the couch clutching our old remote control.*' In this case, the usual relationship is reversed and the long complex clause as in 'when I realized I had fallen asleep on the couch clutching our old remote control' becomes the Rheme. This reversed pattern serves accordingly as a standing-out or marked thematic equative.

Table 3-24: Jinha's Resolution of Text B-10

Title: Remote Control	(Year 5, Age 10:3)
"Wake up! Sleepy head!" that's when I realized I had fallen asleep on the couch clutching our old remote control. 'Phew! It was just a dream." I just noticed what the T.V was advertising. It was a remote control that could control everything. With this I put down the remote control and said to myself 'I don't need that anymore, I've got my hands that I can rely on' and turned off the T.V with my own hands and gave a relieved smile.	

The Resolution of Text B-10 uses another typical conventional pattern of restoration of usuality in the part of Resolution, by waking up the protagonist from his nightmare as in *'Wake up! Sleepy head'*. That means it is time to go back to normal. This Resolution starts with an imperative mood of Mum's shouting as in *'Wake up!'*, signaling to return to the normal life. Such a beginning pattern in this Resolution is significantly in parallel with the start of Orientation in this Narrative, in which mum gave an unpleasant lecture to the protagonist. The protagonist's monologue, *'I don't need that anymore. I've got my hands that I can rely on'*, reveals the change in his thinking which is linked with the protagonist's previous thought about the remote control in the Complication; *'At first I thought having a remote control that could control even human was very fascinating and so I brought it along to school.'* So, at a text level, this Resolution can be considered an example of a more mature writing in the sense that the writer quite successfully uses an embryonic Foreshadowing technique, some Evaluative elements and a recycling or repeating technique.

Additionally, this text makes use of more complicated nominal groups including the above mentioned 'thematic equative' one. Thus in *'what the T.V was advertising'*, *'a remote control that could control everything'* and *'my hands that I can rely on'*, the head nouns are followed by a defining relative clause. Considering all the above analysis, the Resolution of Text B-10 is the most developed of all Resolutions in Jinha's Narrative texts.

3.1.6. Summary of Jinha's Narrative Writing

So far we have examined Jinha's increasing control of Narrative writing from Year 1 to Year 5 by selecting some sample texts of each year and analyzing them at each stage of Narrative generic structure. As shown through the text analysis, overall over the five years, Jinha has developed a range of written language in building up the semantic properties of Narrative writing. Particularly, his Year 5 Narrative writing shows a remarkable growth in orchestrating important features of Narrative writing. In this section, we shall finally summarize our thoughts on his growth in control of each specific aspect of Narrative writing such as 'the Schematic Structure of Narrative', 'Transitivity', 'Nominal Groups', 'Theme' and 'Mood'.

Control of the Schematic Structure of Narrative
Firstly, in regard to the Orientation stage in which the story context is created in respect of settings, participants and their behavioural situation, Jinha's attempts at using conventional expressions such as '*Once upon a time*' or '*One day*' in the beginning period had been getting more specific as time passed. Compared to the other stages (Complication or Resolution), the Orientation element seems to be successful in following some conventional patterns. From Year 4 Jinha attempts more varied styles of Orientation such as dialogue style and, later on, first person perspective novel type (in Year 5). He successfully introduces or personalizes characters in the Narratives by using dialogue exchanges. In addition, and more importantly, his awareness of the element of 'Foreshadowing' can be traced in his Narrative writing.

In specific regard to the Complication stage in which the effect of suspense or sense of crisis is built, Jinha's early Narratives show immaturity in constructing the semantic property of Complication, with some initial texts lacking the distinctive features of the Complication. However, from Year 3, there emerge Evaluative elements which give significance to the Complication events and begin to expand the range of its realization through use of mental processes, relational processes and the technique of 'Dual perspective' and 'presupposition'. In Year 4, more mature Complication elements can be found including a chain of Complications and dialogic exchanges. Finally in Year 5, he is able to construct an overall quite competent Text B-10 in which multiple Evaluative elements are interspersed in building cumulative sense of crisis successfully (although still in a rather explicit manner).

Finally, whereas in earlier texts the problem gets resolved without active efforts of the protagonists, from Year 3, the Resolution becomes more effectively constructed. The sense of crisis gets overcome and the usuality is restored due to active intervention of the protagonists. Sometimes he uses typical conventional happy endings to restore usuality (Text B-8 and B-10). Particularly in Text B-10, the attempt to link the Foreshadowing element in the Orientation and the Evaluative ones in the Complication and Resolution in the parallel pattern is successfully implemented.

Transitivity

In constructing the experiential meaning of Field, Jinha has employed a broadening range of process types throughout his Narrative texts. In particular, in the Orientation he demonstrates an ability to construct both an existential context mainly using existential processes and a behavioural situation, with mostly material processes in his initial texts. Along with the choices of process types, he has expanded his repertoire of circumstantial usages by prepositional phrase and non-finite dependent clauses in order to elaborate or specify temporal and location settings. Over time, his usage of mental processes and attributive relational processes has increased; and from Year 5, verbal processes along with material processes come to be successfully used in construction of the semantic property of the Orientation stage.

In the Complication of the earlier texts, process types are mostly material, mental and relational ones. In Text B-4, some verbal processes are used symbolically as a signal of starting a metaphorical expression. The external world of actions and internal world (inner states) are largely depicted through a range of material and mental processes. Finally, in Text B-10, the three process types of material, mental and relational come to be employed successfully in constructing the sense of urgency in the Complication. In the Resolution stage, the semantic property of restoring usuality is realized mainly by material processes, along with interspersed mental processes (*realized, noticed, rely on*: Text B-10) and identifying relational processes (related to the thematic equative patterns: Texts B-6, B-8, B-10).

Nominal Groups

In line with the range of process and circumstantial choices, the description of participants (e.g. Actor, Goal, Phenomenon, Senser) is realized mostly by the nominal groups. In Jinha's Narrative texts, his developing control of the nominal group structure has been analyzed tracing through each stage. In Orientation stage texts initially he uses the simple structure of nominal group (one word, or two words) such as 'Deictic + Thing' or 'Numerative + Thing'. Then, in the Text B-3 he constructs some nominal groups using a more typical written mode as in '*Ragbag chewing on my uncle's shoe*', which have the functions of post-modifier using non-finite clause. The nominal groups tend to be less elaborate in the text segments that construct dialogic exchanges. Their purpose is to bring into text some of the spoken language flavor, and thus, they reflect more spoken mode features.

In the Complication stage texts, overall, the range of Epithets has semantically expanded to convey the mood of suspense or crisis (e.g. *a dark shadowy figure*). Also, using more complex nominal groups (embedded post-modifier, a defining relative clause) with Qualifiers has enabled him to effectively compress more information in the written mode. In the Resolution stage texts, as mentioned earlier, more complicated nominal groups using thematic equative patterns and defining relative clause are constructed. Even though the growth of control of the nominal group in Jinha's Narrative texts reflects his written language development, as different from the spoken mode, Jinha's developing control of the nominal group structure is further revealed in his factual writing, which will be explored in the next chapter.

101

Theme

In general, the choices of Themes in each stage play an important role in satisfying the purpose of the semantic properties of the Orientation, Complication and Resolution. Throughout Jinha's Narrative texts, a range of Theme choices has been selected to meet the purpose of each schematic structure. In the Orientation stage, the conventional Theme choices such as *'once upon a time'*, *'one day'*, and *'one million years ago'* are chosen in the opening clauses in the earlier texts, becoming more varied to include unmarked topical Themes (*I, they, it, someone*) and textual Themes (*just then, in addition, but*) and interpersonal Themes (in dialogic exchanges). In the Complication stage, in order to create the sequence of events in an urgent manner, Jinha uses temporal connective words including structural conjunctions (*so, and, but, then*) as marked Themes in the earlier texts. Then, to create the mood of 'emergency', a marked clause Theme (e.g. *just as the knife went down*) or a marked prepositional phrase (e.g. *in a blink of an eye*) come to be selected in many cases. Also the marked adverbial group Themes which are largely related to the temporal locations contributed to signaling the next movement or bringing in a change. In Text B-10 (Year 5), particularly, temporal adverbial groups and structural conjunctions as marked Themes such as *'at first'*, *'firstly'*, *'then'*, *'after class'*, *'just then'* and *'in the blink of an eye'* cumulate the sense of urgency, and by the use of the negative conjunction *'but'* at the end of the Complication stage the sense of crisis successfully reaches its flood mark.

Finally, in the Resolution stage, some adverbial phrase Themes (e.g. *in a blink of an eye*) are used to provide a turning point in the resolution of the problem in Complication. Circumstantial clause Theme as in *'When the spy had found'* contributes to building up the mood of settling down the Complication. Lastly, and very importantly, in Jinha's Resolution element in Years 4 and 5, emerge thematic equative cases, which enables the writer to control his emphatic point in the Theme structure (e.g. *And the next thing the white blood cell knew was ...*). This can be evaluated as an evidence of more mature writing.

Mood

The interpersonal meanings realized by the Mood system can be mostly found in the Narrative texts (B-7, B-8) inclusive of dialogic exchanges. Throughout the range of different mood types, the area of Tenor is successfully built up. In other words, the dialogic exchanges among characters such as questioning, commanding, requesting, declaring and suggesting naturally build up the portrait of characters, including their inner conflicts; through the dialogic expressions, we can follow how the protagonist has changed his mind. In the beginning of Resolution part, an imperative mood clause '*Wake up!*' functions as signaler to return to the normal life. In addition to the range of mood clauses, Jinha demonstrated a reasonable usage of modality system mainly through auxiliary verbs (*be used to, seem to be, would, could, will, need to, shall*) and modal adverbs (*not just, never, still*): e.g. '*You shall be destroyed*' contributes to creating the sense of urgency and heroic bravery.

3.2. Sunyoung's Narrative Writing (in English)

3.2.1. The Brief Overview of Sunyoung's Narrative Writing: The Classroom and Home Context

Most of Sunyoung's Narrative writing in English was composed in the school setting, similarly to Jinha's, from Kindergarten to Year 3, but, in contrast to Jinha, Sunyoung wrote several Narratives at home as well, due to her own strong motivation and interest in story writing. During that period, Sunyoung read a great number of storybooks and novels in English at school, home and a community library. Like her brother, Sunyoung learnt basic Korean literacy from the researcher during her preschool years (from age 3 to 5) and enjoyed reading story books in Korean. Subsequently she started learning English literacy, mainly through reading books. The home environment where she spent a lot of time with her older brother Jinha seemed to have influenced her literacy development very positively, by stimulating her interest in reading and writing.

At school, from the very start (Kindergarten), Sunyoung was

exposed to writing lessons that were based mostly on Genre pedagogy (although elements of the Whole Language Approach were used in teaching reading). Over the four-year period of observed, the teachers appeared to be changing their writing pedagogy, from more Process-driven towards the use of more structured formats in teaching Narrative writing and storybook reading sessions.[23]

Initially, Sunyoung wrote stories about animals and as time passed, her story themes spread out to 'insects', 'universe' and 'family relationships', in accordance with the themes studied in school. Even though Sunyoung's storylines are not as varied as Jinha's, in general, her control of Narrative writing had been developing remarkably from her initial period (in Kindergarten) through the next year (in Year 1) up to Years 2 and 3. Her strong motivation has always led her to have many chances to practise Narrative writing at school and home as well as reading a lot of picture books, story books and novels. Roald Dahl, Judy Blume and Meg Cabot were Sunyoung's favorite novel authors who seem to have particularly influenced her Narrative writing style, in the way of constructing dialogue or using humor. In the

---

[23] Particularly, Sunyoung's class teacher (in Year 1) always prepared a range of worksheets to be handed out to students, in order to help them understand the text structure and key elements. As pre-writing activities, the worksheets were aimed to some support for the young writers in handling Narrative writing. For instance, one worksheet might have had a goal of making the students recognize the generic structure of Narrative through the explicit questions: Orientation – setting: who, when, where, what and why, Initiating Events – What began the event? How did the characters get involved? Also, in another worksheet, the students were supposed to fill in blanks even for 'multi problems, Complications and solution'. There are some other worksheets such as 'Character Grid' and 'Plot Profile' which meant to be useful for practicing each element (e.g. character, plot, Resolution) of the Narrative writing. In the worksheet titled 'Narrative Choices', more specifically the teacher could help students learn lexical items commonly used in Narrative writing through the task of choosing proper words, phrases or clauses. In this case, the young learners had a chance to familiarize themselves with phrases commonly used at the start of a sentence in Narrative, such as 'A long time ago' 'Last week' or 'in the past' for Orientation starter. Also the class teacher often handed out some sampling reading material during the Narrative writing sessions. Comparatively, Sunyoung appeared to have been given more structured lessons on Narrative writing than Jinha. Based on the researcher's classroom observation in Sunyoung's Year 1 class, the class teacher often used an overhead projector to demonstrate more effectively the content of the various worksheets, and the young writers seemed to concentrate on her teaching. At home, whenever Sunyoung wanted to write Narratives, she tried to do story-mapping activities along with some noting about characters and settings before writing up the stories. Sunyoung's numerous worksheets seem to indicate that those school works must have influenced Sunyoung's development of awareness of the Narrative structure and elements to a degree.

beginning, her Narratives were often missing the Complication stage, or had it undeveloped. The texts were short, consisting of overall 7 to 10 lines. However, after one year, from Year 1, her Narrative writing started to demonstrate more distinctive generic structure. In many cases, there were the elements of Foreshadowing and Evaluation. At the end of the period, Sunyoung was able to construct a 10 page long story which reveals advanced writing skills and expression. Now we shall explore the aspects of Sunyoung's story writing which reveal her growing control of the written Narrative form Kindergarten (age 5) through to Year 3 (age 8). First, we will examine how Sunyoung has developed her control of the schematic structure and semantic function of the Orientation stage in Narrative writing. As mentioned before, further detailed text analysis for Sunyoung's Narratives by focusing on such several aspects as the range of Theme choices, Mood system, Transitivity system and the use of nominal groups will be provided separately in Sections 3-3 (Orientation stage) and 3-4 (Complication stage).

3.2.2. The Orientation Stage in Sunyoung's Narrative Texts

The Overview of Sunyoung's Orientation Stage Focusing on her Control of Schematic Structure

Sunyoung's initial Narrative writings (age 5) tend to have extended Orientation elements along with an abrupt Complication or sometimes lacking the Complication, and a very brief Resolution. In other words, comparatively, the Orientation stage appears to be more successfully constructed than other structural stages from the early age of 5. For example, even the very first Orientation of Text BB-1 contextualizes participants, temporal setting and behavioural situation like this:

Table 3-25: Sunyoung's Orientation of Text BB-1

(Kindergarten, Age 5:3)
One day I <u>was building</u> a time machine. Because I wanted to take an adventure with the dinosaurs. When <u>I was finished</u> I <u>hoped</u> in it. Then I <u>took off</u> on my time machine. When I <u>arrived</u> I <u>got off.</u>

Note: No title was given by Sunyoung for this Narrative.

Starting with *'One day'* as temporal setting, this Orientation creates a behavioural situation mostly realized by material processes (underlined above). However, this Orientation text does not reveal the participants more effectively than the Orientation of Text BB-3 as below:

Table 3-26: Sunyoung's Orientation of Text BB-3

(Kindergarten, Age 5:9)
Once there <u>was</u> a cat and a dog. They always <u>had a fight</u>. In fact they <u>lived</u> together. Also they <u>lived</u> in a town which <u>was</u> the same as a city, and lots of ghosts <u>were hiding</u> in the town. They <u>came out</u> on some spooky nights. Near it <u>was</u> a beautiful sparkling lake.

Note: No title was given by Sunyoung for this Narrative.

As we can see, the Orientation of Text BB-3 fulfils the primary function of Orientation in the schematic structure of Narrative by creating a more descriptive context in respect of the participants (a cat and a dog, ghosts) and particularly space setting (town, lake) by providing finer detail about them.[24] In terms of Transitivity system, this text is composed of mainly three process types such as existential (e.g. *there <u>was</u> a cat and a dog, Near it <u>was</u> a beautiful lake*), relational (e.g. *which <u>was</u> the same*) and material verbs (e.g. *<u>had</u> a fight, lived, were hiding, came out*).

There are also several marked textual Themes such as *'in fact'*, *'also'* and *'near it'*. As in *'They <u>always</u> had a fight'*, *'always'* as a mood adjunct explicitly expresses the hostile relationship of the two participants in respect to interpersonal functions as well as signaling the forthcoming negative events. This can be claimed as an embryonic Foreshadowing since it makes readers predict that a kind of fighting between the participants might be happening.

---

[24] In terms of generic structure, there can be found all stages such as Orientation, Complication and Resolution more distinctively for the first time during the initial period (in Kindergarten) of Sunyoung's Narrative writing. However, except for Text BB-3, all other Narratives that were composed during Kindergarten (age 5) demonstrate that Sunyoung did not have much difficulty in constructing Orientation part mostly starting with conventional beginning words such as 'Once upon a time', 'One day' and 'One scary night' rather than concrete space setting, even though the other parts of Complication and Resolution did not seem to function as a real Narrative writing but rather made readers think like 'so what?' after their reading the Narratives to the end. For this detail, we shall go further in the section on Complication and Resolution.

During the next period of Year 1 (age 6), Sunyoung's Orientation texts appear to be quite different from those explored before. All the three example texts that belong to this period demonstrate more semantically extended Orientations so that readers can construct the concerned field (context) inclusive of a particular setting, participants and situation building more easily. This whole context building helps familiarize the readers with particular participants or settings as well as arouse their curiosity as to what might happen next. The first example, Orientation of Text BB-6, was composed in the format of a picture book which was both written and illustrated by Sunyoung at home (in Year 1, age 6:3). The title of the picture book is 'My family'. She uses her family members as participants in this story and reconstructs some of the space setting of the house where she lived at that time:

Table 3-27: Sunyoung's Orientation of Text BB-6

Title: My Family	(Year 1, Age 6:2)
Once there was a playful girl who loved her family. Her name was Sunyoung. She had one big brother, her mum and her dad. One day she was out playing in her backyard when she saw a strange man. She didn't talk to him at all. She knew not to talk with strangers.	

As seen above, the Orientation of Text BB-6 starts with a complex clause composed of an existential process (*there was*) and a mental process of affection (*who loved*). Specifically, the principal character, the girl named Sunyoung, is introduced more effectively and conclusively in respect of the story theme or field, by using a Qualifier clause as in '*who loved her family*'. After that, a strange man, another important participant in this story is introduced along with the space setting as in '*playing in her backyard*'. As the name ('*a strange man*') implies, the entrance of a strange man conveys the sense of uneasiness and nervousness to the readers, signaling something unexpected might happen in this family. So in this regard, the above Orientation seems to have achieved its primary semantic function, that of 'Foreshadowing' the problem.

Sunyoung's Narrative texts written in Year 2 appear to be

quite different from earlier ones in many ways. Firstly, she seems to attempt writing from the first person's point of view Narratives rather than more conventional or typical folk tale style, the third person point of view ones. In other words, the narrator coincides with the main character in a Narrative writing. Out of five samples written in Year 2, four Narrative writings demonstrate the first person point of view stories that are likely to invoke more empathy from the readers. Secondly, Sunyoung starts to combine interpersonal functions in Narrative writing by using a lot of dialogic exchanges. Her Narrative texts in this period reveal her better sense of the audience and interactions between the story characters. Overall, from Year 2 onwards, Sunyoung's Narratives demonstrate noticeable development in her control of the interpersonal meanings.

Lastly, even though her Narrative texts in this period do not reveal more control of organizing schematic structure (Orientation, Complication and Resolution), there can be found a different style of Narrative writing, in a more creative way (attempting to escape from the typical and conventional way of Narratives, e.g. from formulaic expressions like 'once upon a time'). For instance, Text BB-9 is an example which combines Narrative and factual writing in a diary style and Text BB-10 is a journal style Narrative with a lot of imaginative elements. Text BB-11 is remarkable in the sense that here for the first time in her Narrative writing, Sunyoung has tried a chapter book style novel (up to chapter 10, about 4 pages long). In this period, the fields of the Narrative writings are related to the school projects (special Theme-based writing) on 'Space and Planets', 'Butterflies' and 'Friendship'. Among them, let's look at the Orientation of Text BB-10 as follows:

Table 3-28: Sunyoung's Orientation of Text BB-10

Title: Space Adventure	(Year 2, Age 7:4)
10, 9, 8, 7, 6 Here I am strapped into the seat of the swift about to blast off into outer space to where, no one knows! To have adventures and meet creatures that are only dreamed about... 5, 4, 3, 2, 1 Blast off! I travel off with my friend (Jamilee) and I enjoy watching stars. I never know where this space rocket might take me. This is my first ever space journey I ever had in my life.	

As mentioned earlier, this text is the Orientation stage of the journal style Narrative. In terms of the schematic structure, this Orientation unfolds the semantic function of Orientation by describing the protagonist's situation and excited inner feeling just before the blast off to space. There is an Evaluative element as in 'This is my first ever space journey *I ever had in my life*' using a relational process '*is*' and a Qualifier (in italics) which emphasizes the significance of the space journey.

From the following Orientation of Text BB-11, we could find out more interpersonal elements than ever before:

Table 3-29: Sunyoung's Orientation of Text BB-11

Title: The Mystery	(Year 2, Age 7:5)
Oh, no!! Sarah, a girl who was fairly smart, cried. "I lost my school homework! The teacher will ground me forever." "Gosh, what am I going to do?" Just then the phone rang. Sarah picked it up sighing. It was Sarah's best friend, Janet. She was a girl who didn't like school and who adored animals. "Oh, it's you." cried Sarah with relief. "Is my homework book there? I lost it." "Well, I lost my dog, Scamper!" They both carefully thought for a while. "Hey, you think we should have a meeting at 2:30?" "OK!" said Janet.	

Throughout the dialogic interactions between the two protagonists and Sarah's monologue, the semantic functions of the Orientation seem to be performed very sensibly in terms of the introduction of protagonists (Sarah and her best friend, Janet) and initiating the forthcoming events (trying to find out the lost dog and the homework notebook). The interpersonal meanings for acting upon others are realized through the system of Mood and Modality. The Tenor of discourse is built up by the degree of informality which is realized through the two protagonists' dialogic exchanges. Even though there is an explicit reference to the social relationship between the two protagonists, Sarah and Janet, as in '*Sarah's best friend Janet*', Sarah's attitude and the degree of affection toward Janet are also effectively supported by the Mood system and Modality as in '*Oh, it's you.*' and '*Hey, you think we should have a meeting at 2:30?*'.

The Orientation of Texts BB-14 to BB-18 written in Year 3 provides evidence of some distinctive growth in terms of Sunyoung's control of the Narrative schematic structure. Out of several points, the element of Foreshadowing has to be highlighted the most. Compared with earlier Orientation texts, Sunyoung appears to have developed or extended her semantic function of Orientation to building up the sense of unusuality and giving some hints about forthcoming events in more implicit ways. Another point is that even in the Orientation stage, Sunyoung seems to include 'Evaluative elements' which can link semantically to the subsequent stages of Complication and Resolution and can perform important roles in building up significant meanings later on in Narrative.[25] The following first example Text BB-14 shows that Sunyoung has tried to construct the field of the protagonist's unwanted space trip along with the sense of situational inevitability:

Table 3-30: Sunyoung's Orientation of Text BB-14

Title: Hannah's Space Trip	(Year 3, Age 8:1)
Hannah was a little girl. She was only 7 and she loved trips. But she hated space. One sunny day Hannah was reading when the door bell rang. A big postman waited impatiently at the door. Hannah raced outside where her parents were reading a message out loud. The headline said 'SPACE' in big black letters. Before Hannah could complain, her mother said, "Hannah, look, it's a draw to have a trip to space!" Hannah half smiled and half frowned. "Everyone is to draw!" winked Hannah's mum. Hannah groaned and faced the wall.	

Even though this Narrative writing was not completed to the Resolution stage, Sunyoung appears to have explored a more novel style of opening, where experiential meanings and interpersonal meanings are combined. The social relationship between Hannah and her mother is revealed through the way of Hannah's mum's suggesting (Mood system) as well as a wide range of behavioural process types such as *'half smiled and half frowned'*, *'winked'*, *'groaned'* and *'faced the wall'*. In a sense, Hannah's attitude to her mum is also displayed along with Hannah's reaction to her mum's suggesting about joining the draw for the space trip. The Orientation helps the readers build up the context for the Narrative writing and helps arouse their curiosity as to what Hannah's final decision and forthcoming events might be. The following Orientation of Text BB-16, which was composed in relation to the special theme of 'Myth' at

---

[25] In this regard, Rothery (1990) explains about 'Evaluative comments' in Complication and common in Resolution but not in Orientation.

school (in Year 3, term 2), is another example of more mature Orientation text in terms of schematic structure:

Table 3-31: Sunyoung's Orientation of Text BB-16

Title: Fred	(Year 3, Age 8:5)
I listened to the rain drumming on my roof. 'Bang'. <u>The silence</u> was broken by a roar. I turned on the light and stared at the atmosphere around me. <u>Sitting under my fireplace</u> was a rather sooty crocodile. 'Er, Hi!' I whispered under my breath. He stared at me with two glary eyes. 'Are you a crocodile?' I asked taking an awfully big risk. He snarled and flapped his huge wings ferociously. 'Oh, No. I had just met an angry dragon.' I wanted to scream. <u>But only</u> a whisper came out. 'Not a dragon. Especially at midnight!' I pinched myself hoping this would be a terrible dream. <u>But still</u>, I stayed where I was, with this dragon...	

As seen above, this Orientation is similar to the previous example, Text BB-14, which well combines experiential and interpersonal meanings. However, in this Orientation, the field creation looks more powerful than in the previous text. In constructing the field in Text BB-16, the writer uses a more effective description of the setting and the unknown creature. In order to construct mysterious and scary mood and setting, Sunyoung uses a range of material and behavioural processes as well as marked textual and topical Themes such as *'But only'*, *'But still'*, *'The silence'* and *'Sitting under my fireplace'*. Also several cases of complex non-finite verbs and nominal groups contribute significantly to creating a more descriptive atmosphere and the sense of uneasiness and fear in the process of identification of the unknown scary and unexpected creature. The use of nominal groups and complex verbs will be addressed in further detail in Section 3-3 (Section 3-3-2 and 3-3-4) and Section 3-4 (Section 3-4-2 and 3-4-4). In line with the Orientation of Text BB-16, there is a text which was written in the third person point of view, similarly building the field of a 'mythical creature' as follows:

Table 3-32: Sunyoung's Orientation of Text BB-17

Title: Cub	(Year 3, Age 8:5)
On a cathedral, a little gargoyle was watching the city below him. He <u>used to be</u> scared of heights but now his hobby <u>was</u> to hang on a wall, or even better high one. The gargoyle's name <u>was called</u> "Cub". It <u>was</u> a pity that people <u>called</u> him 'Cub' because it <u>wasn</u>'t a scary name like 'Blood Thriller' or something along those lines. Cub <u>hated</u> his name. He would do anything to	

change it! Another thing, why didn't he <u>have</u> legs like humans? Cub <u>got</u> so bored thinking about his name, he fell asleep.

In this Orientation, the protagonist 'Cub' is introduced mostly by using mental and relational process types (see the underlined above). The choices within the modality system are also important here, as in '*he would do*...' (which shows Cub's strong intention to have his name changed), and '*he used to*...' (which describes his habitual predisposition in the past). The semantic function of the Orientation of introducing the main characters along with the temporal and space setting is effectively realized in this text, through the contrast between the former and the present personalities of the protagonist. This contrast aspect may help readers anticipate the forthcoming events by knowing that the protagonist is not satisfied with himself only watching the city below like a timid creature (without actually doing anything brave).

Some clauses to provide more significant meaning to the whole situation surrounding the protagonist can be viewed as Evaluative elements: as in '*It was a pity that people called him 'Cub' because it wasn't a scary name like 'Blood Thriller' or something along those lines*' and '*Cub hated his name*', '*He would do anything to change it!*' and '*Another thing, why didn't he have legs like human?*'. The protagonist's dissatisfaction with living as a little gargoyle is quite effectively constructed. This can be linked to the following parts of Complication and Resolution where the gargoyle's heroic action manifests itself and so contrasts with the powerlessly looking gargoyle in the Orientation stage. So, in terms of her control of the Narrative schematic structure, the Orientation in Sunyoung's Narrative texts demonstrates significant development over the four year period, due to the emergence and growing sophistication of the way she constructs Foreshadowing and Evaluation.

The last text to be considered in this section, which was composed at home in Year 3, is quite remarkable as it reveals Sunyoung's significant growth in control of Narrative writing.[26]

Table 3-33: Sunyoung's Orientation of Text BB-18

Title: Face to Face with a Santa Claus	(Year 3, Age 8:6)

Chris was 8 years old and still believed in Santa Claus. Nothing could ever make Chris change his mind. Well, maybe. Chris's big brother Matthew teased Chris and said, "Chris, be more adult type." And besides, Chris' dad was visiting France. It was that day that made Chris suspicious. In the early morning when Chris was sleeping, his mother woke him with a cup of freezing water. "Mum you always....." and before he could say another word, she panicked and said, "Get changed! Matthew has already gone to swimming!" Chris rubbed his sleepy eyes and slowly got changed and ready to go. He went to his mother and said. "I'm all done." His mother just told him to eat some cereal. Chris smiled and thought how the crunchy cornflakes would shimmer into his mouth and he rushed to the kitchen. The kitchen was very small but Chris didn't mind. He thought he had the most beautiful window because he had always seen a lovely swaying of the trees and flowers. This had always been a lovely memory for Chris that he would never forget. As he was eating, he stared out the window half asleep and he saw a red shape sitting on the washing line with a naughty, twisted smile. He dropped his spoon and stared at the red, blurry shape. He knew that he was completely alone in the kitchen with only a spoon to fight with. Chris tried to figure out what the red blurry shape was by staring even harder than before. 'No, it couldn't be', Chris had seen a strange Santa Claus staring at him face to face. Chris faced the other way and then turned and looked at the Santa Claus. He wasn't gone but unfortunately was closer than before....

This text exemplifies the young writer's more mature Orientation. Firstly Sunyoung starts this text by introducing the theme of the Narrative with the technique of Foreshadowing. As in *'Chris was 8 years old and still believed in Santa Claus. Nothing could ever make Chris change his mind'*, the stubbornness of Chris' mind toward Santa is possibly to be a key for Chris in solving his problem which provides for a semantic link to the stages of Complication and Resolution. In addition, in this text, Sunyoung seems to have quite effectively realized all the three important aspects of Register - Field, Tenor and Mode.

---

[26] During the vacation period, she mentioned that she would like to compose a chapter based novel since she got a 'great idea' for it. She tried to jot it down in a hurried manner mostly about story lines. After that, she started to write a 10 page-long Narrative on the computer for only 5 days. The researcher thought that writing a novel on the computer (at that time, her typing skill was good enough) made her keep writing in a speedy manner without any difficulty of being distracted. After finishing it, she looked proud of herself and had spent some time proofreading the whole pages. At these times, she kept on reading novels from a community library. So the researcher thought the reading experience might have had a great influence on Sunyoung's writing proficiency in many aspects.

The selection of process types (including mainly material, relational and mental process) are represented mainly to reveal what the field of this text is about. Also, the interspersed dialogic exchanges which have an interpersonal function assist in characterizing the main participants, along with the Mood system choices as in *'Chris, be more adult type.'*, *'Mum you always....'* and *'Get changed! Matthew has already gone to swimming!'* In realizing the textual meanings the writer does not over-rely on temporal conjunctions or temporal circumstances; instead, topical Themes (see the underlined words in Table 3-33) play a more prominent role in contextualizing the whole Orientation stage with a natural flow of the events. In other words, in this text, there are fewer temporal conjunctions or connectives such as 'and' or 'then' than in the Orientation of Sunyoung's earlier Narratives. The young writer appears to be exploring alternative choices within the Theme system by increasingly using topical Themes as well as giving some variants in the clause patterns as in *'It was the day that...'* Sunyoung's growing control over the textual metafunction as realized in the choices within the Theme system will be further explored in Section 3-3 (Section 3-3-1) and Section 3-4 (Section 3-4-1).

Summary for Sunyoung's Control of the Schematic Structure of Orientation Stage

In terms of her control of the Orientation stage in Narrative, over the four year period, the young writer demonstrates a growing awareness of its critical semantic functions. Thus, the Orientation in Sunyoung's early Narrative texts concentrates mostly on experiential meanings to fulfill the basic semantic function of Orientation such as the introduction of participants along with spatial and temporal setting. The Orientation in most early Narratives tends to prolong to the stage of Complication, the distinction between the Orientation and Complication stages often being very vague. Over time, Sunyoung seems to have grown in her control of the schematic structure of the Orientation, Complication and Resolution which has resulted in her constructing the stages more distinctly, along with using more conventional expressions. Also most texts composed during the Year 1 period demonstrate a more semantically rich characterization. The next year products (in Year 2) look very different from the earlier texts in many ways but overall, it is quite obvious that Sunyoung really attempts to create an Orientation which is not like a conventional folk tale Orientation. She explores writing from the first person perspective and demonstrates her growing control of the semantically important functions of the Field and Tenor. Quite successfully, she includes dialogic exchanges (interpersonal function) in realizing the main function of the Orientation. During the final period (in Year 3), Sunyoung seems to unfold the Orientation stage more smoothly, or implicitly, using the technique of Foreshadowing and Evaluative elements. Although the property of Foreshadowing, in its embryonic form, emerges earlier, it gets a more satisfying realization in the child's Year 3 Narrative texts. In later texts, Sunyoung moves on to more implicit ways of constructing the 'Foreshadowing' so that the readers can retain their curiosity about what will happen with the thought that there will be something related to the given Foreshadowing elements.

Overall, in her growing control over the Orientation stage, even though Sunyoung has been exposed to explicit teaching of Narrative writing (via the schematic structure of Narrative being modeled by the teacher), her writing patterns go through conventional Narrative writing and then beyond the models to which she has been explicitly exposed. To her later Narrative writing, she seems to bring what she knows about Narratives from the books she has read/ had read to her, and what she knows about the possibilities of written English more generally. The explicit teaching about Narrative does not appear to have stifled Sunyoung's writing, contrary to what is often claimed by the opponents of the Genre-based Pedagogy. On the contrary, it appears to have worked as a 'spring-board' for the child's Narrative writing development.

3.2.3. Complication in Sunyoung's Narrative texts

The Overview of Sunyoung's Complication Stage
Focusing on the Control of Schematic Structure [27]

The Complication stage in Sunyoung's Narrative texts seems to have developed significantly over the four-year period (from the beginning period of Kindergarten (age 5) to Year 3 (age 8)). Compared to the stage of Orientation which has been reasonably successful from the early period, the Complication during the Kindergarten year is very incomplete being rather abruptly, followed by the Resolution. The following examples in Table 3-34 demonstrate this:

Table 3-34: Sunyoung's Early Complication Texts (Text BB-2 and Text BB-4)

Elements of the schematic structure	Sunyoung's Texts
Text BB-2 (age 5:7) Complication	I ran to my dad and mum. Dad helped me sleep. Next night I heard the noises again. Mum and dad looked out the window. They saw a ghost. They said let go in my room
Resolution	In my dad and mums room it was peaceful.
Text BB-4 (age 5:10) Complication	One day I was cleaning the floor with my broom and I didn't recognize the button and I pressed it and I was flying!
Resolution	And I believed in my mum.

In the Complication of Text BB-2, the sense of unusuality is initially constructed by the appearance of a ghost in the protagonist's room. Yet, the sense of fear does not seem to be really communicated to the readers since the Resolution by the mum and dad's help follows too soon. There is a distinct lack of creating the inner conflict which could be expected as a result of this unusual event. At the end of the story, the readers can be left feeling very indifferent and distant as if they had read through a simple Recount, without being emotionally involved in the story. The example Text BB-4 also shows a similarity with the former Text BB-2 in regard to the incomplete shortened Complication. The unusual event of flying with a magic broom is likely to need

---

[27] Further detailed text analysis for Sunyoung's Complication texts (focusing on Transitivity, Theme, Mood and Nominal groups) is provided in Section 3-4.

more adventures which can be followed by a climax point. In terms of the schematic structure, both texts are lacking in detail of description of unusual events and there are no climax points in the Complications. Also the Resolution parts as in '*In my dad and mums room it was peaceful*' and '*And I believed in my mum*' do not seem to satisfy the readers as the solutions related to the events of the Complications. This unsatisfied Resolution parts should be understood not only by the incomplete part of Resolution itself but also by the insignificant Complications which fail to build up enough context for the conflicting elements. It is also noteworthy that these two Complications are lacking Evaluative elements which make the Complication more significant for the readers. Without the Evaluative elements, the climax point and detailed description of events, the Complication stage would not really be satisfactory.

Whereas most Complication texts of the early period (Kindergarten, age 5) tend to be simply arranging a series of actions in a row rather than providing readers with some room to get involved in the events, the Complications produced in the following year (Year 1, age 6) illustrate a significant growth in Sunyoung's control of writing the stage of Complication. In terms of the length of the whole Narrative texts, she manages to write more extended texts than in the previous year and, importantly, the Complication element is rather lengthy and elaborate. There also emerge instances of multi-complications in that the young writer attempts to construct two or three minor Complications and Resolutions. The following example of Text BB-6 (Year 1, Age 6:2) demonstrates well Sunyoung's initial attempt at the multi-Complications:

Table 3-35: Sunyoung's Initial Attempt of the Multi-Complications (Text BB-6)

Elements of the schematic structure	Title: My Family (Year 1, Age 6:2)
Complication 1 + Resolution 1	He was shouting at the old Granny next door who was always kind to us. I said, "Stop" in a very loud voice. Suddenly he looked straight at me. His eyes were big and round and fierce. <u>I tried to run away but he was too fast</u>. /I ran into my house and slammed the door. <u>I was home all alone. My heart was beating faster and faster.</u> I looked out of the

	window. <u>The man's eyes were glooming in the sun.</u> <u>So I was terrified</u>
Complication 2 + Resolution 2	He was so angry he decided to dress up into a postman. He knocked on the door very loud. <u>It was like one elephant jumping in our house</u>. He said in the keyhole. "Please take this parcel." / <u>She thought it was a stranger so this is what she said</u>, "Put it on the steps and I'll pick it up later."
Complication 3 + Resolution 3	<u>He was angry because he couldn't trick her</u>. He had another idea. He wanted to make a trap. <u>The man was very sneaky and very very bad</u>. He made the trap where he put the parcel and put dirt over it. Then he waited behind a rock. / I saw the man hiding behind a rock. I waited until it was night, and then I picked up my parcel and took it home

Note: '/' is used to mark a boundary of Complication and Resolution; Underlined refers to Evaluative elements

In Table 3-35, the Complication stage can be divided into three minor Complications along with Resolutions of each Complication. The first Complication of the protagonist shouting at the villain in an attempt of helping the Granny next door temporarily gets resolved by the protagonist running away to her house. The episode about the angry villain's disguise as a postman makes up another Complication and the protagonist's calm and wise reaction helps to handle another crisis. The third Complication is composed of the villain making a trap against her and the protagonist's thoughtful solution of waiting until night rather than picking up the parcel right away.

With regards to the schematic structure of the child's Narrative texts, it can be argued that there has been a significant development over the one year period. Throughout the multi-Complication stages the readers get prepared to learn about the seriousness of the subsequent events and the persistent villain's character and possibly have expectation of the protagonist's wise reaction against the tricks. In addition, in this Complication text there are several Evaluative elements (which are underlined). Compared to the texts written in Kindergarten, the Evaluative elements in Text BB-6 reveals the protagonist's and villain's inner states or plans and negative comments on villain's appearance, which seems to have contributed a lot to making the Complication stage more significant and to adding the situational seriousness to the context.

Another example of Narrative with multi-complications in this period is Text BB-7 which has a more satisfying Resolution:

Table 3-36. Another Example of Sunyoung's Multi-Complications in Year 1
(Text BB-7)

Elements of the schematic structure	Title: The Rainbow Polar Bear (Year 1, Age 6:7)
Complication 1 + Resolution 1	So that night the rainbow Polar bear went to kill the queen. <u>But it was cold and creepy but the rainbow polar bear kept going. The polar bear didn't know it was raining and the polar bear wasn't rainbow it was just that the polar bear wanted to be beautiful to be the queen.</u> So she painted herself. So the rain washed the paint off. "<u>I can't go in this plain old white fur to be the queen.</u>" / So she ran as fast as she could back to her home.
Complication 2	It was hard painting herself again so she poured some paint onto her. <u>All different colors washed about her like star falling down. It will not rain in the morning.</u> I'll go to kill the queen now. The sun shined bright and dried the polar bear's paint. "<u>This time I'm not going to fail.</u>" But she did fail the guards saw her angrily stomping with the knife and blocked the way.
Final Resolution2	While the Polar bear was stomping home, she saw a man with a long beard and dragged clothes just standing still. "Hey, big fellow want to come with me to Canada there is lots of Polar bears there." "OK". So they left to Canada and met the Polar bears and lived happily ever after.

Note: '/' is used to mark a boundary of Complication and Resolution; Underlined refers to Evaluative elements.

The jealous Polar bear who is ambitious to become a queen sets out to kill the real queen, and the protagonist's inner conflict is depicted throughout the trial and error in the two subsequent Complications. Even though there are several grammatical errors in the clause composition, this text demonstrates Sunyoung's efforts in highlighting the unusual sequences of events and in using dialogic expressions revealing the protagonist's disappointment and determination as in '*I can't go in this plain old white fur to be the queen*' and '*This time I'm not going to fail*'. In this regard, the Evaluative elements (underlined) seem to contribute a great deal to making this Complication more remarkable and unusual. Particularly, in this Complication text, Sunyoung appears to have attempted Bruner's 'Dual perspectives' (Bruner, 1986). This involves the readers being able to experience the Complication events through the protagonist's eyes and thoughts as well as the reader's special position whereby he or she is aware of some critical information which is not available to the protagonist. As in *'the polar bear didn't know it was raining'*, the readers can predict what will be happening to the protagonist by knowing that it was raining and it will make the readers get more involved in the forthcoming event.

In terms of the schematic structure, the next period, during Year 2 (age 7), can be called 'time for variation' in which Sunyoung attempts different styles of Narrative writing inclusive of journal style Narrative with imaginative elements (Text BB-10), a chapter book style Narrative (Text BB-11), science Theme based Narrative (Text BB-12) and a Narrative imitating a fantasy novel (Text BB-13). As mentioned earlier in the section on Orientation, the majority of Narrative texts produced during this period do not seem to have the typical, or conventional, Narrative structure, with clearly identifiable stages of Orientation, Complication and Resolution. Mainly because Sunyoung attempts different styles of Narrative during this period, certain texts (e.g. Text BB-10) look more likely a journal combined with a letter format. In these texts it is quite hard to see where the stage of Complication starts and ends. The Complication in Year 2 appears to have constructed quite interesting fields. However there is a distinct lack of climax elements which would lead the readers to feel the sense of urgency. The following examples of selected Complication texts will illustrate some features of the schematic structure during the period of Year 2. Firstly let's take a look at the example of Text BB-10:

Table 3-37: Sunyoung's Complication of Text BB-10

Title: Space Adventure	(Year 2, Age 7:4)
Suddenly I crash into something. This is not very good... but on the other hand, it might just be a huge rock. I slowly shiver out of the space rocket with Jamile. We are in luck because we have landed on the moon. Then we sink down into	

a strange room. Two slimy creatures slither up to me and I back away. The slimy creatures lead me and Jamilee to a kitchen. They eat goey slimy bugs. Jamilee is about to be sick. The beds are also slimy but very soft. We stay here for one night. As we say goodbye the next day, they seem to look poor. We travel back to our real planet (Earth). Just then a comet shoots and <u>we are the only ones to save earth.</u> We push it another direction. Luckily the comet was small. When we land on planet Earth, <u>I suppose slimy stuff compared to dry stuff are very different indeed.</u> I get out and the people gasp! I say "Why" and I was covered in mud and slime. At home I should have taken a bath but I didn't because .... Mum had made oranges for us and I peeled one and threw at mum and Jamilee! We will have an orange fight! The oranges squelched and squeezed as they splat on people's faces! <u>It was very fun. I think that my special adventure starts now!!</u>

This Complication stage comprises three minor events. Firstly the protagonists' landing on the moon leads them to meet slimy creatures. After that, in the attempt of traveling back to the Earth, there is comet shooting. Lastly at home, there was an orange fight in the spirit of celebration. Since this text was constructed in the line with Sunyoung's theme based work (with the specific theme of 'Space') at school, the field itself was all related to the space adventure. Even though it can be claimed as a new try with a different field creation and multi-complications, this text looks like a rather recount writing without no peak point or further conflicting development which is quite important for the state of Complication.

Another example of the Complication texts in Year 2 is the Text BB-11 which was constructed as a chapter book style Narrative writing at home. Sunyoung's writing Narratives had been self-motivated in most cases and this Narrative was also written during the term break time by hand-writing. Although this text contains many punctuation errors and spelling errors, this must be a turning point for her to step ahead for more mature Narrative writing:

Table 3-38: The First Part of Complication of Text BB-11

Title: The Mystery	(Year 2, Age 7:5)
Sarah ran over to Janet's place sharp two thirty. Janet was there waiting for her. "Why were you so late?" She frowned. Sarah was out of breath. <u>She tried to speak but she was so tired of out of breath that no words came out as she opened her mouth.</u> Janet pasted Sarah a cup of water. "Thanks" panted Sarah. Anyway, "how did you exactly lose Scamper?" said Sarah. "Well, first of all I would like to say..." Sarah shouted in her ears, "You are not doing an	

interview. We are just going to say the words!!" "Well, sorry." H<u>er voice was</u>
<u>now a whisper since she was so frightened so much</u>. Suddenly Janet spoke up.
<u>She was angry now</u>! "Oh, you are so perfect!!!" <u>Sarah was now too angry</u>.
"Well, how about you!! You have dog hairs all over your nose. Now for
heaven's sake, let's start the meeting. OK? How Scamper ran away on my lead"
<u>She was talking fast purposely so Sarah couldn't hear</u>. "What she said?" "Fine,
you have no ears at all, maybe you are death" said Janet. "Oh, so Scamper
might not like you any more." And with that Sarah slammed to door shut. Janet
stuck her tongue out at the door. Then her mum came in. Janet quickly slipped
her tongue back in her mouth. Sarah was stomping out. "Is there a problem
with you two?" "Nothing!" she said.

The above text is only part of the Complication in Text BB-
11. The whole Narrative deals with the relationship between
two friends and the main complications (problems) are about
the lost Scamper (a pet dog) and a homework book. The first
part of the Complication starts with the trivial conflict
between the two protagonists, Sarah and Janet who are the
close friends. The whole Complication element reveals
Sunyoung's better developed application of the dialogic
exchanges in representing the characters' personalities and
the flow of the subsequent events than her earlier texts. This
kind of Narrative writing seems to have been influenced by
Sunyoung having started to read chapter books where
dialogue is commonly used to represent the mental plane of
the events, including revealing the characters' personalities.
A significant development in control of the Narrative
structure is the child's learning to link the characters and
events constructed in the Orientation to help build up the
sense of a problem. Even though this Complication element
includes some detail which is not necessary for the main
story line (or problem-solving process), it can be claimed
that throughout the whole text, she has been quite successful
in constructing characterization.

During the final period of Year 3 (age 8), the Complication
of Sunyoung's Narratives demonstrates increasingly
developed context building with descriptive images. The
next examples (Complications of Texts BB-16 and BB-17)
which were constructed in line with the school theme 'Greek
Myths' illustrate more sophisticated techniques in
developing the Complication stage such as involving further
Evaluative elements (Text BB-16) and linking the element

of 'Foreshadowing' to Complication stage more successfully (Text BB-17), than in earlier texts.

Title: Fred (Year 3, Age 8:5)
I ran to the kitchen and quickly fed some meat to it. That seemed to settle him down a bit... He waddled into the bathroom making stomps like earthquakes. Luckily Mum and Dad wear earmuffs. When I was day dreaming, a sprinkle of water woke me up. 'Oh, darn, Mum's going to kill me!' When I ran to the bathroom, the door was locked. 'Gee, I thought that this dragon was clever.' I pulled out my clip and unlocked the door. The dragon was having a bath with my sparkle shampoo! One minute, I'm totally scared of this beast and another minute I'm mad at him! I punch in the air forcing the dragon to back off. But he doesn't budge! He just stalks, I mean stomps to my room! Then my worst nightmare comes. I hear a groan from mum's room! I ran to my room and pushed the dragon in a huge closet. I can barely shove his fat body in! I turn off the light and tuck myself in bed. Mum comes in. she yawns and glares around my room with narrowed eyes that look like needles.

Table 3-40: Sunyoung's Complication of Text BB-17

Title: Cub (Year 3, Age 8:5)
Cub woke up soon enough. A few seconds later, three men came barging in the cathedral. They stared at Cub, so he gave them a warning glare and shouted, "Go away!" That almost worked. They were just about to faint! Perhaps they had never seen a talking gargoyle before. Then the three men tried to knock me down the wall! Cub turned into stone and they punched him. The gargoyle just stared at them full of wonder whilst the men were sucking their fists and howling with pain. Cub jumped down his wall and hopped – well he had to hop, to a small door. He butted the door with his head and the door slowly opened little by little. And inside, was a squirming figure of the priest! Cub found the key on the ceiling. Cub hopped as high as he could but somehow the key just didn't seem to come into his hands. So he went out, jumped on the main roof of the room the priest was in and used his horns to cut a small circle and it fell on to the ground with an ear-bursting 'bang!' Cub ran back into the room and found the key under the priest's foot. Cub quickly picked the key up and turned the lock on the priest.

At first, the above Complication text BB-16 reasonably well constructed the field of encountering unknown creature by presenting the protagonist's embarrassing feeling and reactions to handle with the creature. In respect to the schematic structure, this Complication stage builds up the sense of unusuality and urgency and this makes the stage clearly distinguishable from the stages of Orientation and Resolution. While reading this text, the readers might have been sharing the apprehension about the event on the part of the protagonist and feeling uneasiness in trying to hide the unknown creature from mum and dad. The Evaluative elements (underlined) seem to help in constructing the expression of attitudes and opinions thus marking the event as remarkable and unusual.

The next Complication example BB-17 also can be analyzed as a more mature Complication even though there are comparatively few Evaluative elements. Instead of highlighting unusuality through the Evaluative elements, Sunyoung uses a lot of material processes contextualizing a tense situation in which the protagonist (Cub) confronts the antagonists (three men intruders). In this Complication, the tension is built through this series of events, following fast one after the next and at the end, the readers are able to appreciate the protagonist's heroic stand against the intruders. At this point, the readers' expectation toward Cub which would have been built through a foreshadowing element in the stage of Orientation change from the timid and powerless-looking Cub's image to a brave, responsible and strong one. By this realization in connection with the foreshadowing element in the Orientation stage, this Complication can be considered as a more mature one among Sunyoung's Complications.

The final example of the Complication texts produced in Year 3 (age 8) as given below is composed of an eight page long Complication text, which was constructed on the computer at home during the term break. The following is the first part of Complication stage of Text BB-18.

Table 3-41: The First Part of Complication in Text BB-18

Title: Face to Face with a Santa Claus   (Year 3, Age 8:7)
Chris didn't know what to do. First he rubbed his sleepy eyes and stared again. It was still there!! He wanted to scream but nothing came out of his dried mouth. His face went white. He ran to his mother as fast as he could. "Mum, mum there is a strange 'Santa Claus' on our washing line!!" But his mother just slammed the door on his face and murmured, "Go do something helpful like eating your cornflakes." Chris slowly tiptoed as if the Santa Claus might hear him. When he reached the kitchen, he took a glimpse of his food and snatched it away so he could eat somewhere else. When Chris had eaten his breakfast, he waited for his mother outside her door. Soon she came out and Chris was trying to tell her what had happened, but she didn't believe him and told him he was saying complete nonsense. As they got in the car, Chris stayed silent with anger. 'How could she not believe him?' The swimming Pool came

> close by. His mother parked the car and Chris ran up to the entrance of the building and got changed into his swimmers.
>
> He waited for his mother to come and then jumped into the freezing water. All he could think of was that nasty Santa Claus. Chris usually took his swimming lessons seriously but not today. He was caught from the swim club teacher for listening inappropriately. Chris' mother gave him a hard stare. Then Chris noticed something strange. A red blurry shape sitting on the lane ropes. Santa Claus had followed him! A shiver went up Chris' spine. Was this rotten old Santa going to follow him everywhere?
>
> Swimming lessons had finished. Chris' mother was going to give him an unpleasant lecture. Matthew was already waiting for Chris with his mother. It seemed as if Matthew was ready to tease the Santa lover. Chris explained to his mother in the car. "There really was a mean Santa Claus sitting on the washing line!" He shouted. His mother told him that he was daydreaming too much. Chris looked down to his feet. Then he looked towards Matthew. He was making a sour face trying hard not to laugh. So was his mum. Chris made up his mind. He wasn't going to put up with his family's disgusting behavior. He was going to show them that rotten Santa Claus face to face. For once and for all!!! Chris's car arrived at his house...

This first part (Chapter 2 in her original division: see Appendix 3-2) of the Complication Text BB-18 can be claimed as a much more developed and mature writing in many aspects. Considering the aspect of the schematic structure, this stage appears to be particularly successful in realizing the function of initiating the main conflict along with elaborate characterization of the participants and building up the setting. In fact, in a short version of Narrative writing, this kind of function is mostly satisfied in the stage of Orientation rather than Complication. Yet, it is not unusual that, as in the case of novel-like Narratives, the same function can be achieved with a prolonged manner in the initial parts of Complication stage. In the Complication of Text BB-18, the first main conflict begins with the appearance of a somewhat nasty looking Santa Claus in front of Chris' eyes. In addition, another conflict between the protagonist (Chris) and the family members ('mum' and Chris' brother Matthew) runs parallel with the main conflict. In other words, the protagonist's apprehension caused by the unexpected encounter of the scary Santa goes side by side with experiencing the negative feelings of disbelief and isolation from his family.

In terms of Evaluative elements, this text seems to highlight "comparisons between usual and unusual sequences of

events in which participants in the Narrative are involved"
(Rothery, 1990: 203). While the protagonist and his family
members are doing the usual, routine things in a daily life
such as eating cornflakes for their breakfast and going to the
swimming pool for swimming lessons, some unusual events
such as encountering the nasty Santa in the washing line and
a red blurry shape sitting on the lane ropes are interspersed
with the protagonist's daily routine. It sometimes causes a
break in his usual life patterns as in *He was caught from the
swim club teacher for listening inappropriately. Chris'
mother gave him a hard stare'*, *'His mother told him that he
was daydreaming too much'* and *'He was making a sour face
trying hard not to laugh. So was his mum'*. The Evaluative
elements (underlined) contribute to representing the
protagonist's inner states and some predictions about
possible courses of action to handle the unexpected events
as in *'Chris made up his mind. He wasn't going to put up
with his family's disgusting behavior. He was going to show
them that rotten Santa Claus face to face. For once and for
all!!!'* These elements help the reader make some
predictions as to what might happen next in the
Complication.

The rest of the Complication of Text BB-18 (refer to the
whole text in Appendix 3-2) can also be evaluated as a
mature one, containing a series of well-constructed story
lines, building for the reader a sense of tension, curiosity
and suspense.

Summary for Sunyoung's control of the schematic structure of Complication Stage

So far we have examined the Complication in Sunyoung's
Narratives in terms of the schematic structure over the
period from Kindergarten (age 5) to Year 3 (age 8), with the
view of tracing her writing development. To sum up, in the
beginning period of Kindergarten, Sunyoung starts with
somewhat incomplete structure of Complication. However,
there is a remarkable change during the period of Year 1 in
writing up the Complication stage. Most texts became
lengthy and started to include some Evaluative elements and
even began to apply Multi-Complications. The next year
(Year 2) can be called 'time for variation'. During this

period, Sunyoung attempts various styles of Narrative writing including a journal type, letter type and novel style Narratives along with different science related Themes. In these attempts at creating different fields and styles, the Complication doesn't seem to be clearly distinguished from the stages of Orientation and Resolution, lacking in climax points or clearly identifiable conflict. Lastly, in Year 3, Sunyoung shows much more mature Complication texts than before. There can be found more sophisticated dialogic exchanges, characterization, descriptive events along with Evaluative elements. Particularly during this period, Sunyoung successfully explored the new field of 'Greek Myth' and the 8-page long Complication texts of 'Face to Face with a Santa Claus' with more skilled conflict development.

3.2.4. Resolution in Sunyoung's Narrative Texts

The main semantic property of the Resolution in Narratives is to regain the sense of usuality and the solution to the problems or conflicts of the Complication stage. As Rothery (1990) argues, the restoration to the usuality by the active participation or involvement of the protagonist contributes to construction of a more significant Resolution. In addition, if the stage of Complication interspersed with Evaluation is developed with more sophistication (if the sense of unusuality and tension has been more effectively constructed), the following Resolution stage can be more satisfactory to the readers (Aidman, 1999: 230).

In this respect, Sunyoung's control of the Resolution stage in Narrative has significantly progressed over the four-year period under consideration. Thus, the generic structure of her early Narratives (Kindergarten, age 5) is closer to that of a Recount text (Orientation ^ Record of Events) than to that of the Narrative, since these early texts are lacking in either build up of activities to a crisis or turning points involving the main characters. Whereas the young writer constructs the restoration to peace and usuality, as in '*then we had a cup of coffee and went to bed*' (Text BB-1; age 5) and '*and I believed in my mum*' (Text BB-4; age 5), these do not appear significant and meaningful enough, mainly because such Resolution is not preceded by a satisfactory Complication stage. A sign of growth in Sunyoung's control of the Resolution stage is her beginning to construct somewhat more active participation in resolving the problem and restoring the usuality. An early example of this is found in her Text BB-6 as follows:

Table 3-42: Sunyoung's Resolution of Text BB-6

Title: My Family	(Year 1, Age 6:2)
My family came back. When it was morning the man found himself in prison. He hated being in prison. We came to see him. We smiled. But the man was sad. We went back home and lived happily ever after. But what about the man? Will he still live as happily as Sun-young's family?	

In this text, the protagonist, Sun-young, had been acting very bravely and wisely against the robber who kept on trying to break in her house. When her family came back to her house in the final Resolution stage, the readers can feel relief and feel proud of her way of dealing with the robber. The conventional phrase *'lived happily ever after'* followed by Coda comments as in *'But what about the man? Will he still live as happily as Sun-young's family?'* provides the effect of 'rounding off' to the readers.[28]

Along with the above Resolution (Table 3-42), Resolutions in Narrative Texts BB-7 and BB-8 composed during the period of Year 1 (age 6) appear more mature examples, compared with those in the earlier period (age 5).[29] Text

---

[28] According to Rothery (1990: 211), Coda is "a concluding stage of Narrative which is optional. It provides a thematic summation of the events of the text retrospectively. Its placement is after the Resolution."

[29] Particularly, Text BB-7 develops as multi-Complications and Resolutions, and from the whole developments of events and tentative Resolutions prior to the final one the readers are made to sympathize with the protagonist's accumulated failure experience and feeling of disappointment at the end. When a mysterious person ('a man with a long beard') suddenly appears and suggests going to Canada with him in the final Resolution stage, the readers can expect the protagonist to accept the suggestion and do the right choice for her life. This expectation seems to be attributed to the effect of the multi-Complications and Resolutions, which allows the readers to get tuned into the protagonist's suffering, and develop sympathy towards her.

Table 3-43: Sunyoung's Resolution of Text BB-7

Title: The Rainbow Polar Bear	(Year 1, Age 6:7)
While the polar bear was stomping home, she saw a man with a long beard and dragged clothes just standing still. "Hey big fellow, want to come with me to Canada? There is lots of Polar Bears there." "OK". So they left to Canada and met the polar bear and lived happily ever after.	

BB-8 shows a different pattern of Resolution with an unexpected ending. The protagonist's mischievous dog had been loved by him even though it kept on doing naughty things. To create such a context, Sunyoung constructs an extended Orientation stage, and, as a result, the readers get a better understanding of how the dog makes mischief and annoys people, but also the dog's master's amazing acceptance and patience. And when one day, the dog goes missing, the dog's master tries his best to find the dog. The Resolution thus is appealing and satisfactory to the readers. Upsetting the reader's anticipation, the dog comes back with a good reputation by saving a boy from a robber. Sunyoung also adds a kind of Coda at the end as in '*the moral of this story is that everything can change*'. This text appears to be more successfully constructed creating the unexpected ending through several marked topical Themes (underlined):

Table 3-44: Sunyoung's Resolution of Text BB-8

Title: The Mischief Dog	(Year 1, Age 6:9)
The boy put up wanted signs and lost signs too. <u>Seven days later</u>, the dog appeared and <u>to his surprise</u>, all the people were hugging him. <u>Soon</u> the boy knew what was going on. <u>Instead of mischief</u>, his dog saved the boy by chasing the robbers out of the town! The moral of this story is that everything can change.	

As she grows older, Sunyoung explores Narrative beyond the canonical picture storybook Narrative for young children. This leads her to exploring other ways of constructing the Resolution. The following Resolution is an example attempted in a journal-style Narrative (Text BB-10):

Table 3-45: Sunyoung's Resolution of Text BB-10

Title: Space Adventure	(Year 2, Age 7:4)
So this is why I have written this Narrative of me and Jamilee traveling around in outer space. I asked mum thoroughly "Mum, will I ever be able to see those slimy friends that I met in outer space on my journey in outer space with Jamilee?' Then my mum answered "In your dreams, you will always see them vividly in your head." That very night, I dreamt of me and Jamilee having a fun party with the slimy creatures.	

The Resolution of Text BB-10 as shown above is more like a journal note finishing off with the writer's reflection of

129

the imaginary traveling around in outer space. On the surface the Resolution in this text is not satisfactory enough; as far as the semantic property is concerned, this text is not quite fit to the protagonist's facing with problems and active involvement and solution. However, it can also be considered that this kind of journal style Narrative might or should not be evaluated by the criteria of typical Narrative texts. In this respect, Text BB-10 Resolution text might be an acceptable alternative fitted to the whole flow of this Narrative itself.

A more elaborate and satisfying Resolution evolves in Sunyoung's Narrative writing in Year 3 (age 8). The Resolution becomes more satisfying partly due to an effectively constructed Complication stage. The Resolution stage itself (e.g. Text BB-18) is constructed so that the problem, well built in the preceding stage, gets resolved through physical involvement of the participants and their cognitive and emotional involvement. The Evaluative elements are built into the Resolution stage, to highlight the sense of problem resolution. The dialogue between the participants and the verbal and behavioural processes projecting it contribute significantly to constructing a sense of the return to the usuality. In fact, this Resolution achieves more than just restoring the status quo. This stage sees further development of the protagonists, with both Chris and Santa becoming better people, more understanding and sympathetic with others. The Resolution of Text BB-18 starts off like this:

Table 3-46: Sunyoung's Resolution of Text BB-18

Title: Face to Face with a Santa Claus	(Year 3, Age 8:6)

Chris began to act very rude to Santa Claus. He just stared at Chris strangely. All of a sudden, Santa Claus disappeared and came back with a piece of paper and a pen. 'That's strange?' thought Chris. Santa Claus started to write down a peculiar sign with the pen. Chris had no idea what the sign was and what it meant. Santa Claus finally placed the pen down and moved aside for Chris to look at it. On the paper was a messy word saying 'sorry.' Chris stared at the word for a couple of minutes and then back at Santa Claus. Chris half believed Santa Claus. Santa Claus sighed and then suddenly started to murmur, "**You see, Santa Claus all have different personalities. Other Santas say that I am annoying and clumsy so I have no friends. I was tired of hearing those words so I tried to prove that I was nice and actually wanted a friend. And then I met you. But I just couldn't help myself from acting differently from** my mind. It's just my undesirable habit. But at least you seemed to understand me, and so I have to say that I want to be friends with you." Chris was flabbergasted to hear Santa's confession. And then he began thinking of the way he had been feeling lonely and left out recently after Santa Claus came. So far Chris had not experienced such a difficult time with no friends and no people believing him. And in that way, Chris began to feel as if he was a strange person compared with all the other people around him. He then realized it was just the same for Santa Claus as well. "It's okay." Chris replied, "I think I understand your feelings. Thank you for letting me know how lonely you were." Chris smiled. "Next Christmas, I will promise to deliver you a nice present!" Santa said, "So far I have been so naughty that I couldn't get a job for delivering presents to little kids like you. But now, I am going to be nice and get that job!" "But please don't sit on the washing line again. Just come down the chimney! That's the traditional way." Chris joked. Expecting the nice present for next Christmas, he was grinning from ear to ear and so was Santa Claus. Looking out the window, incredible white snow was drifting down....

In this Narrative, the main conflict between Santa and the protagonist, Chris, is resolved by Santa's sincere confession (see the bold typed in Table 3-46). At this point, the readers might be able to understand that it cannot be achieved without Chris' endurance and active involvement in the whole process. Furthermore, this stage shows Chris' own reflection on his recent unpleasant experience of being isolated from his own family, and, as a result, his being able to sympathize with the Santa from the bottom of his heart. Constructing this confession part, Sunyoung uses more relational processes than in the Resolution elements of other Narrative texts so that 'Santa' can be described more effectively as in "I _am_ annoying and clumsy so I _have_ no friends." The majority of conjunctions are temporal used for sequencing the events. A number of marked topical Themes (see the underlined words) such as 'all of a sudden', 'on the paper' and 'next Christmas' also seem to contribute to constructing a well-developed text. The last two sentences composed with foregrounded non-finite clause leave the readers with a kind of poetic after-effect by which they can round off the Narrative, lingering a while in their minds.

So far we have examined Sunyoung's developing control of each stage (Orientation, Complication and Resolution) in Narrative writing over the four-year period (Kindergarten to Year 3). As shown in her most developed Narrative Text BB-18 (in Year 3, age 8:6), Sunyoung demonstrates a remarkable growth in Narrative writing by orchestrating critical elements of a successful Narrative such as control of the schematic structure inclusive of 'Evaluation' and building up the setting, characters and events effectively through more elaborate choices in the Transitivity system, control of the nominal group structure and choices within the Theme and Mood systems. In the following section, we will compare Jinha's and Sunyoung's growth in control of Narrative writing in English, which forms one of the major findings of this case study.

3.3. Detailed Text Analysis in the Orientation of Sunyoung's Narratives

3-3-1. Theme System in the Orientation of Narrative Texts

This section will focus on Sunyoung's developing control of the Theme system in constructing the Orientation stage over the four year period. Theme choices are critical in realizing the textual metafunction of language (Halliday, 1994). As Halliday acknowledges, the Theme choice for any individual clause will generally relate to the way information (or message) is being developed over the course of the whole text. As a message starter (or departure point, in other words), the system of Theme organizes the clause to what its local context is in relation to the general context of the text it serves in.

In terms of the Theme system, the first point that Sunyoung's Orientation texts have shown is that the Theme component in a clause may have unfolded from one metafunctional perspective to the other ones. To exemplify this, her earlier Orientation texts (in Kindergarten) are composed mostly by using topical (ideational) Themes and textual Themes. In Text BB-1, Sunyoung chooses several cases of marked topical Themes including a 'hypotactic' clause and the textual Theme 'then'. 'One day' is a marked topical Theme in a declarative clause since it is not the subject and it gains a greater textual prominence. It is quite acceptable that non-subject Themes as marked Themes are often important in structuring the larger discourse. Furthermore, as in 'When I was finished', and 'When I arrived' in the following sentences, the 'when' clause can entirely be regarded as functioning as an orienting context for the rest Rhemes of 'I hopped in it' and 'I got off' (Text BB-1: e.g. 1) When I finished I hopped in it; e.g. 2) When I arrived, I got off). The textual Theme 'then' in the middle of the Orientation text also played an important role to give thematic prominence to textual elements with a linking function. We shall trace more evidence for Sunyoung's usage of topical and textual Theme combination in a text and later it will be shown that the Themes in relation to the other interpersonal metafunction were put together in more mature and complicated manner.

3-3-1-1 Theme Choices in the Opening Clauses of Orientation Texts

Very similarly to Jinha's, most Sunyoung's early Orientations produced in Kindergarten and Year 1 start with temporal topical Themes as in the conventional opening such as in 'One day (BB-1)', 'One scary night (BB-2)', 'Once (BB-3)', 'Once upon a time (BB-4)', 'Once (BB—6)', and 'Once upon a time(BB-7)'. These choices show Sunyoung's control of the marked topical Theme in line with her understanding of the primary function of Orientation in Narrative. However, as Sunyoung explores a range of different narrative styles, including dialogic exchanges and diary style first perspective Narratives, conventional marked topical Themes in the opening clause of the Orientation change to unmarked topical Themes (subjects: 5 cases) or marked topical Themes (temporal or special circumstance: 2 cases), and sometimes to multiple Themes (3 cases) combined with continuative textual Themes and topical Theme.

Table 3-47. Sunyoung's Theme Choice in the Opening Clause of Orientation Stage (BB-9)

Hello	I	am the most beautiful butterfly in the whole world.
continuative	topical (subject: unmarked)	
textual	experiential	
Theme		Rheme

(BB-10)

10,9,8,7,6 here	I	am strapped in the seat of the swift.
continuative	topical (subject: unmarked)	
textual	exper.	
Theme		Rheme

(BB-11)

Oh, no	Sarah	Cried.
continuative	topical (subject: unmarked)	
textual	exper.	
Theme		Rheme

(BB-12)

In the past	there were so many planets.
topical (temporal circumstance: marked)	
Experiential	
Theme	Rheme

(BB-13)

I	finally got to the last step.
topical (subject: unmarked)	
Experiential	
Theme	Rheme

(BB-14)

Hanah	was a little girl.
topical (subject: unmarked)	
Experiential	
Theme	Rheme

(BB-15)

Yesterday	seemed like an ordinary morning at first.
topical (subject: unmarked)	
Experiential	
Theme	Rheme

(BB-16)

I	listened to the rain drumming on my roof.
topical (subject: unmarked)	
Experiential	
Theme	Rheme

(BB-17)

On a cathedral	a little gargoyle was watching the city below him.
topical (spatial circumstance: marked)	
Experiential	
Theme	Rheme

(BB-18)

Chris	was 8 years old.

topical (subject: unmarked)	
Experiential	
Theme	Rheme

As seen above, the different style of thematic choices as an opening clause of the Orientation emerge in Years 2 and 3 and among them, there are found continuative textual Themes (BB-9, BB-10, BB-11). Halliday (1994: 53) defines the 'continuative' as "one of a small set of discourse signalers, *yes, no, well, oh, now*, which signal that a new move is beginning: a response, in dialogue, or a move to the next point if the same speaker is continuing." In Sunyoung's Orientations, these continuative textual Themes as in 'Oh, no' and 'Hello' tend to appear when Sunyoung tries to write dialogue style Narratives (a novel-like Narrative) as in Texts BB-11, BB-14, and BB-18. Also it is quite noticeable from the above Theme-Rheme constitution that the main type of Theme used in the opening clauses of the Orientation in Sunyoung's later texts (in Years 2 and 3) is the unmarked topical Theme as the Subject of the clause. Sunyoung's opening clauses in earlier texts (in Kindergarten to Year 1) start mostly with the conventional temporal marked Theme as in 'Once upon a time' or 'One day'.

3-3-1-2 Topical (Experiential) Themes in Orientation Texts

Apart from the opening clauses, the unmarked topical Themes as subjects, however, are realized in wide range of Orientation texts throughout the whole periods (Kindergarten to Year 3) and play important roles as a participant in thematic function which corresponds to 'topic' in the clauses. The topical Themes as subjects mainly made it clear who is the center of the message in most experiential clauses. In many cases in the early period, the unmarked topical Themes are composed of the names of participants as in 'Hannah', 'Sarah' or 'the Polar bear' and mostly personal pronouns such as 'I', 'she' or 'He' and impersonal pronoun 'it'. With specific regard of 'it', Sunyoung's Orientation texts reveal that the limited usage of impersonal pronoun 'it' had been expanded to several types of 'contentless' Subject 'it' as time passed:

It was very hard to travel to another planet as well. (Text BB-12)

It was also very beautiful to see the smallest planet. (Text BB-12)

It was a pity that people called him 'cub' because it wasn't a scary name like "Blood Thriller' or something along those lines. (Text BB-17)

It was that day that made Chris suspicious. (Text BB-18)

In the first three examples above, 'it' was used as Anticipatory 'it' in mental and relational clauses. As Martin (1992) explains, the anticipatory 'it' serves to anticipate an embedded clause occurring later in the structure. Here 'it' has the potential for serving as unmarked Theme and, when it does, it will give thematic status to the choice of mood – just as any other unmarked topical Theme does in a declarative or yes/no interrogative clause. That means we can convert this into an interrogative clause as in 'Was it very hard to travel to another planet as well?'. Also, this structure has a variant where the embedded clause is Theme. For example, the above first clause can be changed as in 'To travel to another planet as well was very hard'. By these points, this anticipatory 'it' can be sorted as 'unmarked topical Theme'.

On the other hand, the last example from Text BB-18 should be sorted out differently even though 'it' also belongs to the same big category of anticipatory 'it'. According to Martin (1992), it is Anticipatory 'it' in Theme predication. The agnation can be 'That day made Chris suspicious.' And it can not be converted to 'What made Chris suspicious was that day', just like the previous examples. This structure singles out one experiential element to serve as both Theme and New. To indicate the marked status of a predicated Theme, the analysis can be shown as follows:

It was that day	that made Chris suspicious.
Theme	Rheme

As given above, it can be claimed that Sunyoung's usage of 'it' as unmarked and marked Themes develops and expands as she learns to express experiential meanings in a growing range of ways, along with awareness and control of other written language features.

In addition to the usage of 'it' as topical Theme, 'this' as a Reference item is found in Text BB-10 and BB-18 respectively as follows:

(BB-10)

This	is my first ever space journey	I	ever had in my life.
Theme	Rheme	Theme	Rheme

Although 'this' is certainly textual in its function as a cohesive item, it can be classified as a topical Theme because it is a participant in the above clause structure. In the above clauses, the two clauses are supposed to be linked by a structural textual Theme 'that', but Sunyoung omitted the conjunction and as a result, the clauses contain two unmarked topical Themes.

(BB-18)

This	had always been a lovely memory for Chris	that	he would never forget.
Theme	Rheme	Theme	Rheme

Sunyoung's usage of 'this' as unmarked topical Theme is again found in the Orientation Text BB-18 and in this case, the complex clause is organized more grammatically with the structural textual Theme 'that' between the two clauses. Also in the Orientation of Text BB-15, there is another simple usage of 'this' as in 'This was amazing' and 'This was strange'. Comparatively, this usage is very similar to the above two examples in terms of its thematic function. In Text BB-15, 'I' as the main participant comes to recognize the strange situation that the whole family was floating in the air, and while 'I' is wondering about the unbelievable event, 'I' comments at first as in 'This was strange.' And afterwards, 'I' wraps up the Orientation with another Evaluative comment as in 'This was amazing' which signals that 'I' accepts this event as a really exciting one. In many cases, if 'this' is used as the topical Theme as given above, it can be claimed that the usage provides Evaluative elements which make the event or thing being referred to significant or meaningful. In Orientation texts, from Text BB-10 (age 7:4), Sunyoung starts to use 'this' as the thematic function of subjects (topical) by constructing

Evaluative elements which can be seen in more advanced Narrative writing.

In regard to unmarked topical Themes used as subjects, Sunyoung has developed their usage in various ways. One remarkable example is that as alternatives for simple pronouns or the names of nouns, Sunyoung comes to employ more complex nominal groups which are sometimes composed of non-finite verbs as the subjects of the clause. The following example from the Orientation of Text BB-16 illustrates this point:

Sitting under my fireplace	was a rather sooty crocodile.
Theme	Rheme

Sunyoung uses inversion here. The subject is 'a rather sooty crocodile'; the predicate is put upfront, thematically. This (inversion) is usually done for emphasis. Here, she, probably wants to present the 'crocodile' as New, and so, thematically foregrounds the process and its circumstance.

Another example is from the Orientation of Text BB-10:

To have adventures and meet creatures	that	are only dreamed about....
Theme 1	Theme2	Rheme2

The above example shows that the main Theme is composed of the usage of non-finite verb (embedded non-finite clause as Theme) as in 'to have adventures and meet creatures' as the main subject of the complex clauses. In the meantime, the main process part (which can be composed of Rheme 1) was omitted intentionally. By doing this, Sunyoung might have wanted her readers to have more room for their own curiosity on what will be happening next.

To sum up Sunyoung's usage of unmarked topical Theme as subjects of clauses, she noticeably expands the range of possibility in putting various words in the subject position such as 'it', 'this' and non-finite verbs as well as some complex nominal groups as in 'my old dog 'Woof'(Text BB-15)' and 'the smallest planet (Text BB-12)'. Of course, the majority of unmarked Themes in the Subject function have a pronoun as Head such as 'she' or 'I' and a common or proper noun as Head such as 'Hannah' or 'Polar Bear'.

3-3-1-3 Interpersonal Theme Choices in Orientation Texts

An important development in Sunyoung's control of the Orientation in Narrative is the expansion of the range of thematic choices, to include Interpersonal and Textual Themes. As mentioned earlier, Sunyoung attempts to combine dialogic exchange in some Narratives and particularly in the Orientation Texts BB-11 and BB-18, several clauses are realized by interactions among the main participants. So, throughout the whole texts, there can be found many cases of interpersonal aspects, demonstrating the various speech functions such as 'offer', 'command', 'statement', 'question', 'rejection', 'refusal', 'contradiction' and 'disclaimer'. Compared with topical (experiential) Themes explored earlier, interpersonal Themes, as the name itself implies, have the central role in conveying messages in the relationship between the speaker and the addressee. This is closely related to the 'Mood' system that reflects another aspect of the meaning of the clause as exchange (cf. Theme system as a message), but this complicated grammatical system (e.g. finite and subject of Mood) will be addressed in detail in the later section 3.3.2. Now we need to explore more on various examples as interpersonal Themes which can be expressed by the forms of 'vocative', 'modal (adjunct)', 'finite (operator)' and WH- (interrogative) (Halliday, 1994: 54). To borrow Halliday's (1994: 49) explanation, "MODAL ADJUNCTS are those which express the speakers' judgment regarding the relevance of the message." The control of adjusting the speaker's own angle on a certain matter by selecting proper model adjuncts in thematic position can be claimed as one of the indicators of children's growth in control of the interpersonal metafunction of language. Since young children tend to be straightforward and over-generalizing in expressing their judgment, attitude or comment, the usage of modal adjuncts along with modal operators is one of important elements signaling children's language development. In Sunyoung's Orientations, the interpersonal Themes are limited to putting the Finite and Vocative elements in thematic position. The first example from Text BB-11 is as follows:

(Text BB-11)

Is my homework book	there?
Theme	Rheme

As the Finite, typically realized by an auxiliary verb (used in forming tenses and moods), is foregrounded in the thematic position, it signals that a response from an addressee is expected. So, in this clause, the speaker's questioning function is emphasized over any other function as an interpersonal Theme in the thematic position.

(Text BB-11)

Hey	you think	we should have a meeting?
Theme		Rheme

The above example starts with 'Hey' as a vocative element which makes the addressee pay attention to the speaker, followed by another interpersonal aspect of 'you think' as the second person 'mental' clause which seeks the addressee's opinion (Halliday, 1994: 354-363). That is, it can be regarded as comparable with Adjunct such as 'probably' and treated as interpersonal Themes. The following example also demonstrates the Vocative element, which is any item, typically a personal name, used to address, and it is followed by an imperative clause to reveal the relationship between the speaker and the addressee:

(Text BB-18)

Chris, be	more adult type.
Theme (vocative + imperative verb be)	Rheme

3-3-1-4 Textual Themes in Orientation Texts

As far as the analysis of text level elements is concerned, textual Theme choices should be highlighted as it provides us with the big picture of how cohesively the young writer connects the clauses to provide for an overall flow of a text. In other words, the textual Themes give thematic prominence to textual elements with a linking function. According to Halliday's explanation (1994: 53), the constituents of textual Themes include structural conjunctions (linking two clauses in a coordinating relation or marking one clause as dependent on another), relatives (relating a dependent clause to another clause), conjunctives (providing a cohesive link back to previous discourse) and continuatives (indicating a relationship to previous discourse). Now, Sunyoung's overall usage of textual Themes in the Orientation of her Narrative texts is illustrated in the following Table 3-48:

Table 3-48. Sunyoung's Overall Usages of Textual Themes in Orientation Texts

Text (age)	Structural Conjunction	Relatives	Conjunctives	Continuatives
BB-1 (age 5:3)	because, when(2) then			
BB-3 (age 5:9)	and	which	in fact also	
BB-4 (age 5:10)	but			
BB-6 (age 6:2)	when	who		
BB-7 (age 6:7)	but			
BB-9 (age 7:3)	And(2)		anyway, also	hello
BB-10 (age 7:4)	where(1)	where(1)		
BB-11 (age 7:5)	just then	Who(2)		well gosh
BB-12 (age 7:5)	x	x	x	x
BB-13 (age 7:6)	And(4), then, as if			
BB-14 (age 8:1)	And(3), but, when before	where		
BB-15 (age 8:2)	that, if, but(2), , and(4), then, as-as, as if	what	like (likewise)	
BB-16 (age 8:5)	and, but(2)	where		
BB-17 (age 8:5)	but, that			
BB-18 (age 8:6)	and(10), that(1), when, before, but(2), because, as	That(2)		well, maybe

Note: The boxed words signify marking the emergence of new textual Theme

As seen above, in her Orientations (from Kindergarten through Year 3), Sunyoung seems to use mostly structural conjunctions as her choice of textual Themes. Among the range of Structural Conjunctions, she uses 'and', 'then' 'because' and 'when' in order to express a temporal sequence or logical connection. Particularly, the frequent usage of 'but' in the Orientation texts seems to show her control of the semantic function of the Orientation stage which signals the initiation of an unusual event or aspect:

Table 3-49. Sunyoung's Use of the Structural Conjunction 'but' as a Textual Theme in the Orientation

But I didn't believe it. (BB-4)
But there was a brown bear queen already. (BB-7)
But no, I was actually floating. (BB-15).
I asked what was happening a few times but they were just as surprised as I was. (BB-15)
But only a whisper came out. (BB-16)
But still, I stayed where I was with this dragon. (BB-16)
He used to be scared of heights but now his hobby was to hang on a wall, or ever better – a high one. (BB-17)
The kitchen was very small but Chris didn't mind. (BB-18)

From age 7 (at the start of Year 2), Sunyoung expands her range of structural conjunctions to include 'if', 'as if', 'as-as' 'before' 'as' and 'that', alongside the previously mentioned conjunctions such as 'and', 'but', 'then' 'because' and 'when'. The semantic function of 'if' and 'as if' in Sunyoung's Orientations can be interpreted in connection with the Evaluative element which gives further meaning and significance to the events unfolding in Narrative texts. As the following examples illustrate, the clauses followed by the structural conjunctions of 'if' and 'as if' make readers contextualize the Narrative events or situational settings more effectively by supposing some visual imaginative elements:

They all were staring at me as if I was a slimy worm. (BB-13)
(as if: Textual Theme + I : Topical Theme + was a slimy worm : Rheme)
I pondered if it was a dream. (BB-15)
It was as if I had wings. (BB-15)

The structural conjunction 'when', which provides temporal or situational contexts as an important role in the Orientation, emerges early (Kindergarten, age 5), to extend later to other structural conjunctions having similar semantic functions such as 'before' and 'as':

> When I was finished, I hopped in it. (BB-1)
> Before Hannah could complain, her mother said, "Hannah, look, it's a draw to have a trip to space." (BB-14)
> Before he could say another word, she panicked and said ... (BB-18)
> As he was eating, he stared out the window half asleep. (BB-18)

It is remarkable that the clauses opening by structural conjunctions such as 'when', 'before' and 'as' are all positioned initially. That means, the modifying clause is followed by the main clause in above examples. In this case, in terms of the Theme structure, we can analyze these 'hypotactic' (i.e. dependent, modifying) clauses in the following two ways:

As he was eating		he stared out the window half asleep	
Marked Theme (as the whole clause)		Rheme	
As	he was eating	he	stared out the window ..
textual	Rheme	topical	Rheme

Considering that it is only 'hypotactic' clauses which have the possibility of occurring in this initial position as a marked Theme of the clause complex, the above examples seem to prove that Sunyoung has come to control the textual Theme development by selecting marked Themes as the modifying clauses with structural conjunctions. However, in her Orientation Sunyoung does not yet use non-finite clauses functioning as the marked Theme of a clause complex, which are often claimed as more advanced writing patterns (i.e. Blinking nervously, he tried to think of something to say).

If we more closely examine Sunyoung's Orientation texts, however, we are able to trace Sunyoung's writing development in Text BB-16, in relation to the usage of the non-finite verbs:

I asked <u>taking an awfully big risk</u>. (BB-16)
I pinched myself <u>hoping this would be a terrible dream</u>. (BB-16)
Cub got so bored <u>thinking about his name</u>, he fell asleep. (BB-17)

As underlined above, the non-finite verb clauses can have the same function with the foregrounded ones. If so, it can be said that Sunyoung might have been developing already these more advanced verb pattern in Year 2 and 3 in a different position (not as a marked Theme but as a Rheme). Also, it is noticeable that Sunyoung selected these patterns as alternatives to using the structural conjunctions in Texts BB-16 and BB-17. If we change these clauses to clauses with textual Themes (structural conjunctions) they could look as follows:

I asked <u>and I took an awfully big risk.</u>
I pinched myself <u>as I hoped this would be a terrible dream.</u>
Cub got so bored <u>while he thought about his name</u> and he fell asleep.

The usage of 'that' was also expanded to cover several functions as structural conjunctions and relatives which connect two clauses with modifying the precedent (expanding or adding more information) as follows:

I climbed out of bed like I normally do, only to discover <u>that</u> there was no gravity. (BB-15)
It was a pity <u>that</u> people called him 'Cub' because it wasn't a scary name like 'Blood Thriller" or something along those lines. (BB-17)
He knew <u>that</u> he was completely alone in the kitchen with only a spoon to fight with. (BB-18)
It was that day <u>that</u> made Chris suspicious. (BB-18)
This had always been a lovely memory for Chris <u>that</u> he would never forget. (BB-18)

The first three examples given above include 'that' as structural conjunctions which connect dependent clauses. Yet, as we mentioned earlier, the other usage of 'that' as in 'it was that day that made Chris suspicious' is explained in connection with 'predicated Themes' even though it looks like a relative 'that' to define the precedent 'that day'. So in this case, Theme is 'it was that day' and Rheme is 'that made Chris suspicious'. In written English, this kind of thematic structure has particular significance mainly because the Theme can be effectively emphasized as "new or unexpected, or important" information to readers (Halliday, 1994: 59). The other part (Rheme) is the old, or given information. According to Halliday (1994: 59), in spoken English, the 'new' is signaled by the tonic accent, a clear fall or rise (or more complex movement) in pitch, but this accentuation is not marked in writing, "the predication has the additional function in written English of directing the reader to interpret the information structure in the intended way." Such a thematic choice, therefore, would reflect Sunyoung's more advanced way of written text construction. Additionally, the last example as in 'This had always been a lovely memory for Chris that he would never forget.' displays the typical usage of a relative that modifies and defines the precedent 'a lovely memory' as a dependent clause (More specifically, this is an embedded clause). In terms of thematic contribution to the discourse, this kind of down-ranking dependent 'that' clause is said to be minimal (for practical purpose can be ignored) (Halliday, 1994: 63).

In spite of the minimal thematic contribution to the whole discourse, the semantic function of 'relatives' in individual clauses should be recognized as expansion to define, delimit or specify the antecedent (head noun) (Halliday, 1994: 243). Also, constituently, this kind of relatives as embedded expansions are closely related to the function of nominal groups that consist of embedded clause as Postmodifier. It is often claimed that the control of more complicated nominal groups is a sign of more mature writing (Perera, 1984; Aidman, 1999). As Halliday (1994: 242) points out the difference of embedding from 'tactic' relations as follows:

> [I]t is important to distinguish between embedding on the one hand and the 'tactic' relations of parataxis and hypotaxis on the other. Whereas parataxis and hypotaxis are relations BETWEEN clauses... embedding is not. Embedding is a mechanism whereby a clause or phrase comes to function as a constituent WITHIN the structure of a group, which itself is a constituent of a clause.

Relative clauses, in fact, are claimed to be very complicated to learn for young writers (Perera, 1984: 236-239), both native and non-native English speakers. In the sense that relative clauses can be used to pack in more information or modify some word groups with connecting two clauses, they are a more important aspect of written language than of spoken language. Relative clauses emerge in Sunyoung's Narrative at the end of her first year in school (Text BB-3, age 5:9), and increasingly become a feature of her Narrative texts:

> Also, they lived in a town which was the same as city, and lots of ghosts
>   were hiding in the town. (BB-3; age 5:9)
> Once there was a playful girl who loved her family. (BB-6, age 6:2)
> ... blast off into outer space to where no one knows! (BB-10; age 7:4)
> Hannah raced outside where her parents were reading a message out loud.
>   (BB-14, age 8:1)
> I asked what was happening a few times... (BB-15, age 8:2)
> But still, I stayed where I was with this dragon. (BB-16, age 8:5)

The first two examples above demonstrate typical defining relative clauses, introduced by 'which' and 'who'. The relative elements in the embedded clauses elaborate or restate the nominal antecedents, 'a town' and 'a playful girl'. Of the other examples above, there are usages of 'where' relatives. Such clauses are defining relative clauses, like the elaborating ones (who, which – the previous examples) except that here the information is circumstantial such as time, place, manner, cause or condition (Halliday, 1994: 245).

To briefly sum up Sunyoung's choices of textual Themes in the Orientation of her Narrative texts, overall, she tends to use structural conjunctions and relatives rather than conjunctive adjuncts or connectives as the method of text development. Most structural conjunctions are used as logical and temporal chains for linking clauses in a whole sequence. Particularly, the usage of 'but' should be emphasized again due to its important role in constructing an initiating unusual event or situation in the Orientation stage. In addition, the usage of relatives such as 'who', which' and 'where' can also be regarded as evidence of written language development since they are effectively applied to elaborate contextual situation (spatial setting) and characters (participants).

So far, we have examined Sunyoung's developing control of thematic choices in the Orientation of her Narrative texts mainly in terms of experiential, interpersonal and textual aspects, respectively. As pointed out already, her choice of topical Themes expands to include 'it' and 'this', which is significant since some usages of 'it' and 'this' contribute to construction of Evaluative elements in the Orientation. Also, some topical Themes which consist of longer units such as infinite verbs and noun groups with pre- or post-modifiers demonstrate Sunyoung's development of her written language skills over the period studied. With the inclusion of dialogic exchanges into her Narrative, there emerge interpersonal Theme choices. Thus, the child comes to use finite and vocative elements in the thematic position, implying the underlying mood and the participants' relationships through the interaction. Lastly, the choice of textual Themes in Sunyoung's Orientation reveals the young writer's appropriate use of a range of textual Themes including structural conjunctions and relatives in order to knit her Narrative texture more cohesively at a text level. Overall, the range of Sunyoung's Theme choices has expanded to include a variety of experiential, interpersonal and textual Themes. This expansion of the range of thematic choices typical of Narrative genre is evidence of the child's written language development in relation to textual coherence.

3-3-2. The Analysis of Mood System in Orientation Elements

The interpersonal structure of the clause comprises Mood + Residue (Halliday, 1994). The Mood element grounds the proposition or proposal by providing a modally responsible element – the Subject – and by providing terms for negotiation in choices of TENSE/MODALITY and POLARITY carried by the Finite and/or mood Adjunct(s). In addition, there may be interpersonal elements that fall outside this modal structure: e.g. the Vocative element, which addresses the listener (Halliday, 1994: 71-92). The following examples from Sunyoung's Orientations (Text BB-7, Text BB-17) illustrate the above explanation of the basic structure of the Mood system:

147

I	'll	kill	the queen	at midnight.
Subject	Finite	Predicator	Complement	Adjunct
Mood		Residue		

Why	didn't	he	have	legs like human?
Adjunct/ WH-	Finite	Subject	Predicator	Complement
Residue	Mood		Residue	

In the first example, the basic Mood structure of Subject + Finite introduces a statement, and the finite ('ll) presents future tense + median modality + positive choices in the clause. Meanwhile, in the second example, the positions of Subject and Finite were swapped, which means the semantic function of questioning, and the finite element of 'didn't' embodies past tense + negative component in the clause.

In the analysis of the Theme system above, some limited parts of Mood elements were presented as interpersonal Themes which are mostly comprised of finite verbs in interrogative clauses. Even though the limited usage of Mood Adjuncts was pointed out in the analysis, we still need to explore the Mood system realized in Sunyoung's Orientations in a more systematic way in order to understand the underlying clause structures of development of dialogue or exchange. Considering that this Mood system is closely related the area of 'Tenor' representing social relations, the way of interaction or speakers' attitudinal elements should be regarded as another important point for interpretation of dialogic texts. As children grow, the way of interaction or their attitude toward something or someone tends to be more subtle and implicit rather than abrupt, direct and congruent as with very young children. In other words, young children's negotiation skills can be developing through dialogue by adapting themselves to the addressees who can be more strict adults, or the child's close friends or an unknown person. They will need to learn that there is a range of ways to express the degree of their politeness and that there are some occasions on which their parents require them to act and speak more formally. In written language, the same tendency seems to apply, but it is noticeable that it is not easy, and it is not a fast process for young writers to prepare themselves as more confident social members by controlling this delicacy through showing finer choices of Mood elements in their writing.

In the semantic categories of the interactive events, the so called 'exchange', Halliday (1994) conceptualizes two domains, of 'proposition' which implies the semantic function of a clause in the exchange of information and 'proposal' which has the semantic function of a clause in the exchange of goods-and-services. As Halliday (1994: 70) points out, in the life of an individual child, the notion of proposal as the entire range of offers and commands develops earlier than the notion of proposition which is realized in the form of questions and statements. The latter one (proposition) comes to gain more general understanding of the clause in its exchange function and to be equipped with more systematic grammatical resources. However, children take quite a while to learn that language is also used for the purpose of exchanging more abstract information rather than concrete and visible (easily acknowledgeable) goods and services. Halliday (1994: 70) explains the semantic range of 'proposition' as follows:

> When language is used to exchange information, the clause takes on the form of a proposition. It becomes something that can be argued about, something that can be affirmed or denied, and also doubted, contradicted, insisted on, accepted with reservation, qualified, tempered, regretted and so on.

Such a multitude of different rhetorical speech functions cannot be mastered in a short period of time but, as young children get more and more involved in various social and cultural activities or get exposed to the related social contexts, they will be learning to control these increasingly diverse speech functions.

From now on, we shall examine Sunyoung's development of control of the Mood system, critical in construction of the Orientation stage in Narrative, throughout the four-year period, by identifying the emergence of some remarkable instances of the mood elements. Firstly, the basic grammatical structure of mood system involving Subject + Finite + Predicator will be focused on. We will examine the range of the Finite verbal operators (temporal & modal operators) used by the child, as well as the choices for the predicator. Through this, we will consider the developing elaboration of the verbal group within the Predicator. Secondly, in terms of the mood system, the usage of modal adjuncts will be examined in detail.

Table 3-50. Sunyoung's Usage of the Mood System in the Orientation of Narrative Texts

Text (age)	Usages of Finite Verbal Operators (bold underlined) + the Components of Predicators (underlined)	Instances of Modal Adjunct (boxed)
BB-3 (age 5:9)		They always had a fight
BB-6 (age 6:2)	She **didn't** talk to him at all.	
BB-7 (age 6:7)	All white and clumsy, **wouldn't make** her stop being jealous of being the queen. I **know** I**'ve got** an idea. I**'ll kill** the queen at midnight.	
BB-8 (age 6:9)		Nobody ever was proud of that dog. All the people always said,
BB-9 (age 7:3)	I **can** live also in your own backyard. Also I **may** live in bushes.	
BB-10 (age 7:4)	I never know where this space rocket **might** take me.	I ever had in my life. I never know where ...
BB-11 (age 7:5)	The teacher **will** ground me forever. Gosh, what **am** I going to do? **Is** my homework book there? Hey, you think we **should** have a meeting?	
BB-12 (age 7:5)	It **was** also very beautiful to see the star forming around the universe.	
BB-13 (age 7:6)	They all **were** staring at me.	I finally got to the last step and I accidentally slapped my face. And quickly dug my way through the grass. I was so scared.
BB-14	...where her parents **were**	

150

(age 8:1)	reading a message out loud. Before Hannah **could** complain,	
BB-15 (age 8:2)	Yesterday **seemed** like an ordinary morning at first. It **was** as if I had wing.	I normally do. But no, I was actually floating. But they were just as surprised as I was.
BB-16 (age 8:5)	The silence **was broken** by a roar. I **asked** taking an awfully big risk. I **pinched** myself hoping this **would** be a terrible dream.	I had just met an angry dragon. But still I stayed where I was with this dragon.
BB-17 (age 8:5)	He **used to be scared** of heights but now his hobby was to **hang** on a wall, or even better high one. He **would do** anything to change it. Why **didn't** he **have** legs like humans?	
BB-18 (age 8:6)	Nothing **could** ever **make** Chris change his mind. Chris, **be** more adult type! Before he **could say** another word, Chris smiled and thought how the crunchy cornflakes **would shimmer** into his mouth. The kitchen was very small but Chris **didn't** mind. No, it **couldn't be.**	and still believed in Santa Claus. Matthew has already gone to swimming. His mother just told him to eat some cereal. Because he had always seen a lovely swaying of the trees and flowers. This had always been a lovely memory for Chris that he would never forget. He wasn't gone but unfortunately was closer than before...

In specific regard to the usage of 'Finite verbal operators', the selected examples above show that Sunyoung employs several different modal auxiliaries such as 'will', 'would', 'can', 'could', 'may', 'might' and 'should' in order to express degrees of certainty or uncertainty. Particularly, 'will' and 'would' are used frequently as a marker of intention as in 'He would do anything to change it' and prediction or simple futurity as in 'The teacher will ground me forever'. Obviously there is a majority of statements or questions which express two poles of certainty or uncertainty as in 'she didn't talk to him at all.' or 'Is my homework book there?'. However, we can see that Sunyoung has developed a way of marking the speaker's degree of certainty about the information over the four-year period. Apart from using the modal auxiliaries, there can be found some variants to express a degree of certainty (so called 'modality') as in 'I know I've got an idea.', 'You think we should have a meeting?' 'Yesterday seemed like an ordinary morning at first.' and 'He used to be scared of heights but now his hobby was to hang on a wall, or even better high one.'

Another semantic function of finite verbal operators, that of imposing an obligation on someone (to include command as well as request, warning, advice, instruction and seeking permission), is known as 'modulation'. This notion should be explained in the degree of politeness and formality which are other aspects of the interpersonal meaning. Although the modulation examples involve an interrogative structure, they function as requests rather than questions. Also many patterns can be seen as variants on a basic imperative structure. For instance, in the Orientation of her Narrative texts, we find examples of the modulation expressed in a most straightforward and explicit way of the typical imperative structure as in 'Chris, be more adult type!' (BB-18). However, there can be many variants which are by an expansion of the predicator (typically by a passive verb or by an adjective) as follows: 'Chris, you are supposed to be more adult type' and 'Chris, it's necessary for you to be more adult type'. Or, it can be expressed by a finite modal operator as in 'You should be more adult type'. Even though we do not see these variants of modulation in Sunyoung's Orientation texts, this aspect of development should be continuously traced in the next part of Complication stage since we need to know how she expands the usage of modulation to express a more considerate attitude on the part of speaker.

Even though the modality of Sunyoung's Orientation texts is mostly exemplified by modal auxiliaries, it is also supplemented by the usages of modal adjuncts. The modal adjuncts are distinguished from conjunctive adjuncts which occur at starting points in the clause and are significant for its textual organization. Also they are different from the circumstantial adjuncts which are metafunctionally experiential and can be seen in the Residue (in the mood structure). For the most part, Sunyoung's examples indicate that her choices of modal adjuncts are mainly limited to the area of 'usuality' such as 'always', 'ever' and 'normally' along with the area of 'temporality (time)' such as 'finally', 'quickly', 'just' and 'still'. There are also a few more examples representing the area of intensity such as 'actually' and typicality such as 'accidentally'. It can be noted that in the Orientation texts, Sunyoung's typical realization of modal adjuncts mostly realizes on the semantic function of proposition which embodies the areas of probability and usuality. Also the usages tend to be rather congruent and explicit rather than metaphorical and implicit. The issue of explicit or implicit and objective or subjective way will be readdressed further on when analyzing Sunyoung's control of the elements of the Complication and Resolution which shows an increase in the range of modal adjuncts and finite verbal operators.

3-3-3. The Analysis of Transitivity in Orientation Texts

So far, we have explored Sunyoung's growing control of the textual and interpersonal metafunctions of language as realized in her choices within the Theme and Mood system. When we consider the clause from the perspective of the experiential metafuncton, the relevant systems are collectively known as Transitivity and the clause itself interpreted as a process configuration. The main three types of components in this configuration are the process itself, participants involved in the process and circumstance. In this section, we will examine the range of different process types in Sunyoung's Orientation texts, demonstrating the expansion of the Transitivity choices the child makes.

In terms of the Transitivity system, Sunyoung's Orientations demonstrate the prevalence of material (87/219) and relational processes (65/219). There are some Orientations composed of mainly material processes and, on the other hand, some texts construed largely through relational processes. However, the majority of texts use both material and relational processes, interspersed with mental (33/219), behavioural (19/219), verbal (13/219) and existential (2/219) processes.

3-3-3-1. Verbal Processes in Orientations

When Sunyoung starts to combine interpersonal functions as dialogic exchange, she uses more projected clauses with verbal processes rather than reporting clauses (indirect speech). Sunyoung's attempts to include a semantically wide range of different verbs as the verbs used in quoting clauses can be claimed as evidence of her growing control of writing fictional Narrative. The verbal processes 'said' or 'asked' and the mental process 'think- thought' tend to be over-represented in young children's Narratives and as they develop as writers, there can be found an increasingly varied range of choices to replace the 'representative' verbs, the term which Halliday (1994: 252) uses to refer to verbal processes generally. As can be seen from the examples below, Sunyoung attempts to include several verbal processes, in addition to 'said' and 'asked' as in 'cry', 'complained' and 'whispered'.

In addition, Sunyoung expands her usage as projecting verbs to combine behavioural and mental processes as in 'I wanted to scream' (BB-16). In other cases, as in 'Matthew teased Chris and said,' and 'she panicked and said,' (BB-18), the verbal processes are adjoined by mostly behavioural processes to maximize the contextualization surrounding the projecting clauses or "to suggest sayer's attitudes, emotions or expressive gestures that accompanied the act of speaking" (Halliday, 1994: 252). Such choices of semantically enhanced verbs are likely to help the reader's understanding of the situational contexts.

Moreover, further examples display Sunyoung's effort to elaborate the verbal processes with some circumstantial element such as 'cried Sarah with relief' (BB-11), 'I whispered under my breath' (BB-16) and 'I asked taking an awfully big risk' (BB-16). As in 'The headline said 'SPACE' in big block letters' (BB-14), even an unconscious being is used as the sayer of verb 'said'.

Table 3-51. The Use of the Verbal Processes in connection with Behavioural
Processes in Sunyoung's Orientation Texts

Text	Examples
BB-4	My mum said it was magic.
BB-8	All the people always said, "Bother that dog."
BB-11	"Oh, it's you." cried Sarah with relief
BB-14	The headline said 'SPACE' in big block letters
	Before Hannah could complain, her mother said, "Hannah, look, it's a draw to have a trip to space."
	Hannah half smiled and half frowned. "Everyone is to draw." winked Hannah's mum. Hannah groaned and faced the wall.
BB-15	I asked what was happening a few times but they were just as surprised as I was.
BB-16	'Er hi!' I whispered under my breath
	'Oh, no, I had just met an angry dragon.' I wanted to scream.
BB-18	Chris' big brother Matthew teased Chris and said, "Chris, be more adult type."
	"Mum, you always..." and before he could say another word, she panicked and said, "Get changed! ..."
	His mother just told him to eat some cereal

Note: Verbal Processes underlined; Behavioural Processes in italic words

3-3-3-2. Mental Processes in Orientations

The use of mental processes in Narrative is critical as the Narrative is concerned with the interaction between the material and mental planes of events (Bruner, 1986; Toolan, 1988). Sunyoung's Orientation texts indicate that many clauses reflect participants' inner experience by using mental processes, the processes of feeling, thinking and seeing. To represent the semantic areas of perception (seeing, hearing), affection (liking, fearing) and cognition (thinking, knowing, understanding), Sunyoung uses the typical pattern of hypotactic clauses (complex clauses) for a projected meaning in many cases as well as simple clauses as follows:

Table 3-52. The Examples of Mental Processes used in Sunyoung's Orientation
Texts

Text	Examples
BB-1	I wanted to take an adventure with the dinosaurs
BB-2	I heard scary noises.
BB-4	But I didn't believe it.
BB-6	Once there was a playful girl (who loved her family)
	One day she was out playing in her backyard (when she saw a strange man).
	She knew not to talk with strangers

BB-7	I know (I've got an idea).
BB-8	All the people didn't like that dog
BB-10	To have adventures and meet creatures (that are only dreamed about...).
	I enjoy watching stars
BB-11	Hey, you think (we should have a meeting?)
	She was a girl (who didn't like school and who adored animals)
BB-12	It was also very beautiful (to see the star forming around the universe).
BB-13	I thought about how small I was.
BB-14	She loved trips
	But she hated space
BB-15	I pondered (if it was a dream).
BB-16	I listened to the rain drumming on my roof
	I wanted to scream
BB-17	Cub hated his name
	Cub got so bored thinking about his name
BB-18	Chris was 8 years old and still believed in Santa Claus
	Chris smiled and thought (how the crunch cornflakes would shimmer into his mouth).
	The kitchen was very small but Chris didn't mind
	He thought (he had the most beautiful window because he had always seen a lovely swaying of the trees and flowers).
	This had always been a lovely memory for Chris (that he would never forget).
	He knew (that he was completely alone in the kitchen with only a spoon to fight with).

Some mental processes of affection are applied to elaborate the explanation about protagonists, as in 'She was a girl who didn't like school and who adored animals (BB-11)', 'Once there was a playful girl who loved her family (BB-6)', 'She loved trips (BB-14)', 'But she hated space (BB-14)', 'Cub hated his name (BB-17)' and 'I wanted to take an adventure with the dinosaur (BB-1)'. Also these mental processes contribute to providing Evaluative elements in the Orientation, which means that they can provide significant clues or points in understanding the whole Narrative texts including the Complication and Resolution stages. Moreover, the mental processes of cognition (thinking, knowing and understanding) come to be more frequently used over time and particularly, in Text BB-18 (Year 3), Sunyoung construes more sophisticated examples exposing the protagonist's inner thoughts and conflicts, by using hypotactic clauses along with the mental processes of cognition such as 'thought', 'knew' and 'forget':

He thought (he had the most beautiful window because he had always seen a lovely swaying of the trees and flowers). (BB-18)

This had always been a lovely memory for Chris (that he would never forget). (BB-18)

He knew (that he was completely alone in the kitchen with only a spoon to fight with). (BB-18)

Also, the mental processes of perception (seeing, hearing) come to play an important role in initiating unusual elements in the Orientation stage along with creating some sense of tension, which might be linked successfully to the stage of Complication. Thus, in 'I heard scary noises (BB-2)', and 'One day she was out playing in her backyard when she saw a strange man (BB-6)', the clauses with the mental processes ('heard' and 'saw') successfully signal in the Orientation that something unexpected is about to happen. As a whole, the effective usage of mental processes including all three semantic areas of affection, cognition and perception contribute to making the Orientation more meaningful by exposing the other side of the participants' experiential world, namely, the inner world of the protagonists. It should be noted that the usage of mental processes becomes more elaborate as Sunyoung grows older, and as her control of Narrative writing develops.

3-3-3-3. Behavioural Processes in Orientation Texts

Behavioural processes play a critical role in Narrative. Along with the mental processes, the behavioural processes help to represent physiological processes manifesting states of protagonists' consciousness such as 'smile', 'frown', 'stare' and 'wink'. These behavioural processes make readers understand the participants' reaction or attitudes toward events or situations and overall, contributes to the concerned field creation. Behavioural processes in Sunyoung's Orientation texts emerge at age 6 (Year 1) and mostly in Year 2 and 3, her repertories of behavioural processes expands to include about 20 different processes (see the examples in Table 4-1-7). Also, as mentioned before in the section on verbal processes, "while behavioural processes do not 'project' indirect speech or thought, they often appear in fictional Narrative introducing direct speech, as a means of attaching a behavioural feature to the verbal process of 'saying'" (Halliday, 1994: 139) as in *"Everybody is to draw," winked Hannah's mum* (Text BB-14). As she matures as a writer, the Orientation in Sunyoung's Narratives makes use of behavioural processes, which, in addition to material processes, allow the writer to represent the participants' 'symbolic or metaphoric doing'. The use of behavioural processes in her Narratives is another important indicator of the child's developing control over this written genre.

Table 3-53. The Examples of Behavioural Processes in Sunyoung's Orientation Texts

Text	Examples
BB-6	She didn't talk to him at all
BB-13	They all were staring at me as if I was a slimy worm
BB-14	Hannah half smiled and half frowned
	"Everybody is to draw." winked Hannah's mum.
	Hannah groaned and faced the wall
BB-16	He stared at me with two glary eyes
	He snarled and flapped his huge wings ferociously.
BB-17	On a cathedral, a little gargoyle was watching the city below him
BB-18	She panicked and said, "Get changed..."
	Chris smiled and thought how the crunchy cornflakes would shimmer into his mouth and he rushed to the kitchen.
	Chris faced the other way and then turned and looked at the Santa Claus

3-3-3-4. Relational Processes in Orientation Texts

In the Orientation stage of Narrative, most relational processes are used to build up the context for the events, similarly to the use of material processes. Particularly to examine the usage and scope of relational processes is likely to be valid for checking Sunyoung's control of Narrative writing, more focusing on Orientation texts. On the whole, Sunyoung has used more than 60 relational processes in her Orientation texts, which is the second largest class of processes after Material one (more than 80). The semantic area of Relational processes includes naming, defining, assigning, classifying, identifying and attributing and it can be related to expressing something or someone symbolically which appears more complicated than the usage of material processes. To develop the variety of identifying or attributive verb patterns, young writers might have more linguistic exercise by expanding their repertoire of verb variants through the control of somewhat symbolic or metaphorical expressions. The specific examples for these variants will be illustrated as we trace through the usage of relational processes represented in Sunyoung's Orientation texts as follows:

Table 3-54. The Examples of Relational Processes in Sunyoung's Orientation Texts

Text	Examples
BB-3 (age 5:9)	Also there lived in a town which <u>was</u> the same as a city,
BB-4 (age 5:10)	Mum said, it <u>was</u> magic It <u>was</u> a broom
BB-6 (age 6:2)	Her name <u>was</u> Sun-young. She <u>had</u> one brother, her mum and her dad.
BB-8 (age 6:9)	He <u>had</u> no friends except for a dog. The boy <u>was</u> an orphan. All his parents <u>were</u> dead.
BB-9 (age 7:3)	Hello, I <u>am</u> the most beautiful butterfly in the whole world. Anyway to get on me, I <u>have</u> brightly colored wings and I <u>have</u> six legs. I <u>have</u> four wings and two antenna
BB-10 (age 7:4)	This <u>is</u> my first ever space journey [[I ever <u>had</u> in my life]]
BB-11 (age 7:5)	It <u>was</u> Sarah's best friend, Janet A girl who <u>was</u> fairly smart She <u>was</u> a girl who didn't like school and who adored animals
BB-12 (age 7:5)	It <u>was</u> very hard to travel to another planet as well It <u>was</u> also very beautiful to see the star forming around the universe The smallest planet <u>had</u> 15 animals on it.
BB-13 (age 7:6)	It <u>was</u> just like I <u>was</u> in the opposite land. Then I thought about how small I <u>was</u>... I <u>was</u> so scared
BB-14 (age 8:1)	Hannah <u>was</u> a little girl. She <u>was</u> only 7 ... It<u>'s</u> a draw <u>to have a trip</u> to space.
BB-15 (age 8:2)	Yesterday <u>seemed</u> like an ordinary morning at first. This <u>was</u> strange. I pondered if it <u>was</u> a dream. I asked what was happening a few times but they <u>were</u> just as surprised as I <u>was.</u> It <u>was</u> as if I <u>had</u> wings. This <u>was</u> amazing.
BB-16 (age 8:5)	Sitting under my fireplace <u>was</u> a rather sooty crocodile. <u>Are</u> you a crocodile? I pinched myself hoping this would <u>be</u> a terrible dream. But still, I stayed where I <u>was</u> with this dragon.
BB-17 (age 8:5)	He <u>used to be</u> scared of heights but now his hobby <u>was</u> to hang on a wall or even better high one.

159

	The gargoyle's name <u>was</u> called 'Cub'.
	It <u>was</u> a pity that people <u>called</u> him 'cub' because it <u>wasn't</u> a scary name like 'Blood Thriller' or something along those lines.
	Another thing, why didn't he <u>have</u> legs like humans?
	Cub <u>got so bored</u> thinking about his name, he fell asleep.
BB-18 (age 8:6)	Chris <u>was</u> 8 years old...
	Chirs, <u>be</u> more adult type.
	It <u>was</u> that day that made Chris suspicious.
	The kitchen <u>was</u> very small but Chris didn't mind.
	He thought he <u>had</u> the most beautiful window.
	This <u>had always been</u> a lovely memory for Chris that he would never forget.
	He knew that he <u>was</u> completely alone in the kitchen with only a spoon to fight with.
	Chris tried to figure out what the red blurry shape <u>was</u> by staring even harder than ever.
	No, it couldn't <u>be</u>.
	He wasn't gone but unfortunately <u>was</u> closer than before.

In Table 3-54, the usage of 'identifying' relational processes appears only a few times as in 'Her name <u>was</u> Sun-young (BB-3)', 'I <u>am</u> the most beautiful butterfly in the whole world.(BB-9)', 'This <u>is</u> my first space journey that I ever had in my life.(BB-10)', 'It <u>was</u> Sarah's best friend, Janet.(BB-11)' and 'People <u>called</u> him 'Cub' (BB-17)'. 'Her name' as identified (token) can be reversible with the position of 'Sun-young' as identifier (value). As in 'people called him 'Cub', 'him' is identified and 'Cub' serves as identifier.

Compared with the identifying relational processes, 'attributive' relational processes are widely used throughout the Sunyoung's Orientation texts. Even though the range of attributive relational processes appears quite limited to the 'be-verb' and possessive 'have-verb', there are examples in Sunyoung's Orientation texts which demonstrate grammatical structures of the 'Carrier' and 'Attribute' increasingly grammatically varied from just adjective or noun Attributes. Overtime, the variants of the attribute position increase in length and become grammatically more complex: to illustrate, as in

It *was very hard to travel to another planet as well* (BB-12)

It was *just like I was in the opposite land* (BB-13)

Then I thought *how small I was* (BB-13)

I asked what was happening a few times but they *were just as surprised as I was*. (BB-15)

It *was as if I had wings*. (BB-15)

I stayed where I *was with this dragon*. (BB-16)

His hobby *was to hang on a wall or even better high one*. (BB-17)

It *was a pity that people called him 'cub' because it wasn't a scary name like 'Blood Thriller' or something along those lines*. (BB-17)

It *was that day that made Chris suspicious*. (BB-18)

This *had always been a lovely memory for Chris that he would never forget*. (BB-18)

He knew that he *was completely alone in the kitchen with only a spoon to fight with* (BB-18)

Chris tried to figure out *what the red blurry shape was by staring even harder than ever*. (BB-18)

He wasn't gone but unfortunately *was closer than before*. (BB-18)

In addition, some variants of verb types were also found as in 'Yesterday <u>seemed</u> like an ordinary morning at first. (BB-15)', 'I pinched myself hoping this <u>would be</u> a terrible dream. (BB-16)', 'He <u>used to be</u> scared of heights but now his hobby was to hang on a wall or even better high one. (BB-17)', 'Cub <u>got so bored</u> thinking about his name, he fell asleep. (BB-17)', 'This <u>had always been</u> a lovely memory (BB-18)', and 'No, it <u>couldn't be.</u> (BB-18)'.

'Ascriptive' verbs (Halliday, 1994: 120) such as 'seem', 'appear', 'get' 'turn into' and 'remain' appear in Sunyoung's Narrative at a later period. The combining verb patterns with auxiliary verb such as 'would', 'have' or 'could' contribute significantly to representing further semantic delicacy. Also, such expressions as 'as if..', 'just like', 'seemed like', 'would be' or 'it was a pity that ..', reveal Sunyoung's employment of attributive and identifying relational processes in metaphorical use of language. As pointed out above, overall, the use of relational processes in Sunyoung's Orientation texts show her developing Narrative writing skills to be able to express the significant semantic areas more efficiently, and this particularly contributes to constructing the description or contextualization of Narrative setting and characters in the Orientation element of her Narrative texts. Many clauses of relational processes are likely to be linked to Evaluative elements and some of them also play an important role of 'Foreshadowing' which implicitly indicates what will be happening in the

Complication or Resolution parts.

For instance, as in 'I pinched myself hoping this <u>would be</u> a terrible dream. (BB-16)', the readers might expect at this point that something unpleasant would be happening to the protagonist, while, concurrently, they notice that the protagonist does not want to face up to fearing that something terrible might happen. And, in this manner, the sense of tension created for the readers. Although the Foreshadowing elements are not sophisticated enough, the young writer reveals her awareness of the significance of this aspect of Narrative.

3-3-3-5. Material Processes in Orientation Texts

Finally, the material processes ('doing' verbs) should be emphasized in their role of field creation along with the semantic relationship of 'actor' and 'goal'. In Orientation in Sunyoung's Narratives, there are more than 80 material processes used to represent the protagonists' actions and reactions toward 'goals' in relation to the concerned Narrative fields such as 'take', 'kill', 'bother', 'ground', 'lose', 'search' and 'float'. As we look at her use of material processes, we notice that the range of material processes has significantly expanded. Thus, some visual or audio oriented verbs are effectively used in Sunyoung's later texts as in 'He snarled and <u>flapped</u> his huge wings ferociously (BB-16).' Another point is that in the position of 'actor' appeared not only living creatures but also non-living creatures; '<u>The silence</u> was broken by a roar. (BB-16)', 'But <u>only a whisper</u> came out. (BB-16)'.

3-3-4. The Analysis of Nominal Groups in Orientation Texts

So far we have examined Sunyoung's control of the developing Transitivity system in the Orientation of Narrative texts, focusing on the range of process types used. As we have seen above, the range of process types used contributes to constructing a semantic foundation in different Narrative fields. In terms of other elements of the Transitivity system, however, we need to consider 'Participants' which are realized in 'Nominal groups'. While

162

the verb groups play the central role in constructing experiential meaning in the clause level, the participants construct such semantically important key elements as 'who' did 'what' 'to whom'. This reminds us of playing a seesaw where there are two spots at each end for the roles of participants which can make more weight pushing depending on who is sitting. When one side has more semantic weight than the other, the seesaw will be tipped down to the heavier side. This analogy can be used when considering the linguistic prominence at the clause level. Using different patterns of nominal groups, some participants' positions can be emphasized or made prominent semantically in the concerned clauses. Sunyoung as a young writer seems to have developed her control of elaborating nominal groups in the Orientation stage of her Narratives, by attempting more complicated modifying structures. In this section, we shall examine the kinds of nominal groups used in Sunyoung's Orientations over the period under consideration, with a view of tracing her Narrative writing development.

Table 3-55. Selected Examples of Nominal Groups in Sunyoung's Orientation Texts

Text	Selected Examples of Nominal groups
BB-3 (age 5:9)	Near it was a beautiful sparkling **lake**.
BB-6 (age 6:2)	Once there was a playful **girl** [[who loved her family]].
BB-8 (age 6:9)	He had no **friends** [except for a dog]. All the **people** didn't like that **dog**.
BB-9 (age 7:3)	I am the most beautiful **butterfly** [in the whole world]. Anyway to get on with me, I have brightly colored **wings** and I have six **legs**. I better get up and get some **nectar** [[for me to eat]].
BB-10 (age 7:4)	To have adventures and meet **creatures** [[that are only dreamed about...]] This is my first ever space **journey** [[I ever had in my life]].
BB-11 (age 7:5)	She was a **girl** [[who didn't like school and who adored animals]].
BB-14 (age 8:1)	It's a **draw** [[to have a trip to space]]!
BB-15 (age 8:2)	It took me a few minutes to turn the **doorknob** [[leading to the corridor]].
BB-16 (age 8:5)	I listened to the **rain** [[drumming on my roof]]. Sitting under my fireplace was a rather sooty **crocodile**.. I asked taking an awfully big **risk**. But only a **whisper** came out.

| BB-17 (age 8:5) | It was a pity that people called him 'Cub' because it wasn't a scary **name** [like 'Blood Thriller' or something along those lines].
He would do **anything** [[to change it]]. |
| BB-18 (age 8:6) | It was that **day** [[that made Chris suspicious.]].
He thought he had the most beautiful **window** because he had always seen a lovely **swaying** [of the trees and flowers].
This had always been a lovely **memory** for Chris [[that he would never forget]].
As he was eating, he stared out the window half asleep and he saw a red **shape** [[sitting on the washing line with a naughty, twisted smile]].
He knew that he was completely alone in the kitchen with only a **spoon** [[to fight with]].
Chris had seen a strange **Santa Claus** [[staring at him face to face]]. |

Note: Nominal groups – underlined; its Thing – bold typed; Embedded clauses – [[ ]]; Embedded phrases – [].

The complexity of Nominal groups signifies young writers' use of lexical expansion. Consequently, Sunyoung's writing development in Narratives can also be traced by identifying how she plays with modification of the 'Thing' or 'Head', the semantic core of the nominal group. Firstly, in terms of the logical structure of nominal groups, there can be found both 'univariate' structure, a structure generated by the recurrence of the same function, and 'multivariate' structure, the type of structure exemplified by Deictic + Numerative + Epithet + Classifier + Thing + Qualifier (Halliday, 1994: 193). For instance, as in 'a beautiful sparkling lake' (BB-3), some of Sunyoung's nominal groups generate long strings of univariate structure which reflects the recursive aspect of the modifying relation. Also the nominal group 'the most beautiful butterfly in the whole world' (BB-9) is an example of a more distinct multivariate structure in which there is a constellation of elements each having a distinct function. This phrase contains the noun 'butterfly' preceded and followed by various other items, all of which in some way characterizing the noun in question.

In specific regard to the usage of 'Epithet', there can be found some examples of past participle form of Epithet such as 'brightly colored wings' (BB-9), 'a red shape sitting on the washing line with a naughty, twisted smile' (BB-18).

Also over time, Sunyoung tends to use more frequently such attitudinal Epithets as 'lovely', 'naughty', and 'strange'.

Moreover, the patterns of 'Qualifier' (also known as post-modifier) have become more complicated in Sunyoung's Orientation texts. In English, a Qualifier is almost always a prepositional phrase or a relative clause and is an example of embedding. In many cases of Sunyoung's Orientation texts, there can be also found the usages of defining relative clauses which are embedded (rank-shifted) in nominal groups. As in 'a playful girl who loved her family'(BB-6), 'creatures that are only dreamed about...' (BB-10), 'my first ever space journey I had in my life' (BB-10), 'a girl who didn't like school and who adored animals' (BB-11), 'that day that made Chris suspicious'(BB-18), and 'a lovely memory for Chris that he would never forget'(BB-18), all the head nouns which are modified by the embedded relative clauses are more specifically characterized and elaborated, which may increase the readers' involvement in the events being constructed. The use of Qualifier realized in an embedded clause emerges in Year 1 (age 6:2). Over time, such clauses become more frequent in Sunyoung's Narratives, and their structure more elaborate.

Another pattern of a post-modifying structure is that of the nominal groups using infinite verbs. As in 'some nectar for me to eat' (BB-9), 'a draw to have a trip to space' (BB-14), 'the doorknob leading to the corridor' (BB-15), 'the rain drumming on my roof' (BB-16), 'anything to change it' (BB-17), 'a red shape sitting on the washing line with a naughty, twisted smile' (BB-18), 'only a spoon to fight with' (BB-18) and 'a strange Santa Claus staring at him face to face' (BB-18), Sunyoung demonstrates her lexical expansion through using non-finite embedded clauses as time passes. These elements as post-modifier (to provide additional defining or circumstantial information about the thing) can hardly be applied in Korean lexical structures, which is one of apparent differences between English and Korean languages.

As stated above, the nominal groups used in Sunyoung's Orientations seem to incorporate a range of components and variously expandable sub-structures in the nominal group modification. It can thus be claimed that Sunyoung's written language has developed to package a large amount of information in one grammatical unit (particularly as a nominal group), by using post-modifiers (Qualifier) and pre-modifiers (Epithets). If we consider the difference between written language and spoken language, one of the critical features of written language is its higher lexical density than spoken versions. The above examples of nominal groups contribute to increasing in lexical density by using a long string of various Epithets and Qualifiers to allow a large-scale expansion of the amount of information that can be fitted into a nominal group.

An important sign of growth in control of written English is the emergence of a projected clause realizing the Participant roles of Phenomenon within the mental processes of cognition. The first example of these appears at age 7:4 in the Orientation of Text BB-13 and after that, we can find out similar examples in later texts as follows:

> I never know where this space rocket might take me. (BB-10; age 7:4)
> Then I thought about how small I was. (BB-13; age 7:6)
> Chris smiled and thought how the crunchy cornflakes would shimmer into his month. (BB-18; age 8:6)
> Chris tried to figure out what the red blurry shape was by staring even harder than ever. (BB-18; age 8:6)

Even though the above examples do not belong to the category of nominal groups, they contribute to performing a Participant role (similar to nominal groups) in a projected clause of mental process, revealing the protagonists' mental state or thought which is usually linked to Evaluative elements. Thus, in addition to the development of nominal groups, this can also be claimed as a sign of Sunyoung's growing control of the written English language in Narrative writing.

3.4. Detailed Text Analysis in the Complication of Sunyoung's Narratives

3-4-1. The Analysis of Themes in the Complication of Narrative Texts

3-4-1-1. Theme choices in the Opening Clauses of Complication Texts

Now in this section, we shall further examine Sunyoung's Complication elements by focusing on the thematic structure in order to track the changes in her control over the text organization, constituting the message structure of the Complication and highlighting some of its prominent elements. Firstly, the opening clauses of each Complication text will be presented in comparison with the Orientation texts. Then, in line with the Theme analysis of Sunyoung's Orientation stages, the three kinds of Themes that Sunyoung uses in the Complication such as topical (experiential), interpersonal and textual Themes, will be explored individually.

Table 3-56. Theme Choices in the Opening Clauses of Complication Texts

(BB-1)

When I arrived	I got off and saw a Brachiosaurus standing right next to me.
clause as theme (dependent clause)	
textual + topical (When + I ...)	
Theme	Rheme

(BB-2)

I	ran to my day and mum.
topical (subject: unmarked)	
Experiential	
Theme	Rheme

(BB-3)

One day	they were fighting.
topical (temporal circumstance: marked)	
Experiential	
Theme	Rheme

(BB-4)

One day	I was cleaning the floor with my broom.
Topical (temporal circumstance: marked)	
Experiential	

Theme	Rheme

(BB-5)

She	met two hairy creatures on the way home.
topical (unmarked)	
Experiential	
Theme	**Rheme**

(BB-6)

He	was shouting at the old Granny next door.
topical (unmarked)	
Experiential	
Theme	**Rheme**

(BB-7)

So	that night	the rainbow polar bear went to kill the queen.
conjunction	topical (temporal circumstance: marked)	
textual	experiential	
Theme		**Rheme**

(BB-8)

I	'll tell you why.
topical (unmarked)	
experiential	
Theme	**Rheme**

(BB-9)

I	spend most of my time just pollinating flowers and flying around.
topical (unmarked)	
experiential	
Theme	**Rheme**

(BB-10)

Suddenly	I crash into something.
modal adjunct	
interpersonal	
Theme	**Rheme**

(BB-11)

Sarah	ran over to Janet's place two thirty.
topical (unmarked)	
experiential	
Theme	**Rheme**

(BB-12)

It	was one day when all the animals on the smallest planet had run out of food.
topical	
experiential	
Theme	**Rheme**

(BB-13)

Just then	I heard my mother's voice.

conjunction (obligatorily thematic)	
Textual	
Theme	Rheme

(BB-14)

It	took a long time for Hannah to decide if she was going to space or not.
topical	
experiential	
Theme	Rheme

(BB-15)

Soon	mum and dad said
conjunctive adjunct (temporal)	
Textual	
Theme	Rheme

(BB-16)

I	ran to the kitchen.
Topical	
Experiential	
Theme	Rheme

(BB-17)

Cub	woke up soon enough.
Topical	
Experiential	
Theme	Rheme

(BB-18)

Chris	didn't know what to do.
Topical	
Experiential	
Theme	Rheme

As seen in Table 3-56, the Sunyoung's opening clauses of Complication texts mostly start with unmarked topical Themes (11 out of 18) such as the person's names and pronouns including 'it'. There are only two cases of 'marked' ones in topical Themes as in 'One day they were fighting (BB-3, Age 5:9)' and 'One day, I was cleaning the floor with my broom (BB-4, age 5:10)', which both cases have the same temporal circumstantial word in a thematic position. The rest of opening clauses use textual Themes of conjunctions such as 'when (BB-1)', 'so (BB-7)' and 'just then (BB-13)' and a conjunctive adjunct such as 'soon (BB-15). Lastly, there is only one case of interpersonal Theme as a modal adjunct as in 'suddenly (BB-10)'.

3-4-1-2. Topical Themes in Complication Texts

In terms of topical Themes in the Complication, it is noticeable that there had been a majority of unmarked subject Themes. From the early age (Kindergarten, age 5), Sunyoung's Complication stages mostly use unmarked subject Themes such as personal pronouns (he, she, I) and nominal groups (e.g. The wise elephant, mum and dad) in the thematic positions. It appears that the overall discourse Themes in the Sunyoung's Complication texts are selected to track the main participants. The following Table 3-57 provides examples of the range of usages of topical Themes inclusive of marked ones:

Table 3-57. The Examples of Topical Themes in Sunyoung's Complication Texts

Period	Marked Theme	Unmarked Theme		
		Usage of 'It'	Noun groups	Others
Kinderg arten (age 5)	Next night (BB-2) In my dad and mum's room (BB-2) One day (BB-3, BB-4)		A wise elephant who lived next door (BB-3) Three tall and skinny goblins (BB-5)	
Year 1 (age 6)	One dark night (BB-7)	It was like one elephant jumping in our house. (BB-6) She thought it was a stranger. (BB-6) The polar bear didn't know it was raining. (BB-6) It was hard painting herself again...(BB-6) It's all because he always lands in mischief. (BB-7)	My heart (BB-6) The man's eyes (BB-6) Most dogs (BB-70	There is lots of polar bear there. (BB-6) That tells other insects that I am not that tasty. (BB-9)
Year 2 (age 7)	At home (BB-10) The very next day (BB-11) One day (BB-11) That day (BB-11) For weeks (BB-12) Until one day (BB-12) With the galaxy's help (BB-12)	It's not funny (BB-11) It was not a very long time for the ambulance came. (BB-11) It was getting dark and very dim to see her way. (BB-11) It was one day when all the	Two slimy creatures (BB-10) All the other kids except for Janet and Sarah (BB-11) Both kids' faces (BB-11) The king of the land (BB-11) A prick from the	This is not very good (BB-10)

170

		animals on the planet had run out of food. (BB-11) It was about 27 twice as long as me. (BB-13) It took me one whole hour. (BB-13)	rosebush (BB-13)	
Year 3 (age 8)	A few minutes later (BB-17) A few seconds later (BB-18) To Chris, it wasn't pleasant. (BB-18) There, lying was a strange black model. (BB-18) For the first time of his life, Chris thought that Santa was nice. (BB-18) But on the trunk was Santa Claus (BB-18) And down below was a scribbled word saying 'mum'. (BB-18)	It took a long time for Hannah to decide if she was going to space or not. (BB-14) It was now a disaster. (BB-15) It seemed as if Matthew was ready to tease the Santa lover. (BB-18) It was Christmas. (BB-18) It looked like a remote control but smaller. (BB-18)	Darkness should love the rocket ... (BB-14) As redness poured the sky... (BB-15) Suddenly a gust of wind blew by ... (BB-15) A sprinkle of water woke me up(BB-16) All he could think of was that nasty Santa Claus. (BB-18) A red blurry shape sitting on the lane ropes (BB-18) A shiver went up Chris' spine. (BB-18) Then a brainwave swooped into his mind. (BB-18) All Chris wanted was to leave him alone... (BB-18) Maybe lying on comfy spots would help thinking of a plan... (BB-18) A kind, Santa's voice drifted inside the thing... (BB-18 None of them was as realistic as the toy that Santa had given him. (BB-18) Nothing was there. (BB-18) Everything was silent. (BB-18) Something was poking his	This is a good opportunity for you to know and like space. (BB-14) There still was no gravity. (BB-15) That seemed to settle him down a bit.. (BB-16)

			back. (BB-18) His mouth was dry (BB-18)) Chris' head seemed to by saying. (BB-18) Anger was boiling inside Chris' mind. (BB-18)	

As given in the Table 3-57, Sunyoung's use of marked Themes in the Complication of early Narratives is limited to expressions of temporal and space circumstances as in 'the very next day' and 'at home'. Yet, in Text BB-18 (age 8), she seems to attempt a different style of 'marked Theme' that can put more emphasis intentionally on certain circumstantial phrases as in 'To Chris, it wasn't pleasant', 'There, lying was a strange black model' and 'For the first time of his life, Chris thought that Santa was nice'. Also, as in 'there, lying was a strange black model', Sunyoung inverted the word order of 'process (lying)' and 'participant (a strange black model)' after putting 'there' in the thematic position. There can be found two similar examples in Text BB-18 as in 'But on the trunk was Santa Claus' and 'And down there was a scribbled word saying 'mum''. So it seems that Sunyoung purposely locates circumstantial phrases in the thematic positions (even though there are the textual Themes of 'but' and 'and' prior to the circumstantial phrases of 'on the trunk' and 'down there', they are still regarded as marked Themes within the multiple Theme structure. These cases are less common in English writing and can therefore achieve their roles to be prominent (more significant) in conveying the clause messages. This can be related to the 'most marked' type of Theme as a 'thematic Complement', when considered Halliday's explanation (Halliday, 1994: 44). These are examples of multiple Theme choices, which is also a sign of Sunyoung's developing control of the written language.

As to the use of 'it' in the Complication element of her Narrative texts, Sunyoung starts to use 'it' in the thematic position from Year 1 (age 6) mostly as a representational 'it' (pronoun) and meteorological 'it' as in 'it was raining'. Then she expands the use of 'it' to the anticipatory 'it' (in

Theme predication) as in 'it was one day when all the animals on the planet had run out of food' (BB-11). Also there can be found impersonal projection 'it' as in 'it seemed as if Matthew was ready to tease the Santa lover (BB-18)'. More importantly, the overall usages of 'it' as unmarked Themes have significantly contributed to constructing Evaluative elements in the Complication texts; e.g. 'it was now a disaster' (BB-15), 'it took a long time for Hannah to decide if she was going to space or not' (BB-14). This thematic function of 'it' can be found in further examples of the clauses starting with 'this' and 'that': 'This is a good opportunity for you to know and like space' (BB-14), 'That seemed to settle him down a bit' (BB-16). In Years 2 and 3, the usages of 'it' also help to create important circumstantial details such as temporal settings which play a role in connecting the development of events: e.g. 'it was not a very long time for the ambulance came' (BB-11). This trend of development, in specific regard to the use of 'it' and 'this', parallels the developmental pattern found in the Orientation stage of Sunyoung's Narrative texts.

In addition, the nominal groups used as unmarked Themes (mostly in Year 3) appear to be significant in building the development of the Complication stage. On a number of occasions, Sunyoung selects non-living noun groups constructing non-living things placed in the Theme position. The meanings constructed are metaphorical; in many cases, the thematic choices add further tension to the Complication, or refreshing effects. Sometimes it can be a signal of turning points in the course of events: e.g. A sprinkle of water woke me up (BB-16); A shiver went up Chris' spine (BB-18); A brainwave swooped into his mind (BB-18); Anger was boiling inside Chris' mind (BB-18). Lastly as in 'All he could think of was that nasty Santa Claus (BB-18)' and 'All Chris wanted was to leave him alone' (BB-18), the embedded 'that' clauses (in here, 'that' was elapsed) serve as subject Theme as a whole. Considering that in Sunyoung's earlier texts, nominal groups are mostly composed of group and phrase complexes in Theme positions, these clause complex Themes can be considered a sign of development in Sunyoung's Theme choice.

3-4-1-3. Interpersonal Themes in the Complication of Narratives

The Complication elements in Sunyoung's Narrative texts also demonstrate her control of interpersonal Themes which mainly serve the function of exchanging messages between the participants. As mentioned earlier in the analysis section of the Orientation, Sunyoung's Narratives (particularly in Texts BB-11 and BB-18) employ dialogic exchanges throughout the texts. This has resulted in the various usages of interpersonal Themes, including the Finite element (typically realized by an auxiliary verb), a Wh-element signaling that an 'answer' is required from the addressee, a Vocative identifying the addressee in the exchange and a Modal Adjunct typically realized by an adverb. Among them, the Finite element and a Wh-element as in 'Would you like to explore?' 'Is there a problem with you two? (BB-11)' 'Go and do something helpful like eating your cornflakes.' and 'Why are you here? (BB-18)' are used to express the speaker's opinion or seek that of the addressee's, revealing the relationship between the participants, their personalities as well as inviting the readers to participate in the flow of their conversations.

Interpersonal Themes also play a significant role in monologue which emerges in later Narratives (Text BB-18, Year 3, age 8:6). Text BB-18 includes many cases of monologue in which the protagonist, Chris, expresses his feelings and inner states of mind of confusion, despair, doubt and disappointment very effectively. As in 'Had this all been a dream?', 'Can't I ever get some peace?' and 'How could she not believe him? (BB-18)', Sunyoung seems to have been expanding her applications of dialogic exchanges from the usual conversation between the participants to monologue styles. In Text BB-18, Sunyoung shows her control of combining the two elements of usual conversation and monologue in a balanced manner. In this respect, it needs to be acknowledged that this kind of more advanced manner of using interpersonal Themes has significantly contributed to knitting the whole Narrative texture. In many cases, these monologue expressions serve as Evaluative elements in the Complication stage as well, which contributes to intensification of the readers' appreciation of the protagonist's inner feelings or attitudes toward the significant events.

Another example of the expanding repertoire of the child's use of interpersonal Themes is the emergence of the Theme realized in a vocative as in '<u>Mum, Matthew,</u> I told you I was right (BB-18)' and Connectives which occur before interpersonal Themes as textual Themes. They can be found in many cases throughout the Sunyoung's Complication texts as in '<u>Oh,</u> so Scamper might not like you any more (BB-11)' and '<u>Well,</u> I will teach that Santa how to treat people nice! (BB-18)'. Lastly, Sunyoung's usages of Modal Adjuncts, which "express the speakers' judgment regarding the relevance of the message" (Halliday, 1994: 49), have to be considered. In the thematic structure of the clause, the modal adjuncts tend to be the point of departure of the message in English which seems to be quite natural. Even though there can not be found the various types of modal adjuncts in the Sunyoung's Complication texts, in some cases, she certainly showed her choice of modal adjuncts in the Theme position such as 'maybe', 'perhaps', 'of course', 'luckily', 'somehow', 'at first', 'unfortunately' and 'suddenly' (Halliday, 1994: 49, Table 3(3)). Sunyoung's use of Modal adjuncts will be examined further on, when considering the developments within the Mood system. Since the thematic position of the modal adjuncts is not obligatory but still a matter of choice, they can be put in the Rheme position as in 'the draw unfortunately ended up'. So in the analysis of Mood system, we shall consider further examples of 'modal adjuncts' in the Complication of Sunyoung's Narratives.

One final type of interpersonal Theme consists of first and second person 'mental' clauses which express the speaker's opinion or seek the addressee's (Halliday, 1994: 102). The followings are the example clauses. These examples are expressed by applying various kinds of mental verbs in some dialogic exchanges and protagonists' thoughts:

> <u>I suppose</u> slimy stuff compared to dry stuff are very different indeed. (BB-10)
> <u>You mean</u> you're an orphan! (BB-11)

I thought that this dragon was clever. (BB-16)
I guess I failed that plan as well (BB-18)
I recon you could find them quicker. (BB-11)

This choice emerges somewhat later in Sunyoung's texts (this is not of feature of her early Narratives), with Sunyoung's constructing more elaborate Evaluative elements. The 'mental' clause introduces the reader to the characters' inner world and their thinking processes. The characters' qualified judgments of the other characters and the story events get thus constructed.

To sum up, in the Complication stage, Sunyoung demonstrates her expanding repertoire of interpersonal Themes along with the earlier emergence of finite elements and Wh- elements realized mainly through dialogic exchanges (as well as a group of Modal Adjuncts). In most instances, she seems to use the Theme choices which would help her construct a more satisfying Narrative text. More importantly, she further develops a range of Evaluative elements throughout the use of 'monologue' and the first and second person 'mental' clauses, trying to involve the reader in the characters' emotional and mental world. Thus, it can be argued that these are important examples showing Sunyoung's growing control over the Narrative writing.

3-4-1-4. Textual Themes in the Complication Texts of Narratives

Textual Themes also play very important roles in the development of the whole texts by mainly performing the linking functions. These are realized in structural conjunctions, relatives, conjunctive adjuncts and continuatives. The Table 3-58 shows what kinds of textual Themes are used and how frequently (by the numbers in the brackets) they occur in the Complication stage of Sunyoung's Narratives.

Table 3-58. Textual Themes in Sunyoung's Complication Texts

Text	Structural Conjunction	Relatives	Conjunctives	Continuatives
BB-1 (age 5:3)	when(2), and			

BB-3 (age 5:9)	because, or, and(2), but, so(3)	Who		
BB-4 (age 5:10)	And(4)			
BB-6 (age 6:2)	but, because, until, and(4), then, and then, so(2)	Who, where		
BB-7 (age 6:7)	but(3), and(6), while, so(2)	that		
BB-8 (age 6:9)	because, and(3), but(4), when(2), so(2)			
BB-9 (age 7:4)	but, because, that			
BB-10 (age 7:4)	but, because(2), then, and(6), as(2), just then, when, that		on the other hand	
BB-11 (age 7:5)	but(5), that(5), as(2), since(2), just then, and then(3), when(2), as long as, so(2)	what(2), that	Anyway, also	well(2), oh(2), now, for heaven's sake, fine
BB-12 (age 7:5)	When(2), and, but,	which(2), that		
BB-13 (age 7:6)	just then, then, until, but		Soon	
BB-14 (age 8:1)	If, that, as,		Soon	
BB-15 (age 8:2)	and, but(3), as, that		Soon	
BB-16 (age 8:5)	And(4), when(2), that, but, then	that	Soon	
BB-17 (age 8:5)	and(8), then, while, as– as, but, so(2)			
BB-18 (age 8:6)	and(45), but(17), as-as(2), as if(5), when(12), as (4), and then(7), then(15), that(8), until, if(4), just then(2), after,	what(3), whom, that(2), where,(10)	soon(3), meanwhile	

177

| | whenever, in case, what if, once, so | | | |

Note: The boxed words signify marking the emergence of new textual Theme choice in the Complication stage of Narrative texts.

Overall, as shown in Table 3-58, the structural conjunctions such as 'and', 'but' and 'when' which constitute a distinct class in the grammar are in thematic positions as textual Themes in most cases of Complications in Sunyoung's texts. This trend parallels Jinha's case. Particularly, in Text BB-11 and Text BB-18 which are novel-like Narratives, Sunyoung seems to expand the range of structural conjunctions (both co-ordinators and subordinators). Of these conjunctions, temporal ones (when, as, until, just then, after, while) emerge relatively early period in Sunyoung's texts. While unfolding the Complication discourse, the temporal structural conjunctions contribute to signaling the important moments of event developments in the Complication stage by explicitly marking the temporal relationship between the preceding clause and the following clause. The child heavily relies on the use of temporal conjunctions (structural) as textual Themes throughout the Complication. In a sense, this would be expected in Narrative where the event development is commonly based on the temporal order. There are also other examples of temporal conjunctive adjuncts used in the thematic positions, such as 'soon' and 'meanwhile'.

As analyzed earlier in the Orientation section, Sunyoung's usage of textual Themes looks limited to temporal conjunctions and a few conjunctive adjuncts in the Complication texts as well. However, as pointed out earlier in the analysis of the Orientation in Sunyoung's Narratives, Sunyoung seems to attempt to replace the structural conjunctions by dependent non-finite clauses in many cases (mostly in her later Narratives). Remarkably, this trend emerges after Year 2 (age 7) and seems to be expanding the logical-semantic functions from temporal to other categories. The followings are examples of the non-finite dependent clauses in the Complication texts:

Table 3-59. Examples of the Non-Finite Dependent Clauses in Sunyoung's
Complication Texts

She stomped away, <u>muttering some dry, unintelligent words to herself</u>. (BB-11)
<u>Suddenly hearing this</u>, both kids' faces brightened. (BB-11)
"There's no hope!" cried Janet, <u>tears coming out of her eyes</u>. (BB-11)
He waddled into the bathroom, <u>making stomps like earthquakes</u>. (BB-16: age 8:5)
I punch in the air, <u>forcing the dragon to back up</u>. (BB-16: age 8:5)
A few seconds later, three men came, <u>barging in the cathedral</u>. (BB-17, age 8:5)
Chris' mother and Mathew leaped out of the car and hurried off into the house, <u>leaving Chris behind to hold the swimming bags</u>. (BB-18, age 8:6)
Chris whimpered sadly<u> thinking that they still didn't believe him</u>. (BB-18, age 8:6)
She was pulling a sour face, <u>trying hard not to laugh</u>. (BB-18, age 8:6)
Santa came down <u>pulling a twisted, mean smile on his face</u>. (BB-18, age 8:6)
He sat down on the concrete <u>crying and thinking of a new plan he could work on</u>. (BB-18, age 8:6)
Chris frowned at her and went into the lounge and sat there for a few minutes <u>thinking about another plan he could try</u>. (BB-18, age 8:6)
Chris made his way to his room <u>snarling again</u>. (BB-18, age 8:6)
This time Chris dreamt about himself, <u>playing happily with the evil Santa Claus</u> (BB-18, age 8:6)
When he reached his door, he sat down on his chair and drank his water <u>making slapping and sucking noises</u>. (BB-18, age 8:6)
He almost chocked on his drink once he saw Santa Claus sitting beside him, <u>sticking his tongue out as well</u>. (BB-18, age 8:6)

These non-finite clauses are mostly used to provide additional information as a coordinate clause starting with 'and' or 'and then'. For example, 'Chris frowned at her and went into the lounge and sat there for a few minutes <u>thinking about another plan he could try</u>' can be interpreted as 'and thought about another plan he could try'. Also there are a few cases of enhancing clauses which need a subordinator such as 'when', while', 'because', 'if' and 'until'. As in 'when he reached his door, he sat down on his chair and drank his water <u>making slapping and sucking noises</u>', the underlined non-finite clause can be transformed as in 'as he made slapping and sucking noises'. Since there is no indication of its logical-semantic function, there can be no definite interpretation of the dependent non-finite clause. Nevertheless, overall, in the above examples, Sunyoung seems to use non-finite clauses as mainly extending clauses ('and' type additives) and enhancing clauses ('while' type temporal).

Moreover, in this regard, some issues can be raised. Firstly, in Sunyoung's case, she seems to be using dependent non-finite clauses rather than some dependent finite clause (with co-ordinator or sub-ordinator) during her later periods (Year 2-3). Perera (1984: 236-239) points out that the pattern of non-finite clauses in the predicate is found mostly in more advanced writers (in children's writing in average 9 to 10 years). This seems to be characteristic of written English rather than spoken English. According to Halliday (1994: 241), this kind of transfer from dependent finite clause (e.g. When you reach the monument,...) to dependant non-finite clause (e.g. Reaching the monument,...) can be a process of a gradual loss of information since the dependent finite clause shows Transitivity, with Process and Medium; dependent mood, with Subject, and reduced primary tense. Yet the dependent non-finite clause shows Transitivity with Process but no Medium; no mood, no explicit Subject and no primary tense. The dependent non-finite clause also can be simplified to prepositional phrase which shows no Transitivity, no mood, and no tense (e.g. At the monument ...). Halliday (1994) explains that the process of loss of information can be related to 'Grammatical metaphor' which is characteristic of advanced writing skills. So, Sunyoung's development of the dependent non-finite clauses may be explained as an advanced implicit way of written language.

3-4-2. The Analysis of Mood System in the Complication Stage of Narrative Texts

From now on, we shall examine Sunyoung's growth in control of the Mood system throughout the Complication stage of her Narratives. Similarly to the approach used in the analysis of the Orientation, we will consider clause samples which involve a prominent Mood system (Subject + Finite + Predicator) and the instances of Modal Adjuncts.

Table 3-60. Mood System in the Complication of Sunyoung's Narratives

Text (Year, age)	Usages of Finite Verbal Operators (bold underlined) + The Components of Predicators (underlined)	Instances of Modal Adjunct (boxed)
BB-1 (Kinder, age 5:3)	All past (simple) tense	
BB-2 (Kinder, age 5:7)	He told their mum and she said, "Dog **can** stay in our house but cat **can't.**	
BB-6 (Year 1, age 6:2)	He was angry because he **couldn't** trick her.	
BB-7 (Year 1, age 6:7)	It **will not** rain in the morning.	
BB-10 (Year 2, age 7:4)	But on the other hand, it **might** just be a huge rock... They **seem** to look poor. At home, I **should** have taken a bath.	... it might just be a huge rock...
BB-11 (Year 2, age 7:5)	Oh, Scampler **might not** like you any more. As you **might** have known, ... She shouted "we **could** put up signs" 'OK, **should** we find Scamper first?'	
BB-12 (Year 2, age 7:5)	When all the animals on the smallest planet **had** run out of food, ... But no one **was** to be seen ...	I almost nearly drowned.
BB-14 (Year 3, age 8:1)	Darkness **should** love the rocket	
BB-15 (Year 3, age 8:2)	But nothing **would** work. **Was** she lost forever?	
BB-16 (Year 3, age 8:5)	That **seemed** to settle him down a bit ... I **am** totally scared of this beast ...	I can barely shove his fat body in. I am totally scared of this beast...
BB-17 (Year 3, age 8:5)	Perhaps they **had** never seen a talking gargoyle before. Somehow the key just **didn't** seem to come into his hands.	Perhaps they had never seen ... That almost worked. They were just about to faint. The gargoyle just stared at them full of wonder. Somehow the key just didn't seem

		to come into his hands.
BB-18 (Year 3. age 8:6)	As if Santa Claus **might** hear him ... How **could** she not believe him? But he **was** caught from the swim club teacher for listening inappropriately. It **seemed** as if Matthew was ready to tease the Santa lover. There really **was** a mean Santa Claus sitting on the washing line! He **wasn't** going to put up with his families disgusting behavior. He **began** to think how he could prove that there really **was** a Santa Claus. He **must** have escaped. Nothing **would** come into his mind. All Chris wanted **was** to leave him alone and go find .. Maybe lying on comfy spots **would** help thinking of a pain, thought Chris. He **would** talk to the nasty Santa Claus and ask him if he **could** leave!! He **must** have (of) thought that Chris **was** going to pounce... **It's** really nice of you to keep me company ... Nothing **was** to be seen... Then the Santa **must** be invisible.! He **sat** down on the table and **waited** for his food to be delivered on the table. But he still **thought** he **had to** be a lot more careful about Santa Claus. **Would** you like to explore? Chris's head **seemed** to be saying, 'Be Santa Claus's friend!' But Chris **couldn't**, No he **wouldn't**. Chris wished that he **was** never born. He **stared** at one of the kitchen stools where a red jacket **had** been hung.	But his mother just slammed the door on his face ... Chris usually took his swimming lessons seriously ... Matthew was already waiting for Chris with his mother. When Chris saw Santa Claus, he almost jumped at least a foot in the air. Chris just said, ... Chris almost jumped a foot in the air. He had already stepped into the dusty door. He dozed off to sleep as he usually did. Can't I ever get some peace? He almost checked on his drink once he saw Santa Claus sitting beside him sticking his tongue out as well. But he still thought he had to be a lot more careful about Santa Claus. Chris wished that he was never born.

As shown in Table 3-60, the tendency of Sunyoung's

employing Finite verbal operators in the Complication is similar to that in the Orientation. There are mostly past tense verbs in the Complication element as well, along with present perfect and simple future tense. Also the child's use of modal auxiliaries such as 'can', 'can't', 'could', 'couldn't', 'will not', 'would', 'might', 'might not', 'should', 'must have escaped', 'must be invisible', 'had to be' shows that she has developed a range of modal operators from semantically low ('can', 'may') to median ('will', 'was to') and high area ('must' and 'had to') (refer to Halliday, 1994: 76, Table 4(3)).

Among these usages, Sunyoung seems to be attempting to express a type of obligation (modulation) by using 'should have + p.p'. Apart from using the finite modal operator (typical realization), there also can be found some variants of modalization and modulation as in 'no one was to be seen' (BB-12), 'I am totally scared of this beast' (BB-16) and 'It seemed as if ...' (BB-18). Sunyoung begins to use more varied pattern of clauses such as passive voice or infinite verb patterns and this made Sunyoung's Complication texts include more Evaluative elements: 'He stared at one of the kitchen stools where a red jacket had been hung (BB-18)' and 'Nothing was to be seen (BB-18)' and 'All Chris wanted was to leave him alone and go find... (BB-18)'.

As to the modal adjuncts used in the Complication stage, the usage patterns are similar to those in the Orientation stage. In Sunyoung's Complication texts, the first instance of modal adjunct is 'just' in Text BB-10 (age 7:4) to express 'intensity' as adjuncts of mood (later, the use of 'just' is expanded to express temporality), and then in Text BB-12 (age 7:5), 'almost nearly' is used for expression of 'degree'. During later periods (mostly in Year 3), her choices of modal adjuncts increases to the range of 'usuality' ('usually', 'ever', 'never', 'barely'), 'temporality' ('already', 'still' and 'just') and 'degree' ('totally'). The appearance of these modal adjuncts in a child's text is commonly viewed as a sign of an increased control over the written mode of the English language (Perera, 1984).

To sum up, the choices within the Mood systems which

Sunyoung makes in the Complication elements also show her developing control of applying the function of exchange or interaction through various usages of Mood elements such as modal auxiliaries, finite operators and modal adjuncts. In addition, over the four-year period (from Text BB-1 to BB-18), there is a distinct expansion of the range of verb patterns (predicators) used to express meaning in more subtle ways.

3-4-3. The Analysis of Transitivity in Complication Texts

Another important area of the child's growing control of the written Narrative is the choices she makes in the Transitivity system. First, the majority of process types are material and relational ones. In the Orientation element, however, the numbers of material processes and relational processes are almost in the same proportion. Comparatively in the Complication texts, the number of relational verbs is not so big as the portion of the Orientation texts as this trend seems to reflect the characteristics of semantic meaning of each stage in the Narrative writing. While in the Orientation stage, the main function is to introduce the main characters or settings where more relational verbs are necessary, the main function of the Complication is to develop more events or conflicts between the characters. Significantly, the verb pattern (predicator) of attributive relational processes has become more complex over the period. Also, the range of material processes used in the Complication element has expanded significantly with a wide variety of semantic meanings, to include such processes as 'zoomed', 'drowned', 'grounded', 'squeezed' and 'blocked'.

Second, the Complication in Sunyoung's Narrative texts includes a lot of behavioural processes. The nuclear participants in the Complication are more often represented through behaviors revealing their personality and conflicts between the characters. In many cases, these behavioural processes are used to project the participants' utterances (to introduce dialogue), as in 'stomped', 'shivered', 'gulped', 'stared', 'nodded', 'collapsed', 'snarled' and 'tipped'. In addition to using mental processes (of perception, cognition and affection) in order to expose the participants' inner states including conflicts, Sunyoung commonly uses behavioural processes, in combination with material ones. So it can be pointed out that Sunyoung's Complication texts consistently employ a range of behavioural verbs, in addition to verbal and mental processes, so that the role of behavior in the Transitivity system is more emphasized in the semantic meaning of Complication stage.

Lastly, many process types are used in non-finite forms (present continuous, to-infinitive) to add further detail to the semantic elements as in 'came barging', 'came down pulling a twisted, mean smile on his face', and 'tried to knock me down'. Along with this, a significant development in Sunyoung's control of written language is the growing range of circumstances to elaborate on the processes being constructed, as in 'Chris waited for hours and hours with a serious face expression (BB-18)'. Also some material processes such as 'made' or 'gave' were used with a goal like phrase as in 'made a so-what face' and 'gave an unpleasant lesson'. All these exemplify Sunyoung's expansion of usages within the Transitivity system in the Complication of her Narrative texts.

3-4-4. The Analysis of Nominal Groups in Complication texts

A significant area of children's developing control of the written language is their mastery of the expansion of the nominal group. The expansion of a noun can be realized in various ways within the nominal group structure. Sometimes it generates long strings of noun modification or the Thing. The semantic core of the nominal group is modified by Qualifiers which can be embedded (rankshifted) by a clause or phrase. Now we shall examine Sunyoung's growth in control of the nominal group structure in the Complication of her Narrative texts. Table 3-61 shows selected examples of nominal groups used in Sunyoung's Narratives over the four-year period.

Table 3-61. Selected Examples of Nominal Groups in Sunyoung's Complication Texts

Text	Selected Examples of Nominal Groups	Comments
BB-1 (age 5:3)	and saw a **Brachiosaurus** [[standing right next to me]]....	
BB-3 (age 5:9)	A wise **elephant** [[who lived next door]] said not to fight ... The wise elephant had a deep **heart** [same as the lake].	
BB-5 (age 5)	Three tall and skinny **goblins** also said to meet.	
BB-6 (age 6:2)	He was shouting at the old **Granny** next door [[who was always kind to us]]. It was like one **elephant** [[jumping in our house]]. He made the **trap** [[where he put the parcel and put dirt over it]]. I saw the **man** [[hiding behind a rock]].	
BB-7 (age 6:7)	All different **colors** washed about her like star falling down. ... she saw a **man** [[with a long beard and dragged clothes just standing still]].	* a man [[with a long beard and dragged clothes just standing still]]: an embedded phenomenon
BB-9 (age 7:4)	... we are the only **one** [[to save earth]].	
BB-11 (age 7:5)	All the other **kids** except for Janet and Sarah brought in their homework. She stomped away muttering some dry, unintelligent **words** to herself. Sarah tipped over a tree **root** [[that was shaped in a curve]]. ... Sarah was the first **person** [[to put her hand up]]. Janet's mum had to type down all and exactly 30 **signs** each [with a photo of Scamper on it].	
BB-12 (age 7:5)	... when all the **animals** [on the smallest planet] had run out of food, .. The **king** [of the land] sent some brave animals to search for a **planet** [[which had plenty of food]]. Until one day, one **animal** [[that the king had sent]] had flew over to the starving animals. When they came to the **planet** [[which had so much food]], ...	

186

BB-13 (age 7:6)	A **prick** [from the rosebush] had pricked me. Soon I had reached the **top** [of the rose bush]	
BB-14 (age 8:1)	This is a good **opportunity** [[for you to know and like space]].	
BB-15 (age 8;2)	Suddenly, a **gust** [of wind]blew by...	
BB-16 (age 8:5)	... a **sprinkle** [of water] woke me up. I hear a **groan** [from mum's room]. I ran to my **room** and pushed the **dragon** [in a huge closet].	
BB-17 (age8:5)	So he gave them a warning **glare**... And inside was a squirming **figure** [of the priest]!	

BB-18
(age 8:6)
	Go do **something** helpful [like eating your
	    cornflakes.]
	He took a glimpse of his **food**..
	All [[he could think of]] was that nasty **Santa
	    Claus**.
	Chris' mother gave him a hard **stare.**
	A red blurry **shape** [[sitting on the lane ropes]].
	Chris' mother was going to give him an
	    unpleasant **lecture**.
	There really was a mean **Santa Claus** [[sitting
	    on the washing line]].
	He was making a sour **face** trying hard not to
	    laugh.
	Matthew showed a puzzled **face**.
	Santa came down pulling a twisted, mean **smile**
	    [on his face].
	He sat down on the concrete crying and thinking
	    of a new **plan** he could work on.
	In a second, the mysterious Santa was sitting
	    right next to Chris as if he had known the
	    plan [[Chris was plotting on]].
	... so he didn't have a **chance** [[to take a glance
	    at Chris' mysterious present]].
	Chris tiptoed off to his room and took off the
	    wrapper [of the bright red package...]
	Chris' mother was reading a Christmas **recipe**
	    [for pudding].
	None of them was as realistic as the **toy** [[that
	    Santa had given him]].
	Chris made a so-what **face** and frowned.
	Chris tried to push down his angry **thoughts**.
	Chris had a very peculiar **dream** about himself
	    [[becoming friends with the evil and lousy
	    Santa Claus]].
	As Chris ran down the **hallway** [[that was
	    leading to the door]], he could make up a red
	    shape [[guarding the door]].
		* a glimpse
		of his food:
		'food' is
		chosen as
		the Thing to
		highlight in
		the
		experiential
		structure of
		the nominal
		group.

	He sat up straight and headed for the kitchen to help himself to <u>a glass of freezing **water**</u>. He stared at <u>one of kitchen **stools** [[where a red jacket had been hung]]</u>. Chris made <u>a go-away-I-don't –like-you **face**</u> and stuck out <u>his red, pointy **tongue**</u>.	

Note: Nominal groups – underlined; its Thing – bold typed; Embedded clauses – [[ ]]; Embedded phrases – []

Firstly we can notice that there are many modifying elements by V-ing (present in present) as in 'a Brachiosaurus <u>standing</u> right next to me (BB-1)', 'one elephant <u>jumping</u> in our house (BB-6)', 'the man <u>hiding</u> behind a rock (BB-6)', 'a red blurry shape <u>sitting</u> on the lane ropes (BB-18)' and 'a mean Santa Claus <u>sitting</u> on the washing line (BB-18)' from the early age to the Year 3 period. Also as a pre-modifier which is followed by a head noun or thing, the form of V-ing had been used several cases as in 'a <u>warning</u> glare (BB-17)' and 'a <u>squirming</u> figure of the priest (BB-17)'. Also the past participle adjectives such as 'a puzzled face' and 'a twisted, mean smile on his face (BB-18)' can be found as a similar functional pre-modifiers. Similarly, the other structure by infinitive verbs also had been successfully used in some cases as in 'we are the only one <u>to save</u> earth (BB-9)', 'the first person <u>to put</u> her hand up (BB-11)', 'a good opportunity for you <u>to know</u> (BB-14)' and 'a chance <u>to take</u> a glance a Chris' mysterious present (BB-18)'.

Secondly, the Complication elements seem to demonstrate that Sunyoung is using a defining relative clause as an embedding system from an early age. As in 'A wise elephant <u>who lived next door</u>' (BB-3), 'the old Granny next door <u>who was always</u> kind to us' (BB-6), 'the trap <u>where he put the parcel and put dirt over it</u>' (BB-6) and 'a planet <u>which had plenty of food</u>' (BB-12), the embedding clauses contribute to describing important information on the participants or key material which is related to events or setting. In Text BB-18, Sunyoung uses the defining relative clause using 'that' more frequently as in 'the toy <u>that Santa had given him</u>' and 'the hallway <u>that was leading to the door</u>' in order to further qualify the important objects in the events, and in some cases, she omits the relative pronoun 'that' as in 'a new plan he could work on' and 'the plan Chris was plotting on'.

Another type of structure of the nominal group in the Complication stage is the use of the prepositional phrase (with, for, on, from, in) as a post-modifier. This emerges in Year 1 Narratives (age 6:7). As in 'a man with a long beard' (BB-7), 'all the other kids except for Janet and Sarah' (BB-11), '30 signs each with a photo of Scamper on it' (BB-11), 'all the animals on the smallest planet' (BB-12), 'A prick from the rose bush' (BB-13), 'a groan from mum's room' (BB-16) and 'the dragon in a huge closet' (BB-16), the various prepositional phrases modify the core things by clarifying or elaborating the nouns. At the same time, Sunyoung demonstrates successful usages of 'of-prepositional phrase' as in 'the king of the land (BB-12)', 'the top of the rose bush' (BB-13), 'a gust of wind' (BB-15), 'a sprinkle of water' (BB-16), 'a glimpse of his food' (BB-18) and 'a glass of freezing water' (BB-18) in order to provide further detail about the participants or to describe a measuring unit of material uncountable nouns.

Some particular expressions which expose Sunyoung's writing patterns are as in 'gave him a hard stare', 'he gave them a warning glare' (BB-17) and 'to give him an unpleasant lecture' (BB-18). Using hyphens between the words, Sunyoung sometimes creates an univariate structure (long strings of pre-modifiers + head noun) as in 'a go-away-I-don't-like-you face' (BB-18) and 'Chris made a so-what face and frowned' (BB-18). In Complication stage, Sunyoung seems to be using the full potential of the nominal group to pack in information about the participants: she uses both pre- and post-modifiers. As pre-modifiers, experientially she commonly uses the structure of Deictic + Epithet (sometimes, more than one) + Thing. Also, very productively, she uses elaboration in the Qualifier position: she uses both embedded phrases and embedded clauses. The combined nominal groups by pre-modifiers and post-modifiers also can be frequently found as Sunyoung has been developing to control her nominal group writing: e.g. 'a red blurry shape sitting on the lane ropes' (BB-18), 'a twisted, mean smile on his face' (BB-18), and 'a very peculiar dream about himself becoming friends with the evil and lousy Santa Claus' (BB-18).

To sum up, Sunyoung has developed her control of the nominal group structure in many ways, using pre-modifiers and post-modifiers in order to clarify and elaborate the core nouns (Thing), in the experiential structure, which are important or key words in the events of Complication element. These elaborations help to further describe the circumstances of the events in the Narrative, and equally importantly, help construct the feelings of the characters. Thus, this kind of modification of the noun group demonstrates Sunyoung's growing control of the written Narrative, and of the written mode of English more generally.

3.5. Comparative Analysis of Jinha and Sunyoung's Narrative Texts

Throughout the text analysis of Jinha and Sunyoung's Narrative writing, their developmental patterns and characteristics have been disclosed in the aspects of their control of schematic structure, Transitivity, Nominal groups, Theme choice and Mood system, along with consideration of their Narrative writing contexts (both school and home).[30]

3.5.1. Control of Schematic Structure

In terms of their control of the schematic structure, both Jinha and Sunyoung seemed to be more confident in writing

---

[30] Earlier sections have outlined possible variables in the comparative analysis of the two siblings' backgrounds, including their learning style, age, personal preference of special genres, their school and home environment as well as literacy related experiences. Apart from the personal factor variables, their school and home contexts in related literacy experience were very similar. Since Jinha started his school learning earlier in 1997 Kindergarten than Sunyoung, the first two years of Jinha's school literacy experience, which was based on Whole Language Approach and Process Writing, can be another variable factor. When two years later Sunyoung entered the same school as Jinha's, the Genre pedagogy was about to be introduced and Sunyoung started her formal literacy learning during this 'transitional' period. Therefore, for the whole period of research (1999 – 2002, Kindergarten to Year 3) focusing on Narrative writing, Sunyoung was exposed to Genre-based literacy pedagogy both in school and in the home. For Jinha, during the first two years in school (1997-1998: Kindergarten to Year1) he was exposed to the Whole Language approach and then, for the next three years (1999-2002: Year 2 to Year 5), he experienced Genre-based Approach being introduced in literacy pedagogy.

190

the stage of Orientation than Complication and Resolution elements. Their writing products also prove that even in their initial texts the Orientation stage is mostly constructed quite successfully, with its semantic property of introducing the setting, characters and initiating events. The elements of 'Foreshadowing' also emerge in both children's texts in an embryonic manner (explicitly rather than implicitly). Their Complication and Resolution stages are initially not distinctive due to lack of sense of crisis and problem-solution. Distinctly, both children's early Narratives reflect that they had some difficulty in developing the Orientation stage up to the next stages in terms of managing the story line. Since the young writers would have been used to the conventional Orientation and ending elements just like 'Once upon a time' and 'they lived happily ever after', they could start the Narrative texts using such formulaic expressions. As to the Complication stage, however, they seemed to need more systematic practices along with modeling and joint construction.

Both children have demonstrated growth in their control of the Evaluative elements which give significance to the Complication and Resolution stages. In realizing the Evaluative elements, Jinha and Sunyoung have developed their linguistic choices somewhat differently. For instance, initially Jinha uses more relational processes or existential ones (e.g. *There was one major problem. Was it evil?*, *Now it was pretty obvious that this creature was evil*) whereas Sunyoung uses more mental verbs with projection clauses (e.g. *she thought that it was a stranger*). Later Sunyoung expands the ways of realizing Evaluative elements by using 'it' or 'that' in thematic positions. She also uses monologues (revealing protagonist's inner feelings or attitudes toward the significant events) as well as a range of existential and relational processes. In this way, the children's later Complication and Resolution stages could give more room to the readers to retain their curiosity or sense of crisis, not going to the last stage so abruptly. However, as mentioned above, in realizing the Evaluative elements, it is quite obvious that Sunyoung attempts more various ways than Jinha.

Another remarkable fact is that both children have developed their Narrative writing texts to include dialogic exchanges from the middle period (Sunyoung: Year 2, Jinha: Year 4). They seem to attempt another style of Narrative texts which are different from conventional folk tales. In this doing, their interpersonal meanings were practised and they seem to be successful in finding other ways of constructing Narrative texts by effectively using characterization through dialogue exchanges. Particularly in Sunyoung's case, she appears to prefer this kind of Narrative texts (using conversational dialogues) to other types so she extends her Narrative writing to construct a novel-like Narrative (e.g. Text BB-18, Year 3). Her successful case of writing the 10-page Narrative can be attributed to the fact that she has developed the dialogic style along with the exploration of one of her favorite topics, such as friendship. Meanwhile, Jinha has also been able to construct quite a successful Narrative text (B-10) in Year 5, writing from the first person perspective. Sunyoung's most successful Text BB-18 (in Year 3) is the third person perspective inclusive of many dialogue exchanges whereas Jinha's does not have much dialogic exchange (only a few clauses) with different perspective. The children appear to have developed their own style of Narrative texts even though they have been exposed to the same Genre approach at school and in the home. One of the factors influencing their writing style can be the kinds of texts to which they have been exposed in reading.

In this respect, it can be argued that Genre-based Approach to Narrative writing does not result in stereotypical texts lacking creativity, as its opponents would claim. The counter argument that Genre Approach's explicit teaching on the schematic structure and language features might limit the young children's imagination and originality appears to be far from the reality of primary literacy learning. According to the researcher's observation of Jinha and Sunyoung's classrooms for a prolonged period, young children usually do not have sufficient time to practise and develop a range of written genres up to satisfactory level which would approximate the models presented. Without the structured explicit teaching of the schematic structure, a majority of young writers would not progress in their Narrative writing with satisfaction and sense of achievement. In Jinha and Sunyoung's case, the explicit teaching of the schematic structure clearly assisted them to develop further awareness of the Narrative features and made them feel more confident in starting and developing Narrative texts within the limited time allocation. The sense of achievement from their finalizing a Narrative text was important. Even though Jinha was not quite impressive in Narrative writing during the research period, compared with Sunyoung, he commented that he would like to write more Narratives after finishing one of his most successful Narratives, Text B-10. As mentioned before, the development of Narrative writing for primary aged children obviously includes many essential factors such as exposure to oral and reading experience. However, in order to make their reading experience enhance their writing products more effectively, the explicit teaching of at least the Narrative schematic structure through modeling and joint construction as well as worksheet exercises could be beneficial for those who want to write but don't know how to start.

3.5.2. Transitivity

To construct experiential semantic fields in Narrative writing, both Jinha and Sunyoung start to employ material processes and relational processes from early on and later on come to employ a range of mental processes to depict the participants' inner world including their emotional conflicts and attitudes toward the key events. Particularly the mental processes of perception (seeing, hearing) come to play an important role in initiating the unusual element in the Orientation, along with creating some sense of tension, which might be linked successfully to the Complication (e.g. '*I heard scary noises.*', '*when she saw a strange man*').

There are also differences in the children's choices in the Transitivity system. Thus Sunyoung employs verbal and behavioural processes more symbolically and meaningfully in comparison with Jinha's counterparts. For example, Sunyoung has certainly extended the range of verbal processes from some representative verbal ones such as 'say' or 'ask' to a semantically wide range of different verbal ones such as 'complain' or 'whisper' (in quoting clauses). Also some verbal processes are adjoined with behavioural verbs, enhancing situational contexts (e.g. *She panicked and said,*) or are used with some circumstantial elements as in '*I whispered under my breath*'. In many cases of Sunyoung's Narrative texts, behavioural processes contribute to representing the participants' symbolic or metaphorical action which can not be realized in material processes only. The significant usages of verbal and behavioural processes in Sunyoung's Narratives outnumber Jinha's counterparts and it can be claimed that this kind of difference might have significantly contributed to Sunyoung's control and development in Narrative texts. In addition, she also demonstrates a range of grammatically complex verb patterns to convey subtle meanings effectively. If we think of the experiential characteristics of Narrative writing in terms of lexical range and grammatical complexity, control of verbal groups appears to be one of the key factors in successful writing in this genre.

3.5.3. Nominal Groups

The development of nominal groups is also closely related to the young children's control of written language mode. In Narrative texts, nominal groups are mostly found in the positions of participants which depict characters or key events. Therefore, the successful usage of nominal groups is directly linked to the essential Transitivity system along with the role of the 'process'. In specific terms of Nominal groups, overall, Jinha and Sunyoung's Narrative texts demonstrate a range of nominal groups with both elements of pre-modifiers and post-modifiers. Even in their early texts, both children employ an embedded clause as Qualifier in their nominal group structure, and to provide additional defining or circumstantial information about the Thing (Head noun), both children use the pattern of 'V- ing' as post-modifier frequently (e.g. *I saw the man hiding behind a rock*).

Also, the range of Epithet (adjectives) has also semantically expanded over time. Some further patterns of modification in nominal groups can be found in Sunyoung's Narrative texts. The nominal groups using infinitive verb (e.g. *Sarah was the first person to put her hand up*.) or past participle as pre- or post modifier (e.g. *a puzzled look, a twisted, mean smile*) are much more frequently found in Sunyoung's texts. In addition, in many cases, there are nominal groups which use prepositional phrases as post –modifier as well as '-of prepositional phrase' (e.g. *a man with a long beard, the wrapper of the bright red package*). Since Sunyoung constructs morel lengthy Narratives in her later periods than Jinha, and also the Sunyoung's total production of Narrative texts outnumbers Jinha's, more varied application of nominal groups might have been possible for Sunyoung's Narrative texts. However, it appears quite obvious that Sunyoung has developed her lexico-grammar related to the nominal groups at a remarkable rate and at a younger age than Jinha.

3.5.4. Theme Choices

For effective text development and contextual coherence, the Theme choice of written texts is generally accepted as an important factor in constructing textual meanings. However, in Narrative texts, thematic choices seem to perform more than the normal function by making special effects to create the sense of emergency, a turning point or a feeling of settling down in each stage of Orientation, Complication and Resolution. In Jinha's and Sunyoung's Narrative texts, both of them demonstrate growth in control of the range of thematic choices (topical, interpersonal and textual) throughout the research period. This kind of controlling thematic choices can be claimed as the evidence of written language development in connection with contextual coherence and emphasis.

The tendency of extending the range of thematic choices is very similar in both children. The unmarked topical Theme (e.g. *I, Chris*) and textual Themes (mainly structural conjunctions – *and, but, because, when*) are selected in most cases in earlier texts, and temporal circumstantial clauses or adverbial phrases are frequently added as thematic choices in both subjects' later Narratives. When they start to write the Narrative texts which include dialogic exchanges, interpersonal Themes (finite verbs, connectives, vocatives) emerge but there are relatively a few modal adjuncts as Theme choices. In later periods, both children include some cases of 'thematic equatives' (e.g. *All Chris wanted was ...*) which have the focal emphasis effect (exclusiveness). This appears to be further evidence of their development of the written language mode.

Along with the similarity in their development patterns in Theme choices, there are also some special points in Sunyoung's Narrative texts. In her later Narratives, the choice of unmarked subject Themes begins to include more abstract nouns such as '*a brainwave*', '*a gust of wind*', '*darkness*' and '*anger*', and they actually contribute to constructing symbolic meanings in connection with Evaluative elements. Also the impersonal pronouns such as '*it*' and '*that*' realize many different semantic meanings. Also, in many cases, Sunyoung uses dependent non-finite clauses in her later Narrative texts rather than structural conjunctions realizing textual Themes (e.g. *She was pulling a sour face, <u>trying hard not to laugh</u>*).

3.5.5. Interpersonal Meanings – The Mood System

Mood system is closely related to the area of 'Tenor' in the register of text representing social relations, the way of interaction or speakers' attitudinal elements. Therefore, the choices within Mood system in Jinha and Sunyoung's Narrative texts should be examined mostly in their dialogic Narrative texts (interactive events) inclusive of different mood clauses and modality system. Overall, both Jinha and Sunyoung's dialogic Narrative texts show that they have definitely developed their control of applying the function of exchange or interaction through various usages of mood elements such as modal auxiliaries, finite operators and modal adjuncts.

In particular, Sunyoung has extended her Narrative writing to more lengthy dialogue style texts in later periods, thus having had more opportunities to develop her Mood system. As a result, in many cases, her growth in control of the increasing variety of different rhetorical speech functions are represented by more varied ways of modalizaton and modulation using passive voice choices or more complicated modal operators (to express more subtle ways of language use as a more confident social member). The growth in control of interpersonal meanings as realized in the choices in the Mood system in Sunyoung's case can be claimed to have influenced her diary and E-mail texts writing in Korean.

As shown above, in the Narrative writing during the research period, Sunyoung has demonstrated more competent Narrative texts in terms of their schematic structure, the choices within Transitivity, Theme, Mood and nominal group structure. Judging from their age factors, she must have developed far advanced writing ability in relation to Narrative texts. However, Jinha has also developed his Narrative writing skills very steadily particularly from Year 2 to Year 5 (the period when Genre-based Approach was being introduced in the school). Considering the fact that both children had already built up sufficient reading input and familiarity in Narrative texts before they started Narrative writing, the explicit teaching of its schematic structure and opportunities to practise Narrative texts must have contributed to developing their writing more effectively and at a relatively faster rate. Especially for these ESL children who had limited exposure to spoken English in the home environment, the Genre-based Approach with explicit teaching really contributed to the children getting equipped with the essential guidance and assistance tools in their Genre writing development.

Chapter 4. Jinha's Factual Writing in English

4.0. Introduction

Parallel with Narrative writing (fiction), Jinha developed writing literacy in the area of factual texts (non-fiction).[31] He appeared more interested in constructing factual texts rather than Narrative writing over the period under consideration (from Kindergarten to Year 5). Even though factual text types were not as familiar as Narrative writing to Jinha during his lower primary grades (Kindergarten to Year 2), his overall patterns of writing development in factual texts show that he was quite successful, and confident in the process of controlling or constructing a range of factual text types such as Report, Explanation, Procedure and even Argument. Among those factual texts, Jinha constructed many science related Reports and also texts in the area of social studies from the early grades. The choice of content was most commonly related to his school curriculum which used a 'Theme-based Approach' (will be elaborated later).

From the functional linguistic perspective, factual texts can be significant for children who are in the middle of experiencing and developing the general features and lexico-grammatical elements of written language (Halliday and Martin, 1993). Apart from creating an imaginative world through Narrative writing, young children also need to know the real world outside that is composed of a number of objects, things, facts and ideas. This different kind of discourse, to inform or provide knowledge, is supposed to

---

[31] In this chapter the term 'factual text' is used to refer to "those texts that present factual information, ideas or issues in ways that either: inform, persuade, instruct or enhance the knowledge of the reader" (Wing Jan, 2001: 35). Wing Jan also points out that factual texts are "functional" in the sense that they "have identifiable structures, features and purposes which enable the user to conduct effectively the reading and writing demands required in everyday life." According to Halliday (1996: 340), becoming literate embodies broader concept than the traditional that is limited to pure activities of reading and writing. He explains the process of becoming literate by emphasizing that it includes obtaining "the more elaborated forms of language that are used in writing- and the system of social values that goes with them".

be rather difficult due to its specific features by young children.

In this chapter, Jinha's written language development is examined through analyzing his factual texts from a Systemic Functional Grammar perspective. Before that, however, the contexts of school and home and their influence on the construction of factual writings will be discussed in detail, and a general overview of the range of his factual texts will be provided. Both the 'Genre-based Approach' and 'Scaffolding Literacy' which were adopted at school and home as complementary supporting methods will be explained. Then, the reason why the five particular text types of such as Report, Explanation, Review, Argument and Procedure were chosen for detailed analysis is explained.

4.1. The Contexts of Jinha's Factual Writing (School and Home)

Jinha's factual writing developed successfully over the period under consideration, occurring both in the school and home contexts. Unlike the situation in literacy education in some Australian primary schools through the 1990s, with all the problems of 'Whole Language Approach' and 'Process Writing', Jinha's primary school subscribed to a pedagogy that involved more explicit teaching of literacy. From Jinha's Year 2 the approach to reaching literacy in his class was increasingly a combination of the 'Whole Language Approach' and the 'Genre-based Approach'.

The literacy curriculum was built around a specific theme per term that was related to a topic in the area of science or social studies, such as water, fire, the planet, the Olympics, Federation and such like. This kind of 'Theme-based Whole Language Program' was conducted in Jinha's school with an aim of eliminating unnecessary artificial barriers between subjects and providing a means by which a child can integrate and use what s/he has learned (Cambourne, 1988). Under the specific themes, Jinha was also given valuable reading and writing sessions along with some project type homework. In the literacy sessions over the period, there was a gradual change in the pattern toward more structured ways by using more modeled reading texts and guided writing along with reference worksheets.[32]

Among Jinha's writing activities at school, the 'learning journal' should be mentioned in relation to the development of some types of factual writing such as Report and Explanation. He had been writing a free style journal or learning journal from Kindergarten to Year 5 at school and this writing seems to have been influential for Jinha's writing development even though it was not structured by the teachers' instruction. In many cases of the learning journal, Jinha combined the Recount writing with Report or Explanation texts by reflecting on what he had learnt in the classes at school. The learning journal might have provided good opportunities to practice the factual writing's language features and subject-specific terms in a natural way.

Another significant environment for Jinha's factual writing was the home. As stated above, from Year 2 Jinha seems to have been enhanced and empowered by modeling through example texts and more explicit teaching along with guided worksheets and discussions on a particular text. The teachers encouraged the students to further practice these factual genres and this he did through homework in which he constructed the text types introduced in class. Since the researcher was aware of the efficiency of the Genre Approach, the scaffolding literacy that involved discussion

---

[32] For example, when the class (in Year 1) needed to learn about 'the Bilby', the class teacher sequenced the teaching/learning events in a way which seemed to be particularly suitable for lower graders. She prepared handouts of a worksheet that involved students completing a 'filling in the blanks' task. The handout was an example of a Report text. The children were asked to fill in the key words (mostly subject specific words or technical terms) from the word lists and, after that they would read the whole, a sample 'Report-like' text about the Bilby. The worksheet was used as a model for writing before the children individually constructed their own Report text. In addition, guide worksheets (mostly for upper graders from Year 2) such as 'Report Plan' or 'Explanation Plan', which consisted of several structural sections, were used in many cases before students were asked to do factual writing.

Also, to develop the students' research skills, the library teacher explicitly provided useful instructions with the title of 'Non-fiction books in the library' at least once a week even in the Year 1 class. This is a very different approach from the 'Process Writing' orientation in literacy teaching which involved minimal teacher intervention. The balanced literacy program with the 'Genre Approach' components that was adopted in Jinha's school provided children with opportunities to write different factual text types.

on the structure, language features and lexico-grammar of each factual text seems to have worked as supplementary teaching at home. Some books and workbooks about the Genre Approach (from libraries and bookstores) were referenced during this process and the instruction or discussion was made in the mother tongue (Korean) but, if necessary, English was also used.[33]

4.2. Overview on Jinha's Factual Writing

As explained above, Jinha's factual writing was gradually developing in the context of the balanced literacy approach at school and the Genre-based Approach at home. The range of factual text types that Jinha constructed between Kindergarten and Year 5 can be classified variously but consistently the structurally distinctive ones in factual writings were Report (on natural science and social science), Explanation, Procedure, Review and Argument. The text type Report emerged the earliest, in Kindergarten. During

---

[33] At home, 8 Explanation texts from Years 3 to 5 were jointly constructed through oral discussion on the given writing titles (see Table 4-3). During the entire process of the Explanation text construction done for homework, Jinha seems to have developed an awareness and confidence in writing this particular type of text. Even though there were sometimes difficult issues for Jinha, the process of joint-construction through pre-discussion probably lessened the burden of writing for him.

Another type of factual writing, 'Book or Film Review' was routinely practiced as part of his writing activities at home from Year 2 to Year 5. Book or Film Review can combine elements of the two different text types Recount and Judgment. Since Jinha was familiar with Recount writing from Kindergarten, summing up the storyline of a book or a film was not too challenging for him. However, composing the judgmental comments, analysis or evaluative thoughts on books and films was writing that Jinha was not familiar with. He could learn this effectively through model writing and joint construction. An external motivation for writing the Reviews was the announcement of the 'NSW Writing Competition' when Jinha was in Year 5 (age 10). The text type selected for the competition was known to be a book or TV/ film Review. As preparation for the competition, Jinha was encouraged by the researcher to practice Review writing at home.

In addition, over the 4 year period (from Year 2 to Year 5), the researcher encouraged Jinha to keep writing this kind of Review text type because this text could be naturally integrated in his daily literacy routine such as reading books and watching TV programs and films. Whenever he read books or films, the researcher tried to have discussions with him about them, and then suggested he write a Review of the piece. In the beginning, a considerable amount of guidance on the text structure or evaluative points or language features was provided by the researcher but after several writings, he seemed to be more confident and, as a result, many pieces of Review writing were constructed quite successfully, with appropriate evaluative comments (positive and negative points were made in a balanced manner).

the period Kindergarten to Year 5 aspects of natural science were explored (kangaroos, killer whales, frogs and toads, red back spiders, Saturn, Neptune). The first Report on social sciences was constructed in Year 1 (on Papua New Guinea), with quite a few more to follow in that year and in subsequent years (on Anzac day in Year 2, on 'democracy' in Year 3, on 'mediator' in Year 5, among others). As for Procedure and Review, Jinha started to write these text types from Year 2 and continued to develop them up to Year 5. Explanation and Argument text types emerged in Year 3 and 4 respectively. Explanation and Argumentative writing seem to be more challenging for young children to construct than other text types. Partially, this could be related to the fact that reasoning skills (such as cause-effect relationships) take some time to develop (Painter, 1993). Perera (1984: 245) also comments on children's ability to articulate cause-effect relationships in writing emerging after they are comfortable with providing additional information and using temporal sequencing. The challenge of constructing a reasoned Argument may relate, at least partly, to the fact that this is a text type much less commonly occurring in children's lives compared to recounts of events (personal recount), for example, and even descriptions of living creatures (science Report).

The following Table 4-1 shows the overall range of Jinha's factual writings from Kindergarten to Year 5:

Table 4-1. Jinha's Factual Texts in English over the Six Years of Schooling

Years in school / Type of text	Kinder (1997)	Year 1 (1998)	Year 2 (1999)	Year 3 (2000)	Year 4 (2001)	Year 5 (2002)	Total Numbers
Explanation				5	2	3	10
Procedure			1	1	2	6	10
Report (Science)	3	2	1			8	14
Report (Social study)		1	1	3		2	7
Argument					10		10
Review (Books and TV programs / Films)			3	2	5	13	23

From the factual texts that Jinha had constructed, the focus here is placed on five text types, namely, Report, Procedure, Explanation, Argument and Review. These factual types were chosen mainly because they were all what he mostly constructed (21, 10, 10, 10, 23) throughout his time in primary school. An examination of these allows us to follow Jinha's developing awareness of written language features in each of the text types. Also, most examples of the chosen text types were constructed both in the school and home contexts which means they provide more reliable and objective data for evaluation. The examination of the chosen five text types allows us to identify the patterns of Jinha's growing control over constructing of taxonomies, definitions and judgmental texts and to map out this developing control of uncommon sense and the patterns of his growing ability to differentiate between narrative fields and factual writing.

We shall figure out how Jinha established a wide range of taxonomies, definitions and judgmental texts to control uncommon sense in his factual writings and how he differentiated his writing patterns from Narrative writings. Some aspects of the written mode of language such as tense, reference, conjunction choices, abstract language and nominalization will be demonstrated and highlighted through the detailed text analysis. The analysis of Jinha's factual texts will also demonstrate his growing awareness of the difference between speech and writing. Thus, there is a tendency towards a significant decrease overtime in the language choices he considered appropriate in an informal conversation, but which were not expected in the above written genres. For a detailed overall view on how Jinha constructed the five factual text writings (when, where, topic and etc), the following tables are provided and then this is followed by a detailed text analysis of the factual writing.

Table 4-2. Jinha's Report Texts

	Title	Year in school	Place	Further detail of context; elements of generic structure, field and etc.
1	Kangaroos	K	School	Science Report
2	Saturn	K	School	Science Report
3	Neptune	K	School	Science Report
4	Killer Whales	Year 1	Home	Science Report
5	Frogs and Toads	Year 1	School	Science Report
6	Redback Spiders	Year 2	School	Science Report
7	Microscope	Year 5	Home	Science Report
8	Storage System	Year 5	Home	Science Report
9	System Unit	Year 5	Home	Science Report
10	Medicine	Year 5	Home	Science Report
11	Infections	Year 5	Home	Science Report: introduction + Body
12	Water	Year 5	School	Science Report, Theme-based Approach
13	Fire	Year 5	School	Science Report, Theme-based Approach
14	Tasmanian Devil	Year 5	Home	Science Report: Definition + Description – One paragraph, taking notes
15	Papua New Guinea	Year 1	School	Social studies
16	Anzac Day	Year 2	School	Social studies
17	Democracy	Year 3	Home	Social studies
18	Vietnam	Year 3	Home	Social studies
19	Olympic Torch	Year 3	Home	Social studies
20	First Aid Kit	Year 5	Home	Social studies
21	Mediator	Year 5	School	Social studies

Table 4-3. Jinha's Explanation Texts

	Title	Year in school	Place	Further details of context; elements of generic structure, field and etc.
1	I know where my food goes...	Year 3	Home	how
2	How you grow	Year 3	Home	Learning journal
3	Canberra became the Capital city	Year 3	Home	How
4	How crocodiles survive in the dry season	Year 3	Home	How-, watching after a TV documentary program
5	How England became a very rich and strong	Year 3	Home	Written in the part of learning journal

	country about 500 years ago			
6	Terrorist attack in the U.S.A.	Year 4	Home	Recount + How text
7	Queen Elizabeth II on the five dollar note	Year 4	Home	Report + Why text
8	How fire engines works	Year 5	School	Multi-draft writing, well structured. Teacher's comments "Great Jinha, a very clear Explanation"
9	How a kite works	Year 5	School	
10	How to play "Yute"	Year 5	Home	

Table 4-4. Jinha's Review Texts (Books and Films)

	Title	Year in School	Place	Further Details of Context; elements of generic structure, field and etc.
1	The diary of Neil	Year 2	School	Book Review: the reasons why this book is recommendable
2	Bug's Life	Year 2	School	Film Review: why I like this film
3	How the camel got this	Year 2	School	Book Report (positive and negative points)
4	The Newspaper kids	Year 3	Home	Book Review (Recount +)
5	Just Crazy	Year 4	School	Book Review: elaborate evaluative comments
6	Cockroach War	Year 4	School	Multi-drafts
7	Architecture	Year 4	Home	Multi-drafts : non-fiction book
8	My favorite Authors – Why?	Year 3	School	
9	Deltora Quest II	Year 4	Home	Book Review (Recount +)
10	King of the Dragons	Year 4	Home	Book Review
11	Review	Year 5	Home	Preparing for NSW Writing Test, Scaffolding example about Review text type
12	The Lord of the Rings	Year 5	Home	Film Review
13	Won Gon	Year 5	Home	TV Review : Why the TV program was good
14	"Y"	Year 5	Home	TV Review (evaluation)
15	Spy Kids	Year 5	Home	Film Review
16	Nips XI	Year 5	Home	Book Review
17	ET	Year 5	Home	Film Review
18	Star Wars	Year 5	Home	Film Review

19	Deltora Quest	Year 5	Home	Book Review
20	Jimmy Newtron	Year 5	Home	Film Review
21	Matilda	Year 5	Home	Book Review
22	Star Wars #2	Year 5	Home	Film Review (+ second draft)
23	Harry Potter #2	Year 5	Home	Along with negative points

Table 4-5. Jinha's Argument Texts

	Title	Year in School	Place	Further details of context; elements of generic structure, field and etc.
1	School uniform should be compulsory	Year 4	School	With Argument plan (Argument for/against)
2	Sing a song of season	Year 4	School	With supporting evidence, paragraphs explaining reasons
3	Choose wisely	Year 4	School	With supporting evidence
4	Sport and us	Year 4	School	Using concept map, supporting reasons
5	Exposition – Taking one point of view "We should stop every 10 minutes for a game"	Year 4	School	Worksheet to help constructing the Argument text. Including the whole process of drafting
6	The better sport	Year 4	School	First Draft + Good copy
7	Should zoos be destroyed?	Year 4	Home	Preparing NSW Test
8	One nation of Australia (100 years ago and today)	Year 4	Home	After discussion with parents
9	Should bullying in school be punished seriously?	Year 4	Home	Preparing NSW Test
10	Should parents let their children climb trees?	Year 4	Home	Preparing NSW Test

Table 4-6. Jinha's Procedure Texts

	Title	Year in School	Place	Further details of context; elements of generic structure, field and etc.
1	Slap	Year 2	School	Using numbered sentences
2	Violet crumble	Year 3	School	Guided writing with a

	recipe (Cooking)			structured worksheet: Equipment, Ingredient, Method. Subheading set up
3	Games and puzzles	Year 4	School	Set up a game (3 Procedure for setting up)
4	Making a tube (Math)	Year 4	Home	With drawing, homework
5	Evaporation (Science experiment)	Year 5	School	Procedure + Materials (with drawing)
6	Making toast (Cooking)	Year 5	School	Ingredient, Introduction, Method
7	Aim or What you are doing	Year 5	School	
8	How to make the water clock	Year 5	School	
9	What materials absorbs water	Year 5	School	
10	Newspaper stand	Year 5	School	

4.3. Report Writing

The term Report here will be defined broadly as in the text type "used to organize and present factual information in a concise and accurate form within a specific structure" (Wing Jan, 2001: 46). According to Wing Jan (2001), Report texts will commonly comprise of logically organized sequences of statements about facts, and will usually have some or all of the specific features of classification, generalization, description, definitions and comparisons. Also, Martin (1985) explains that the Report most likely provides some general characterization of things or phenomenon, in contrast to description which focuses on one particular thing. Since the text itself seems to require the writers to have developed the logical concepts (such as generalization, classification and comparison) in their cognitive ability as well as the literacy skill of writing, more mature examples of 'Report' writing are more likely to be found in upper primary children rather than lower graders.[34]

---

[34] This idea can be based on the view of Cognitive linguists in the sense that they aim at a balanced account of the relationship between language and human cognition. They claim that there is the general character of conceptual structure for language in human cognition (Talmy, 1988: 49-100). It also should be added

On the other hand, researchers have found that, with explicit teaching and scaffolding of the genre, even early primary-aged children can produce appropriate examples of Report texts (Stead, 1995; 2002). Apart from a requirement for the basic structure and features of Report writing, successful construction of the genre requires a knowledge of the topic of the Report, and suitable terminology for building this topic. To be able to write up more successful Report texts, young children should be able to obtain any proper channels through which they can make meaning about the topic. In this regard, particularly ESL children like Jinha and Sunyoung needed to negotiate the difficult terms or specific content with the researcher, mostly in Korean, when they did the Report writing as homework. Whenever this kind of parent-child interaction occurred, the researcher became confident about the importance and usefulness of sharing language of mother tongue. This issue shall be elaborated further in this chapter.

Report can frequently be classified as being either 'natural science report' or 'social science report' depending on the subject dealt with. In another way, according to Wing Jan (2001: 46), information reports include three different types such as scientific reports, technological reports and social studies reports. Even though the definition of 'Report writing' and its types can vary according to scholars, in Jinha's case most of his Report writings were classified as science report and social one. There are about 20 texts that can broadly be referred to as Report-like writing throughout his primary years. These texts fall into two groups: the first involves constructing information on natural sciences (living species - especially animals such as 'kangaroos', 'killer whales' 'frogs and toads', 'redback spiders' and 'Tasmanian devil', medical science such as 'medicine' and 'infections', computer science such as 'microscope', 'storage system' and 'system unit' and other science areas such as 'Saturn'. 'Neptune', 'water' and 'fire'); and the

---

as the theory of developmental cognitive linguistics that the human cognitive structure for language develops by the various factors such as age maturity, education, environmental element and etc.

208

second group dealing with social sciences (including geography – different countries such as 'Vietnam' and 'Papua New Guinea', sociology such as 'Anzac day', 'democracy', 'Olympic torch', 'first aid kit' and 'mediator') (refer to Table 4-2).

Out of the total number (21) of Report texts that Jinha constructed from Kindergarten to Year 5, 10 texts were written at school, mostly as part of Theme-based Approach. Many were entries Jinha made in his learning journal. The remaining 11 texts were constructed at home as homework or as an extra writing activity that followed after reading factual books (mostly upon the request of the researcher). It is necessary to mention that Jinha did not initiate his factual writing at home, but whenever he got involved in the writing activity after factual book reading (mostly chosen by himself from a community library or school one), he seemed to enjoy the Report writing to the end. Particularly in the case of writing about natural science he showed more enthusiasm and endurance to go through the Report writing than did Sunyoung. She was more interested in such texts as story recount or diary journal to include personal involvement (her feeling, thoughts and comments); Jinha was not quite so good at making comments on his personal feelings and thoughts in his journal writing. Jinha looked more confident in getting involved in factual writing on natural science from an early age (Kindergarten).[35] For

---

[35] Table 4-7. Report Text FR-3

Monday 10th November (in Kindergarten)
Neptune's triton is falling apart. Neptune is a gas giant. Neptune has blue clouds and green clouds. Neptune has five rings. Saturn has the most rings. Neptune is cold. Neptune has no water. We will freeze. Pluto is the very smallest planet. The moon is not a planet. A tenth planet may be waiting to be discovered beyond Pluto. Pluto is made out of frozen gas.

Before this writing, Jinha's class had an excursion to a Science Center and then a follow up reading session with a big book about the Solar System. Jinha himself wrote this factual writing in his learning journal at the end of the class session. Even though the above example text does not seem to be logically structured and connected, this Report writing was almost impersonalized with the Themes of each solar system such as 'Neptune', 'the moon', 'Pluto', 'Saturn' and 'A tenth planet', with the exception of the use of the first person pronoun 'we' to refer to people,

instance, at school his class teachers Julieta and Katie commented positively on his factual writing on Neptune and other parts of the solar system like this: "Your wonderful work makes me smile!" (Julieta); or "Julieta, look at how much information they have learnt out of one of the big books already!! Yesterday's trip was well worthwhile." (Katie)

The tendency of boys to be more interested in the real world surrounding them, particularly in scientific knowledge, might explain Jinha's case as well. Also, as Halliday (1996) claims, this kind of factual writing can be considered with the system of social value that goes with literacy education. The factual books on natural science or social science can be linked with the academic world and the researcher was very pleased with Jinha's interests in reading and writing factual texts. Much praise and encouragement was given to Jinha whenever he successfully finished his reading and writing of factual texts. This kind of expectation and positive atmosphere at home toward engaging with factual texts might have contributed to Jinha's interest in and developing control of factual writing. To make this happen the researcher helped him to access some relevant books in the community library and educational CDs on medical science, computer science, animals and etc. The researcher also encouraged Jinha to read the books and use CDs, explaining difficult technical terms and concepts as he was reading. Also, whenever he needed to construct a challenging text in terms of content and vocabulary the researcher gave him more support through child-parent interaction. In some cases of home produced texts, in line with advocates of Genre-based Approach, the researcher would construct a model text and read it together with Jinha.

---

or 'human beings'. In addition, the use of process types and tense (relational verbs such as 'is' and 'has', present tense) is successful in terms of construing a Report text dealing with scientific facts. The logical methods to organize this text are classification, definition and description. More mature writers probably will use the logical relationships of comparison and contrast established through the use of such conjunctions as 'whereas', 'while', and, 'but'. In that case, the paragraphing skill should be needed to organize the related (relevant) sentences together. However, the above text constructed by a Kindergarten child is meaningful; the ideas are expressed clearly, and there is quite a lot of uncommonsense information being constructed. The text seems to be a distinct example of a young writer setting out to Report on the factual world around him.

The researcher explained to Jinha the critical elements (stages of the generic structure) in this text. Often the researcher and Jinha jointly constructed another example of the genre. Jinha made suggestions and the researcher acted as scriber. After explicit teaching of the summary skill, paragraphing, sub-heading and methods of logical sequence such as comparison, generalization, classification and definition as well as the explanation of technical terms, factual writing became familiar to him and, as the result, he did not seem to rely so much on the researcher's support as time passed. Equipped with the conventions of factual writing, he appeared to have a greater control of his own texts at school and home.

Text Analysis on Report Writing from Kindergarten to Year 5

The following Report Text FR-1 and FR-2 are Jinha's earliest works written in the Kindergarten period.[36]

Table 4-8. Jinha's Report Texts in Kindergarten

Text FR-1		Elements of schematic structure
1.	*Kangaroos* <u>are</u> mammals.	Classification
2.	And *Kangaroos* <u>are</u> marsupials.	Classification / Description: habitat
3.	*Opossums* <u>live</u> in America.	Classification
4.	*Kangaroos* <u>are</u> herbivores.	Classification
5.	*Wombats* <u>are</u> herbivores	

Text FR-2		Elements of schematic structure
1.	*Saturn's ring* <u>is made</u> out of dusts.	Description: Constitution / Classification
2.	*Jupiter* <u>is</u> the biggest planet.	Classification
3.	*Venus* <u>is</u> the second biggest planet.	Description: Movement Characteristics
4.	*The moon* <u>does not go</u> around the sun.	Description: Possession / Description: Constitution
5.	*Earth* <u>has</u> a lot of water.	Description: Climate
6.	*Jupiter* <u>is made</u> out of gas.	
7.	*Pluto* <u>is</u> very cold when you are in Pluto.	

[36] The right hand column relates the elements of the generic structure of these Report texts. Jinha's misspelled words are corrected here. Also, for reference convenience, numbering was added by the researcher in front of each sentence.

In terms of text structure, both FR-1 and FR-2 consist of several sentences of Classifications and Descriptions which are features of Report writing. We can consider these texts to be embryonic Reports as, in terms of structure, these texts are not well organized cohesive texts but, rather, texts written sporadically by presenting one bit after another, in the manner of addition. More mature writers could, for example, have written these texts by using comparison. Both texts also successfully employ subject-specific terms such as mammals, marsupials, herbivores, Saturn, Jupiter, Planet and Pluto even though there are some misspelled terms (i.e. huvsze for herbivores) that can be understood as developmental spelling errors. These common nouns are mostly used as unmarked Themes in each clause (see the italic font words in Text FR-1 and FR-2) and tell the reader what the text is about. The choice of person is consistently third person (which is different from Recounts and Journal writing where 1st person is usually chosen). The tense choice made is the timeless present tense (see Text FR-1 and FR-2 verbal groups underlined). In terms of Transitivity, the most typical verb 'be' as relational process is used in both texts' identifying clauses. As far as nominal groups are concerned, in the clauses of 'classification', a common noun as Head is used as 'identified' and 'identifier'. For example, in 'Kangaroos are mammals' (FR-1/1), 'Kangaroos' is 'identified' and 'mammals' is 'identifier'. Since the nominal group realizing the function of identifier is typically definite, the superlative adjective form is often used as in 'Venus is the second biggest planet' (FR-2/3). As pointed out above, overall, the earliest Report texts FR-1 and FR-2 demonstrate that Jinha seems to have attempted the genre of Report, writing along with a reasonable sense of convention and language features.

The following texts are examples of Jinha's science Report writing in Year 1, showing some developmental changes compared to the earlier report texts:

Table 4-9. Jinha's Science Report Texts in Year 1

Text FR-4	
Animal Report: The Killer Whale	Elements of Schematic Structure
1. The killer whale is the member of the dolphin's family.	Classification-a/1
2. The killer whale eats seals, porpoises and fish.	Description-b
3. Dolphins are whales.	Classification-a/2
4. The killer whale is 7 meters long and weighs 4 to 5 tones.	Description-c
5. The killer whale is a fast swimmer.	Description-d
6. The killer whales are very powerful.	Description-e/1
7. The killer whale smash through the ice and grabs the penguin and seals.	Description-e/2
8. The killer whale is found in most oceans.	Description-f
9. I like killer whales because they are cute.	Personal Comments

Text FR-5	
Title: Frogs and Toads	Elements of Schematic Structure
1. Green tree frog jump fifteen meters high.	Description-a
2. All frogs eat flies and mosquitoes.	Description-b
3. Frogs lay about ten eggs when they are laying eggs.	Description-c
4. Some have bright colors to warn them that they are poisonous.	Description-d/1
5. Red frogs are very poisonous.	Description-d/2
6. Toads and frogs look the same but they are different kinds.	Comparison-e/1
7. They have their nostril on the front of their heads.	Comparison-e/2
8. Most of the frogs have very dark colors.	Description-d/3
9. Frogs can stay on land and on water.	Description-f/1
10. Frogs live in dams and lakes and rivers.	Description-f/2
11. Some animals like foxes and snakes eat frogs.	Description-g

Compared with the earliest Report texts FR-1 and FR-2, the above two texts include more information on each of the topics 'killer whale' and 'frogs'. So, the length of the texts is comparatively longer than the previous texts and the range of description areas appears to be wider than before. Particularly in text FR-5, Jinha applies the structural skill of comparison (with toads) to provide a finer description of frogs. Even though the attempt of comparing frogs with toads (FR-5/6-7) does not look very systematic and organized, it can be noted that this text, in general seems to be more analytical due to the application of comparison sentences. Also, in several cases in FR-4 and FR-5 above at least two sentences can be put together to describe a similar feature (please refer to the small case alphabet characters to indicate the similar area of 'description' as in e/1 and e/2 or f/1 and f/2). The former texts FR-1 and FR-2 include more classification sentences, interspersed with stand-alone description sentences. Whereas the text is not conventionally paragraphed and the elements of the schematic structure are often lacking distinct organization, there has been a visible growth in his Report writing, particularly in the area of providing further field details mainly through elaboration of the nominal group and the emergence of circumstantial information, and an increase of complex and compound sentences.

In terms of Theme choices also, the above Text FR-5 demonstrates more specific and descriptive nominal groups than before. As in 'most of the frogs (FR-5/8)', 'some (FR-5/4)', 'all frogs (FR-5/2)', 'Green tree frog (FR-5/1)', and 'Some animals like foxes and snakes (FR-5/11)', the use of Themes becomes more specific in terms of the amount or kind of frogs or animals. The feature of being more specific in description can be indicated as one of necessary points for better Report writing. Considering that younger children tend to over-generalize factual things or phenomenon around them, the application of more specific Themes through more complicated nominal groups seems to reflect one aspect of development in Jinha's written language. In addition, Jinha tries to refer some common nouns to appropriate pronouns in some cases. As in 'I like killer whales because they are cute' (FR-4/9), he avoids using the same noun by the reference of 'they'. Another example can be found in FR-5/6 as follows: 'Toads and frogs look the same but they are different kinds.'

The next period's Report writing, from Year 2 to Year 4, reflects that Jinha was developing more in social studies' Reports rather than science Reports. This is mainly because, during this time period, his class teachers put more emphasis on themes related to social studies such as different countries and social systems (e.g. democracy). His embryonic Report writing (Text FR-15) on social studies written in Year 1 already demonstrates that Jinha was instructed on how to write a social studies' Report by using sub-headings as follows:

Table 4-10. Jinha's Social Studies' Report Text in Year 1

Text FR-15	<Title: Papua New Guinea>
Plants and Animals	
The tree kangaroo came from Australia. The bird of Paradise is a special bird.	
Location	
Papua New Guinea is just below the equator. It is above Australia.	
Land Forms	
In Papua New Guinea, the roads are very rough so they have to fly or walk.	
Climate	
In Papua New Guinea there are two seasons. One is hot and dry and the other is hot and wet.	

Even though the misspelled words were corrected by the class teacher this text shows that, with the guidance of the class teacher, Jinha was able to put together related facts under the sub-headings. This means he could do the skill of grouping which is very significant in factual writing. All four sections are composed of two or three clauses that involve parallel facts under the subheading (in the case of 'Plants and Animals') or related logically (refer to the underlined parts: it, so, One- the other). This kind of guidance on Report writing at school was enhanced through the reading sessions with factual books. The class teacher often emphasized how the organization of factual books can be distinguished from that of fiction books whenever she started reading a new factual book. After the practices on sub-headings or categorizing, Jinha was able to compose more mature Report writing on social studies in Year 3 both at school and at home, expanding his fact organizing skills to cover the range of 'generalization', 'definition', 'exemplification' and 'contrast' types as well as paragraphing. The following two texts (FR-17 and FR-18) are selected to illustrate Jinha's development in social studies' Report writing:

Table 4-11. Jinha's Social Studies' Report Text in Year 3

Text FR-17	<Title: All about Democracy>[37]
1. Definition about 'democracy'	A democracy <u>is a system of government [[in which representatives are voted for by all the people over a certain age, in regular elections]]</u>. In Australia, there are several party and each one has a leader. <u>The most people on party the head</u> gets to be the prime minister.
2. Exemplification by comparing 'democracy' to 'the process of decision-making in my family'	To understand what democracy is, let's think it as a house not a country. When we, our family members including me, my sister, my mum and dad have <u>different</u> suggestions [of going outside]. I think the fair way is <u>to follow the person [[who votes for that the most]]</u>. That's democracy. In addition, <u>saying what you really want to say</u> is also <u>a special point of democracy</u> as well.
3. Contrast with 'Dictatorship'	On the other hand, dictatorship is <u>controlling all the people how he or she wants it</u>. This is <u>some of what the government does</u>. Makes up rules and laws, collect taxes, helps communities, has meetings, protect the country, rules the people, gives us punishments.

In terms of the basic structure of FR-17 (as above), it is mainly composed of three parts: definition, exemplification, and contrast. More precisely, this is a definition text which is then elaborated and enhanced by the later parts of exemplification and contrast. In a definition text of an abstract phenomenon (dealing with 'democracy' here), mature writers depend on the use of grammatical metaphor (as a less congruent version) in identifying clauses. This kind of factual text therefore tends to show higher lexical

---

[37] The above Text FR-17 was constructed at home as school homework. Before writing this text Jinha had studied social systems at school for about two sessions and had read one book about 'democracy'. At the time of Report writing he did not seem to be confident about this issue due to the difficult concept itself for a child of his age (age 8). So, the researcher tried to explain this concept by comparison and contrast which is reflected in his text above. Following the researcher's explanation, he attempted to write down the content in his own words. The word choice appears to reflect what he learnt from his school and the book. Sometimes during writing, Jinha would pause and ask the researcher if he was on the right track. The researcher did not try to correct his writing after he got into his independent writing stage. So, in this text, the content and overall structures were negotiated with the researcher before his writing; during the real writing time, he selected what to write down himself without any further assistance.

Even though Jinha was not as interested in writing social studies' Reports as science Reports, he seemed to get quite involved in writing some pieces on social aspects of life such as history, geography and sociology. Also, this kind of social studies Report allows tracing the pattern of emergent control of writing in the humanities.

216

density as a result of the process of nominalization. The following reflects Halliday's view on nominalising in relation to grammatical metaphor:

> Nominalising is the single most powerful resource for creating grammatical metaphor. By this device, processes (congruently worded as verbs) and properties (congruently worded as adjectives) are reworded metaphorically as nouns; instead of functioning in the clause, as Process or Attribute, they function as Thing in the nominal group. (Halliday 1994:352)

In regard to this matter, it can be said that Jinha, attempting to develop an ability to use a range of different verbs and adjectives in the Narrative writing or recount writing, moves to another stage of 'the noun world' in order to construct an abstract phenomenon in the definition of factual writing. This kind of factual writing practice leads young children to develop their awareness and control of the distinctive features of written language. The use of nominal groups in this text demonstrates Jinha's several attempts in relational Transitivity. As token and value relationships most nominal groups can be found in the position of participants in relational processes 'be' and 'have': e.g. A democracy (Token) is (Process: identifying) a system of government [[in which representatives are voted for by all the people over a certain age]] (Value).

Underlined nominal group phrases in the above text FR-17 can be sorted into three patterns: 1) of + noun phrase; 2) be + to infinitive; and 3) be + ~ ing. The first type (of noun phrase) is thought to be simple and easy for young children to pick up, but in this case Jinha is able to successfully manage the nominal group combined with relative pronoun as post-modifier as in: 'a system of government in which representatives are voted for by all the people over a certain age, in regular election'. It still sounds rough but he certainly manages to compact necessary information in a nominal group in order to define the difficult notion of 'democracy' and does so quite effectively.[38]

---

[38] However, the very next example is a sort of failure for a nominal group because it does not make sense at all: the most people on party the head gets to be the prime minister. He might have intended to compose like this: The head of the party

The other types of nominal group (be + to infinitive, be + ~ ing) can be viewed as being between the characteristics of verbs and nouns, the middle stage toward abstract nominalization. As in 'the fair way is <u>to follow the person who votes for that the most</u>' and 'dictatorship is <u>controlling all the people how he or she wants it</u>', Jinha seems to have confidently used the 'to infinitive' and '~ ing forms' in place of a noun (participant) in the relational processes. These examples signify an emergence of nominalization in Jinha's factual texts. Emergence of nominalization in children's writing is considered to be a critical sign of their developing control over writing (Derewianka, 1995). That there is more use made of nominal groups in Jinha's Report writing is demonstrated through the following text FR-18.

Table 4-12. Jinha's Social Studies' Report Text in Year 3

Text FR-18	<Title: Vietnam>[39]
Introduction	I would like to write down [[what I have been learning about Vietnam]]. In the first paragraph, I would like to write about [[where Vietnam is]], secondly the national days in Vietnam, last of all I would like to introduce the festivals.
Body 1)	Vietnam is in east Asia and shaped <u>something like an S</u>. Mainly <u>three quarters of the land</u> is covered with <u>amazing high mountains</u>. Vietnam is next to many countries. Here's some of them Laos, Thailand, and Cambodia.
Body 2)	Vietnam has <u>many different kinds of national days</u>. May 19th is <u>their great leader Ho Chin Minh's birthday</u>. Also, on September 2nd was [[when Vietnam got their country back from French and Japan]]. September 2nd was also <u>Ho Chin Minh's date of death.</u>
Body 3)	On 15th of the late 8th moon it is <u>the mid Autumn festival</u>. In

<u>that gets the most people</u> gets to be the prime minister. The coexistence of a successful example and a failure for '– of noun phrase' indicates that Jinha was developing confidence in using this kind of complicated noun phrase (a sign of trial and error).

[39] Text FR-18 was constructed at home; it was homework from school after classroom learning about different countries. For the homework, Jinha was asked to choose one of his favorite countries, then to read some relevant reference books and finally to write a Report about the country; at that time, Jinha lived in a two-story house where a couple of a Vietnamese and a Canadian was subletting downstairs. The researcher's family was very close to the couple, which could have influenced Jinha's choice of his 'favorite country, Vietnam'.

The teacher did not state any specific structural requirements but indicated it should be one page in length. The teacher asked the children to prepare a presentation (oral) to accompany the Report. For this reason the text was written in the format of a presentation, particularly in the introduction (spoken mode). Jinha used the personal pronoun "I" in the position of Themes to meet the requirements of the spoken mode.

	the mid-Autumn festival, they eat the moon cakes. And also many other traditional foods. For the fun they wear masks. Vietnamese people like <u>having dragons</u>. And last of all they have <u>water puppetry</u>.

Note: [[ ]]: embedded clause; underlined: nominal groups.

In terms of structure, this text is well organized into four paragraphs. The issues that have been raised in the introduction are all clearly addressed in the body parts and with the division of each paragraph.

As far as nominal groups are concerned, this text has several noun clauses and phrases. They are underlined in the above sample (FR-18). In the text, in the position of 'goal' in material transitivity, Jinha used some relative pronouns and adverbs that are followed by clauses: 'I would like to write down <u>what I have been learning about Vietnam</u>' and 'I would like to write about <u>where Vietnam is</u>'. Also, in the identified-identifier relationship (token and value), he tried to use the relative adverb as in 'on September 2nd was <u>when Vietnam got their country back from French and Japan</u>'. Another example is as in: 'Vietnamese people like <u>having dragons</u>' in the part of Body 3. According to Halliday (1994: 248), this clause can be analyzed as follows:

Table 4-13. An Example of Nominal Group (in Transitivity System)

Vietnamese people	like	having	dragon
Senser	Process: Mental of affection	Phenomenon: Act	
		Having: Relational process of possession	dragon: Attribute Possessed

In this example it is significant that what appears to be the field is realized through construction of participants. The fact that the participants are generalized, and not specific, is important too. Generalization is a significant feature of factual writing but so also is writing about phenomena removed in space from his personal experience.

So far the social studies' Reports which had been scaffolded by the researcher at home have been demonstrated through the analysis of the nominal groups and also the structural features. Parallel with this development, Jinha's science Report writings had also been developing, from short texts with rather short sentences to texts which were much longer, better organized, and packed with significant amount of information within a sentence and a clause. The following Text FR-12 is representative of Report writing that was guided explicitly by class teachers using the Genre-based Approach to teaching writing. During Term 1 of Year 5, Jinha's class learnt the theme of 'Fire and Water'. The theme outline which the class teacher handed out had each section of English, Mathematics, Science and Technology, Studies of Society and the Environment and Information Literacy very carefully designed. In the English section, for the writing tasks the sheet says: 'Writing – text type: Reports, Procedures, Explanations and Narrative', 'Viewing – watch documentaries and news segments about the theme and take notes' and 'Reading – locating information from factual text to research fire and water'. For the purpose of learning on the theme of 'Water and Fire', the class teacher included writing tasks based on the Genre Approach. To complete the first step towards achieving the aim, the children had a time of 'Structured Brainstorm' that was guided by a clarified slip note and explicit Explanation. According to the slip note attached to Jinha's theme book, a 'Structured Brainstorm' involves:

Table 4-14. An Example of Classroom Instruction based on Genre Approach

Structured Brainstorm:	Topic - Water
Outcome: - to make a brainstorm by sharing ideas - to rewrite the information into a paragraph The Task: - Following a modeled brainstorm as a whole class, the students worked individually to layout and began their own brainstorm - With a partner they shared and exchanged ideas. Each student was invited to share ideas with the class. - As a class, we wrote a paragraph of information about Water. - Each student then wrote his or her own paragraph.	

As can be seen in Table 4-14, the task description shows that Jinha's writing class appropriately included the brainstorming and sharing ideas as part of the Genre Approach to modeled writing. The following is the example text of modeled writing and joint construction the class teacher wrote on the white board, as she listened to suggestions from the students:

Table 4-15. An Example Text of Modeled Writing based on Genre Approach

Title: Water (constructed by the class teacher and students together)
Water is a liquid. Water boils at 100 degrees Celsius and freezes at 0 degree Celsius. When water freezes, it expands slightly. When water boils, it evaporates into steam. Water is odorless, colorless and tasteless. All life on earth requires water. Plants and animals are largely made of water.

For the final stage of the writing session each student of Jinha's class was asked to write his/her own Report individually based on the model paragraph provided. Text FR-12 demonstrates Jinha's developing skills in constructing an organized Report text, using several paragraphs joined together with relevant information;

Table 4-16. Jinha's Report Text based on Genre Approach at School

Text FR-12	Title: Water (constructed by Jinha himself, in Year 5)
The definition of Water Description on the usage of Water	*Water* is odorless, tasteless and colorless liquid. *Water* covers about 70% of earth's surface but only 0.01% of that water is drinkable. There are lots of uses for water. Some uses are sometimes used for making electricity. Then the electricity runs down huge wire to people's homes.
Description on the Water Cycle	*The Water Cycle* starts by water flowing into the sea. Firstly the heat from the sun evaporates the water into tiny water droplets [[that we can't see]]. Secondly that forms the clouds. Thirdly the wind blows the clouds across to the rivers and waterfalls down again as rain, hail or snow. *Then the water cycle* starts again.
Description on Sinking and Floating as one of Water related features	Some things when you drop into the water like a brick sinks. This is because it is heavier than water. But a boat does not sink because the air in the boat keeps it floating. Same like people, when people are swimming. The lungs store air in it so it does not sink.
Concluding comment	This is [[why water is very important in our daily life]].

As seen above, Text FR-12 demonstrates that many nominal groups constructing the notion of 'water' are placed in the thematic position – unmarked topic Themes (in italics and bold), along with some connection words (firstly, secondly and thirdly) and a referencing pronoun 'this'. In the

Transitivity, the text is largely constructed through relational and material process. In particular, the second paragraph consists entirely of material processes (starts-evaporates-forms-blows-starts) in order to explain the Water cycle in a sequenced manner. As far as nominal groups are concerned, the clauses underlined should be mentioned. As in 'This is why water is very important in our life', the equative clause with relational process seems to function like noun. Also, as in 'tiny water droplets <u>that</u> we can't see', the head noun 'droplet' is successfully modified by a relative pronoun 'that' along with a pre-modifier. As a whole, the above text FR-12 demonstrates growth in Jinha's Report writing. Two other texts[40] which were composed by the most competent classmates in Jinha's 5/6 composite class are shown below as comparison.

Table 4-17. Two Other Report Texts by Jinha's Competent Classmates

Ref. FR-12d: Report Text A (constructed by a Year 5 classmate)	
Water as the most common substance on earth	Water is the most common substance on earth. 70 percent of earth's surface is covered in water. Water is in the air we breathe. Water is everywhere. Nobody can live without water. The earth consists mostly of water. The human is about two-thirds water. A chicken is three quarters water, and a pineapple is about four fifths water. Scientists believe that life began in the salty water of the sea. With the salty taste of our body sweat and tears that might be true.
Water as the original source for earth's formation	Water began shaping the land thousands of years ago. It hammers against the land and the oceans pound on the shores. The rivers knife and plow the*
Ref. FR-12e: Report Text B (constructed by a Year 6 classmate)	
Water as the common thing on earth and the importance of Water	Water is the common thing on earth. It covers about 70% of the earths. Surface is covered by water. Water is in oceans, lakes and livers and also in the air we breathe. Water is everywhere. Without water, all life will perish. All living things must drink water to survive. All living things consists of mostly water. Your body is about two-thirds water.

Note: *not completed in original.

Jinha's text compares favorably with the texts written by his

---

[40] For the comparison purpose, two other Report texts among the Jinha's competent classmates were selected. Please refer to the FR-12d and FR-12e. These samples were copied through the help of the class teacher by the end of that term.

classmates with regard to overall organization and elaboration of the nominal groups, constructing participants as well as circumstances. Even though the class teacher offered the writing model (see Table 4-15) to all the students, the individual writing varied among the students in terms of its overall length, structure, the selection of fact details and other language features. The above two text samples belong to the students who always got high scores in writing sessions. From this perspective, Jinha seems to have managed his Report writing more confidently than other students in his class, particularly by demonstrating his organizing skills through paragraphing. Starting from the general statements or facts on Water in the first paragraph, he develops his Report by adding more specific details of Water such as 'Water Cycle' (Jinha first came across the information in the earlier organized class activity). He seems to have utilized very well what he had learnt in constructing his second paragraph. Finally, he attempts to present another feature of water (sinking and floating) in his third paragraph. The final statement, as in 'This is why water is very important in our daily life', appears to be a reasonable wrapping up statement to embody all the previous paragraphs. So, it seems Jinha's text largely satisfies the science Report genre criteria, particularly in demonstrating how Reports begin with a general opening statement or classification of the subject matter, and then proceed onto descriptive elements that are organized into interrelated sections or a series of paragraphs.

So far, we have explored how Jinha developed his Report writing from Kindergarten to Year 5. With the supportive context at school and home prompting a Genre Approach and Scaffolding literacy, Jinha's Report writing seemed to be empowered. As did the school curriculum, he put more work on science Reports (Kindergarten to Year 1) at the beginning then proceeded to social studies' Reports (Year 2-Year4) and lastly in Year 5, he was able to develop further in science Report writing with more challenging themes. During this whole process Jinha did not seem to have much difficulty in becoming familiar with the writing convention and text mapping of the Report, especially with the systemic assistance of school and home but also with the related factual reading input experience. The use of specialized vocabulary, timeless present tense, the choices within the Theme and Transitivity were developing and this helped meet the requirements of the Report genre. Jinha's later texts appear to be constructed using a more formal and objective style than his earlier attempts at Report writing. Lastly, specifically in regard to the nominal group, his writing started from simple object nouns in the beginning stage of science Report and developed to more complicated forms. In particular, when constructing social studies' Reports, he learned to use nominalization and elaboration within the nominal groups for constructing participants. This aspect of written language development shall be examined further in the following text type of 'Explanation'.

4.4. Explanation

'Explanations are used to describe how or why things happen' (Wing Jan, 2001: 74). According to Wing Jan (2001), as far as the basic structure is concerned, it is generally divided into three sections: 'opening statement' to orientate the reader about the topic; 'a sequence of paragraphs or statements' that describe how or why something happens and that are linked either through cause and effect or temporal sequence; and a summing up of the Explanation which involves a concluding paragraph or sentence that draw all the information together. If the focus is on how things happen (the emphasis on process), it can be specifically classified as 'sequential Explanation' in which a series of events are introduced to the readers in a temporal and logical manner. According to Veel (1997: 177), the possible structure of the sequential Explanation is as follows:

> Sequential explanations usually comprise a Phenomenon Identification stage, in which the thing to be explained is introduced to the reader, followed by an Explanation Sequence, in which the reader is taken through a sequence of events describing the phenomenon.[41]

---

[41] Even though the definition and its generic structure of 'sequential Explanation' are identified as above, among some scholars from the Genre Approach tradition, it is argued that the genre of 'information Report' sometimes overlaps with sequential Explanation or the Report genre might include the aspect of sequential

After acknowledging the definition of 'sequential Explanation' with its specific regard for time sequence, we need to know the other type of Explanation that focuses more on 'why' things happen. It has been classified by the name of 'causal Explanation'. According to Martin (1985: 11), this kind of text should be distinguished from Personal Judgment that can be found in Recount writing as in 'I like vegetable because it makes me healthy'. In this respect, it is often indicated that Judgment involving generalizations tends to be challenging for young children since it requires impersonal stance and the process of justification (Martin, 1985: 12). Therefore, young children need to be more systematically and explicitly prepared for this kind of genre writing. Aidman (1999: 265) highlights the positive influence of the minority language patterns when used in the home on bilingual children's writing development in the majority language (English), particularly in 'casual Explanations'. She explains that if parents keep trying to make interaction with their children by prompting 'why questions' orally in everyday contexts, children may be better prepared to write judgmental texts.

In Jinha's case, from an early age he had been involved in the home context where parents talked to him to encourage his reflection on how and why things were happening. He often had chances to share his thoughts with his parents and particularly the researcher tried to extend that language by providing a framework to guide him to reflect on the process involved in making things: How does it work? Why does it work? In addition, after reading some non-fiction factual books at home, Jinha was encouraged to write a learning journal. His early Explanation texts were constructed in this 'learning journal' using a less formal (than would be

---

Explanation. When taking into account of the purpose of this sequential Explanation, it is necessary to explain to readers by emphasizing the sequential process of how things occur (along with special emphasis of the function of time conjunction). In this point, we find more reasons why the sequential Explanation should be recognized differently from the information Report. However, distinguishing these two writing types under different names might cause some difficulty to young children when they need to know the difference between the two, because the two share many common things in terms of basic structure and similar language features such as generalized participants (rather than about a specific thing), timeless present tense, and use of specialized and technical terms.

expected in Explanation) writing style. The following text FE-1 is a typical example of Jinha's embryonic Explanation text written in Year 3.

Table 4-18. Jinha's Embryonic Explanation Text in Year 3

Text FE-1	<Title: I know where my food goes>
1. Introduction (Phenomenon)	Today I am going to tell you where your food goes after you swallowed it. I learnt it from a book [[called 'I know where my food goes']].
2. Operation : how it works – the process of digestion	First when you put your food in your mouth, a watery mixture [[called saliva]] mixes with your food. This helps your food to go down to your food tube. There is another name for the food tube [[called the oesophagus]]. In estimation, it is about half as long as a child's arm and only as thick as your thumb. Also even if you eat up side down, the food doesn't just slide down your esophagus because the muscles squeeze the food along just like some toothpaste. Then the food goes down to your stomach [[which is like a sloppy bag]]. It squishes the food until it is sort of liquid. Then it goes down to your small intestine [[which is about 5 meters long]]. And intestine is all folded into like spaghetti. But the waste bits go into something [[that is called a large intestine]] until the leftover bits reach your bottom [[which comes out as poo]]. This is [[how the food travels around your body, which is called digestion]].
3. Interesting comments / Evaluation	I liked this story because it was simple and told me a lot about my body. Even though it is a simple book, I think that I learnt very much. It was sort of wrote in a fiction book way and a non-fiction.

As seen above, Text FE-1 has some features of the spoken mode, making a personal opening statement as in 'Today I am going to tell you where your food goes after you swallowed it'. The concluding part also deviates from the formal conventions of written Explanation texts. This type of conclusion is more likely to be found at the end of a 'Book Review'. In terms of word choices, the text, as a whole, contains many spoken words such as 'goes down', 'come out', 'eat up', 'sort of', and 'bits' (it also includes clichés and slang). However, the section 2 (Operation: how it works) includes information in a logical sequence to explain how the phenomenon of digestion occurs, using temporal conjunctions and linking words (first when, then, until) to signify the appropriate sequence. [42] There are subject specific terms used such as 'saliva', 'esophagi' and 'intestine'. In addition, cohesion is maintained to some degree through anaphoric reference (using the personal pronoun 'it') to refer to a generalized non-human participant (e.g. esophagus and stomach) and anaphoric reference using the demonstrative pronoun 'this' to refer to the preceding description of the process (Halliday, 1994: 315-317). Furthermore, the definitions of these terms are well elaborated through the complex nominal groups containing an embedded clause as part of their structure (as Postmodifier or as Head):

> Then the food goes down to your stomach [[which is like a sloppy bag]][43]
> Then it goes down to your small intestine [[which is about 5 meters long]].
> But the waste bits go into something [[that is called a large intestine]].
> This is [[how the food travels around your body, which is called digestion]].

In addition to the topic of digestion, the Field in Jinha's early Explanation texts ranges from history to current news to natural science (e.g. on crocodile mating). Among these texts, the text FE-3 is examined more closely in order to figure out its availability as an Explanation text. Since it is generally accepted that most historical descriptions tend to be classified as 'Recount Writing', which covers 'what happened', the following text FE-3 may also need to be classified as one type of Recount writing. However, it can be claimed that the content of this text focuses more on 'how Canberra became the capital city', which coincides with the nature of 'Sequential Explanation'. In this regard, even

---

[42] As referred to the underlined conjunctions (in text FE-1), it seems that Jinha overuses these conjunction. Conjunctions 'and' and 'but' occur at the beginning of sentences, which is not appropriate for formal written texts.
[43] The sign of [[ ]] represents embedded clauses (inclusive of finite and non-finite clauses). Halliday (1994: 242) classifies the embedded clause as two groups; one is as Postmodifier in a nominal group and the other function is as Head of a nominal group (i.e. as a nominalization). The last example above (as in 'That is [[how the food travels your body...]]' belongs to the other group of embedded clauses as Head.

though the following text FE-3 has some differences in the language features from other Explanation writings (such as present tense), it seems that it also deserves to be regarded as a sequential Explanation text.

Table 4-19. Jinha's Explanation Text in Year 3

Text FE-3	<Title: How Canberra became the Capital City>
The first European settlement in this area was a grazing property [[established in 1824]]. The owner, Josha Moree named the property Canberry, [[which is an aboriginal word meaning 'meeting place]]'. In 1908 the site for the city of Canberra was selected by C.R. Scrivener, the districted surveyor of New South Wales. The federation Act of Australia required that Australia's capital city be built on Commonwealth land. There was intense rivalry between Sydney and Melbourne [[to become new federal Capital]]. A compromise was reached [[whereby the capital would be build in New South Wales, but more than 160 kilometers from Sydney]]. (the extract from Text FE-3)	

The above text is lacking a time sequence since it does not employ any proper linking words or conjunctions so, the text itself does not seem to satisfy the purpose of the text effectively. Probably at the time Jinha was not familiar with this kind of historical texts either from reading or writing. The subject specific terms would have looked very challenging to him at his age and some attempts to use passive voice are not correct. Nevertheless, this text is a good start on this specific subject area in that Jinha attempted to write this Explanation in an objective manner, excluding personal aspects. Also significant is the use of the conjunction 'whereby' which is only used in written language (commonly by the bureaucrats and the legal profession). As we consider the underlined words above, all the Themes are generalized participants that include some abstract nouns such as 'intense rivalry' and 'a compromise'.

What also appears as significant is the amount of experiential information built in what is quite a short text. This is due, mainly, to elaboration of the nominal group which has an embedded clause as Qualifier (see the boxed words as the Heads of the nominal groups). Also important is the construction of subject specific information. The child must have become familiar with a significant amount of subject specific information detail. In this regard, it can be argued that as the child moves up the grades through primary

228

school, success in writing becomes increasingly dependent on his/her knowledge of the topic, so-called subject specific knowledge. The building of such knowledge thus becomes a critical part of literacy teaching.

While Jinha was practicing his Explanation texts through oral discussion and learning journals in many different subjects from Year 3 to Year 5, his class teachers at school put effort into teaching this text type with more systematic joint construction of the Genre-based Approach. [44] The models of Explanation texts that were demonstrated by the teacher before setting the independent Explanation writing task could have supported the children's organizing the text structurally. They could also have allowed them to focus on the content of the text.

The following text FE-8 (How Fire engines work) demonstrates explicitly how Jinha developed his organization skills in Explanation writing step by step. Jinha practiced this text with sub-headings prior to the final copy. With the class teacher's explicit guidance he was able to plan and organize information using the suggested framework. The reference book was available for children to refer to for subject specific terms in the classroom, but Jinha did not seem to have any help from the reference book since the content already was not difficult for him. The class teacher wrote as feedback on Jinha's text: 'Great Jinha, a very clear Explanation.'

---

[44] 'Joint construction' is explained as follows: "Collaborative or shared writing will help children move towards independent writing of Explanations. Choose a familiar topic in the context of the curriculum and ask children to meet in small groups to brainstorm and compile information they can remember about the topic. They then categorize their information using headings from the Explanation framework planning sheets ... and discuss any points that need to be clarified. The teacher, with help from the children, scribes the first and second paragraph. As the children are contributing ideas the teacher can explicitly discuss aspects of the construction such as the language features or text organization necessary to achieve a clear Explanation. This process may continue over a number of sessions. Alternatively, after the first session children can move back to their groups and jointly construct the remainder of the text. Groups can then share and discuss features of their Explanations. The finished texts can be left for reference." (The Education Department of Western Australia, 1997: 117)

Table 4-20. Jinha's Explanation Texts in Year 5

Text FE-8	<Title: How Fire Engines Works>
Text title	How Fire Engines Works
Definition	A fire engine is a vehicle [[designed to put out fire]].
Components / Parts	Fire engines have lots of part [[to put out fires]]. Like ladders, oxygen tanks, lamps, crowbars and many other items.
Operations	These parts help firemen to do their job. For example, ladders help firemen to get up high to either put out fire from high above and rescue people from high windows. The oxygen tanks help firemen to work in smoke and fumes to help people [[who have breathed into much smoke]].
Applications	Fire engines have been used to put out fires, to transport people quickly and for emergencies.

Text FE-9	<Title: How a Kite Works>
Topic	How a kite works
Definition	A kite is a flying object [[that is heavier than air]].
Components/Parts Description of the parts	A kite consists of a frame, a skin [[covering the frame]] and a long string [[held by the user]].
Operations: How it works (cause and effect)	A kite becomes airborne when the wind pressure between the kite and the ground lifts the structure into the air. The tilt of the plane surface of the kite causes a lesser air pressure to occur behind the kite's upper surface than the pressure [[created by the wind on the under surface]].
Applications: When and where it works or is applied	Kites have been used as signals, experimental instruments in atmospheric measurement and as play objects [[dating back many thousands of years]].
An Interesting Comments: Special Features/ Evaluation	

As support for students' construction of Explanation texts the teacher handed out a pre-arranged sheet with separate boxes for each of the elements of the schematic structure, with the labels of these elements such as Definition, Components, Operations and Applications (in the left-hand column). Jinha's texts seem to have achieved discourse cohesion through thematic continuity. The underlined nominal groups above are all Themes as the first element in a clause and mostly they are concentrated on the topics of the texts, the fire engine and the kite. To achieve this kind of thematic continuity Jinha employed passive forms in the Application element section, as in 'Fire engines have been used to put out fires, to transport people, quickly and for emergencies' and 'Kites have been used as signals, experimental instruments in atmospheric measurement and as play objects dating back many thousands of years'. Jinha successfully uses the passive voice choices in both texts to keep this thematic prominence. The use of the passive voice is a characteristic feature of the Explanation text type so that Jinha's employing this choice in his factual text demonstrates his growing control of the genre.

Another significant feature of these texts is Jinha's use of the potential of the nominal group to pack in information. There are many examples of embedded phrases and clauses used in the Qualifier position within the nominal group structure. These embedded clauses are realized in relative clauses and non-finite clauses. These nominal groups play an important role in achieving lexical density as one feature of written texts:

> vehicle [[designed to put out fire]]
> lots of part [[to put out fires]]
> people [[who have breathed into much smoke]]
> a flying object [[that is heavier than air]]
> a skin [[covering the frame]]
> a long string [[held by the user]]
> the pressure [[created by the wind on the undersurface]]
> play objects [[dating back many thousands of years]]

These nominal groups provide the texts with the necessary clarification and elaboration along with the subject specific terms, and consequently contribute to satisfying the purpose of the informative Explanation text type.

As far as the Transitivity process types are concerned, the range of relational process types has been expanded. The typical type verb 'be' was varied by other verbs such as 'consist of', 'become' and 'cause'.

4.5. Review

Book and film Reviews are another kind of factual writing quite extensively practiced by Jinha over his years in primary school. The earliest, really embryonic examples were written in Kindergarten (age 5). Admittedly, these earlier text examples are more likely 'Recount writing on story books' along with a brief personal comment as in 'it was fun' or 'I liked this story because it was scary'. As a recognizable text type, book Reviews were written on a regular basis, several Reviews per school year, between Years 2 and 5 (age 7-10).

Review texts were constructed both at school and in the home. At school, Review writing was initiated by the classroom teacher who let children write a 'book Report' after their individual reading sessions. The teacher mostly guided the children with some questions as follows: 'On a separate sheet of paper write what you think of the book.' 'What was your favorite part in the story? Why?' 'What are the good points about the book? In the home, Jinha was encouraged by the researcher to write a Review of a book which he had just enjoyed or a movie which he had just seen. Both children seemed happy and willing to share their impressions after having completed reading a book, or having watched a movie or a video. The researcher took this opportunity to channel their expressive efforts towards writing a piece about what they thought of the book or the film. Thus, the researcher often engaged Jinha in an oral discussion of the book/film, and then would suggest that he write down what he had just said. The task seemed to make sense to Jinha as he commonly followed the suggestion. The task was suggested by the researcher so that the text type expected in school could be practiced in an informal context. The task might also help the child further develop his overall control of written English.

Text FRV-6 and Text FRV-14 are examples of Review texts written by Jinha at home. The texts consist of three parts: a brief Introduction, Body (mostly book summary) and Evaluation and Personal Comments in the last section. The Evaluation element includes, as part of it, a 'why'

Explanation.

Table 4-21. Jinha's Review Text in Year 4

Text FRV-6	<Title: The book Review of 'Cockroach War'>
Introduction	Every August in Australia, the authors put all their books [[that they have written]] and the judges read all of these books and the best books get a Children's Book Award, and I think that the book 'Cockroach War' will get one.
Body (book summary)	The problem of the story is that a family [[named the Judges]] lived next to the worst neighbors in the world. I liked the way [[that it's not the adults [[who solve the problem in the story]] but it's their children, Emma and Toby]]. Emma was planning to be an insect scientist and she had discovered a way [[to control insects]]. Using that method, they chase the neighbors out of their house with cockroaches!
Evaluation and Personal Comments	These are some good points about the book [[which I suppose]]. Compared with other children books, this book is firstly interesting because it has lots of funny expressions and the characters have funny characteristics. Also, the story actually forced me to read more and more. Secondly the events were all very exiting and once I read one, I kept on expecting the next. And the setting was well described that I could draw the pictures in my head very clearly and imaginatively. Thirdly I like the book because it is science fiction.

Thus, in more detail, the Evaluation in the Review on the book 'Cockroach' provides three reasons why Jinha liked the book, using the sequential adverbial words – 'firstly', 'secondly' and 'thirdly' along with a cause-effect conjunction 'because' (associated with reasoning). According to Derewianka (1990: 80), the logical relationship of 'cause and effect' can be expressed somewhat differently across the spoken and written modes of language. In the case of the spoken mode, "cause and effect is usually expressed through conjunctions like "because" and "therefore." However, in written texts particularly, cause-effect and other relations are also expressed by using nouns (The first *reason*...) or, as here, verbs (could *result* in...), or prepositions (*through*...), to give more structural choices and often more subtle connections". In this text, Jinha seems to have mixed the spoken and written modes. The technical terms to analyze the storybook are successfully employed as in 'characters', 'characteristics', 'events', 'setting', 'imaginatively' and 'science fiction'. The use of technical terms that are expected in a particular text type is a distinct sign of his developing control of this genre.

The following text, FRV-14, also can be considered a good example of a 'Review' text in that it demonstrates Jinha's insightful evaluation that was constructed after watching a TV program at home and an oral discussion with the researcher for shared understanding on it:

Table 4-22. Jinha's Review Text in Year 5

Text FRV-14	<Title: Review of TV Program "Y?">
Introduction: The program definition	For my Review, I chose the program "Y?" Y? is a learning educational program because it tells you a great deal of information about things.
The content structure of "Y?"	In the show "Y?", it is composed of three sessions, the science, animals and Australians. First there is a science and experiment session. This session lets you to explore experiments about lots of different, interesting things. This chemical science session is also very good because the speaker tells you the reason [[why it happens and how]]. The next session is about endangered species of wild life. This is a session [[that tells you about endangered animals]]. I find this session quite interesting because they explain the animal shortly but clearly. Lastly it is a session with famous people, for example, firefighters etc. I suggest the people [[who come in this session]] are very important in our daily life.
Evaluation on the TV program "Y?"	I consider "Y?" is a very educational and useful program. It uses proper and appropriate language. It is on in a suitable time in the day <u>also</u> it has a good source of information. I <u>also</u> think that there are no negative points about the television program Y? <u>Additionally</u> I would like to say it is an outstanding program because it is interactive. Like at every advertisement stops, it gives you questions to think about. This makes the program fun and interactive. <u>In addition</u> the presenter is always asking you questions, not doing it all **themselves. They** <u>also</u> let the watchers give feedback by mail.

Compared with the former Review Text FRV-6, Text FRV-14 looks similar in terms of the overall text structure, namely introduction, the middle part of content analysis and the last section of evaluation. In a sense, the middle part is weaved in a similar pattern to the logical sequence in the evaluation part of the former text FRV-6, with the use of words like 'first', 'because', 'the next section', 'because' and 'lastly' sequentially. These similar structural patterns and the choice of connective words reflect the influence of the Genre-based Approach under which the researcher introduced Jinha explicitly to the structural characteristics and language features of 'Review' texts using sample writings and workbooks in the home context. The evaluation element appears to be satisfactorily constructed in that the entire content is relevant to the evaluative comments, and the judgments seem well thought-through and well reasoned. However, the text structure does not look organized; various ideas seem to have been added one after the other. There is overuse of connectives such as 'also' (three times), 'in addition', and 'additionally'. Pronoun reference is also not clear in some cases (themselves, they) and is in bold type in the above text. In regard to use of the personal pronoun 'you' (in the middle section mostly), it is worthwhile considering Kroll's (1981: 32-54) explanation about three approaches termed 'subjective, objective and hypothetical'. Kroll (1981) indicates that children's writing tends to develop toward the impersonal tone in factual writing such as instruction. Based on Kroll's study, the use of 'you' in Text FR-14 can be regarded as an 'objective' approach, which projects the relationship between the TV program (each section) and 'you' (the reader). Even though Jinha reflects his view on the TV program mostly with the first pronoun 'I' (as in 'I consider-', 'I find-') throughout the whole text the other pronouns 'you' and 'it gives –' make the Review text more persuasive by inviting the reader into the text. Along with the use of the pronoun 'you', the following sentence patterns contribute to making the tone of the text more objective:

1) This session lets you to explore experiments ...
2) I find this session quite interesting ...
3) It gives you questions to think about.
4) This makes the program fun....

In sentences 1), 3) and 4), the judgment is expressed in an impersonal manner. The unmarked topic Themes (this session, it, this) foreground the events rather than the writer's personal feelings about these events. In example 2), the writer uses the mental process of cognition to project his judgment, which also contributes to a more distanced representation of an opinion.

To sum up, in many ways the Review texts FRV-6 and FRV-14, appear to satisfy the purpose of Review writing. In order to choose a good book, TV program or movie to see, children sometimes need to read book Reviews, TV guides or film Reviews in daily life. Many model texts of this genre are readily available. With the real purpose of choosing the right book or movie for them, children can be encouraged to read or browse through the guide material carefully. Also, children can be exposed to relevant oral discussion on the evaluation of what they have read or watched by doing this with their parents or friends. Through spontaneous or planned opportunities children can be supported in writing this particular text type, 'Review', less effortlessly at home and at school. Finally it is worth pointing out that this kind of Review writing seems to be a good start for critical literacy since children can get accustomed to the evaluative text associated with reasoning. This writing experience might extend to persuasive Argument texts, which requires more challenging cognitive and writing skills later.

4.6. Argument

Argumentative writing has a special standing in the English-speaking cultures, being a highly valued kind of writing. This type of writing is also an expected learning outcome of the mid-to upper-primary school curriculum. Importantly, students are expected to construct Argumentative texts in their secondary and tertiary level schooling. Jinha wrote his first examples of what can be identified as Argumentative texts in Year 4 (age 9), both in school and in the home. However, it is also noteworthy that, before starting his Argument writing, Jinha had been exposed considerably to the convention of justifying his position through relevant oral discussions at school and at home (in his native tongue, Korean as well).

Before analyzing Jinha's Argument texts we need to define

this particular text more clearly.[45] According to Derewianka (1990: 75), "Argument texts belong to a genre group called "Exposition" concerned with the analysis, interpretation and evaluation of the world around us." For more elaboration, the following explanation would be necessary:

> An argument requires the presentation of one point of view on an issue and justification of this with selected supporting evidence so that other people are convinced to accept the point of view on the basis of the information presented. The information is presented in a form appropriate to the audience to be convinced and the writer appears to be well versed in the subject. (Wing Jan, 2001: 84)

Now we shall examine Jinha's Argument text FA-5 that he constructed at school in Year 4 as below:

Table 4-23. Jinha's Argument Text (in Year 4 at School)

Text FA-5	<Title: We should stop every ten minutes for a game to rest our brains>
Opening Statement	While in the classroom, we should stop every ten minutes for a game to rest our brain.
Supporting ideas – point 1	If we have a game at the end of every ten minutes, time will seem faster and we will work harder. Children become restless in hot, airless classrooms.
Supporting ideas – point 2	Secondly I think we should have a game every ten minutes because games are fun to play because I enjoy myself more than anything else when I'm playing games.
Supporting ideas – point 3 and Concluding statement (restating of opinion)	Thirdly because it makes me forget about the bad things [[that I was thinking of]] because the game keeps me concentrated. So this is in the reason [[why we should stop every 10 minutes for a game]].

The above text, FA-5, was constructed with the guidance of the class teacher through several preparatory steps such as

---

[45] Argument text can also be differentiated from 'Discussion' texts in which two opposing points of view (argues for and against an issue) are raised and discussed with supporting evidences. In Jinha's case, the discussion kinds of text was practiced at school as well with the issue of whether school uniform should be compulsory. In a preparatory task, Jinha was required to fill in four sections consisting of 'Argument for' and 'supporting evidence' as well as 'Argument against' and 'supporting evidence'. The worksheet itself looks satisfactory to some degree, but we cannot evaluate it further since follow up writing such as a real discussion text was not produced at that time. Except for this example, Jinha's expository texts were all close to Argument texts that present his own point of view with supporting evidence.

brainstorming on the issue and the exposition framework consisting of 'State Problem and Point of View', 'Assertions and Evidence/Data/References' and 'Conclusion or Summary'. As far as the basic structure is concerned, the text seems to largely satisfy the conventions of the Argument text organization.[46] Also, Jinha is attempting to use generalized participants, as in '<u>Children</u> become restless in hot, airless classroom', and 'if <u>we</u> have a game at the end of every ten minutes, <u>time</u> will seem faster and we will work harder'. Some generalized participants and 'we' were employed in order to make his supporting evidence sound more objective and persuasive. On occasions, however, the young writer switches over to reporting personal experiences.

The other Argument example is a text that Jinha constructed at home. The researcher encouraged Jinha to write a number of Argument texts in the weeks leading up to the announced State-wide testing of writing across the primary grades.[47]

Table 4-24. Jinha's Argument Text (in Year 4 at Home)

Text FA-10	<Title: Should parents let their children climb trees?>
(Section 1) Introduction- Opening Statement	Some parents let their children climb trees, but other parents don't. There are different points of views about this matter. Some people think that their children can climb trees. So they can either agree to the statement or disagree. <u>In my opinion I would like to choose that parents should not let their children climb trees. These are some of my supporting ideas.</u>
(Section 2) Supporting ideas – Two points; 1.children could be	<u>Firstly</u> if children climb, trees and a little twig [[that they're standing on]] snaps, they can easily fall down and get a serious injury or could even die. So it could be a very dangerous thing to do. I have heard

---

[46] Text FA-5 largely satisfies the conventions of the Argument text except for the last part that was not grammatically and syntactically correct: the underlined clauses can be corrected as in 'Lastly it makes me forget about the bad things that I am thinking of and keeps me concentrating.' For this kind of syntactical error occurring, we need to consider Jinha's developmental attempts to get accustomed to or control the connectives and conjunctions in relation to cause and effect.

[47] The exact title of the test in which Jinha participated was 'Australian Schools Writing Competition' sponsored by The University of New South Wales Educational Testing Centre. When Jinha was in Year 4, the text type for the writing task was 'Argument'; 'Imagine that schools do not have rules for using the playground. You have been asked to write an Argument in the school newsletter to convince people that playground rules are good for schools. Write an Argument that persuade people that this is a good idea.' In this competition, Jinha got the award of 'Distinction' which was quite satisfactory.

dangerous. 2. Nature could be dangerous. (with presenting examples)	on the news that a kid from high school was climbing a tree and a branch broke down and unfortunately he died. <u>Secondly</u> it could be harming the nature around us and also the environment in many different kinds of ways. For example, they could accidentally break a very big branch down and it would put the tree into danger and could also crack other creatures' habitats.
(Section 3) Concluding Statements - Restating his view - further advice (giving caution)	<u>As I have pointed out the reasons above, I think that climbing tress should be prohibited in the childhood.</u> But of course some children have climbed lots of trees before and it can give them special pleasure and fun, nevertheless, I think that if they are going to climb trees, I think the people [[who are climbing the trees]] or the people [[who are taking care of them]] should check these things first. For example the height, the thickness of the branches and the creatures [[that are living there]].

As seen above, Text FA-10 demonstrates more lengthy and naturalistic Argument, compared with the former text FA-5 that gives a sort of formatted like impression at first glance. Actually, Jinha constructed this text seemingly effortlessly, and at a much faster speed than any other Argument texts. He did not stop until he came to the end. After finishing the first draft, he was advised by the researcher to revise and do proofreading. In the section of supporting ideas, Jinha seems to show much more developed strategies by using relevant examples. In Section 2 (Supporting Ideas) Jinha uses exemplification (using the phrase of 'For example'). This is a significant development, compared to his earlier written Argument texts. It is also noticeable that in this section Jinha shows a more mature way of using differing degrees of certainty with which he can make claims. In connection with this issue, Derewianka (1990: 80) explains the tendency in using proper certainty words between adults and children as below:

To win an argument, children often exaggerate and make sweeping generalizations. An adult knows that the reader will become skeptical and the argument will be jeopardized if bald statements and unqualified claims are made. An adult leaves room for negotiation by using words such as "nearly" "often", "most", "generally", "tend to" and "might", etc.

In this text, Jinha attempts to qualify his statements. Within the mood system, several times Jinha employs modal operators such as 'can' and 'could' as in 'they can easily fall down', 'could even die', 'it could be a very dangerous thing to do', 'it could be harming...', 'it would put the tree into danger' and 'they could accidentally break...'. This choice of modal operators seems to make this text sound more reasonable and plausible than Text FA-5.

Although the introduction part and the conclusion part show some immaturity of organization, overall this text can be evaluated as a more successful example of Argument, showing Jinha's control of Argument texts.

So far we have examined some selected of 'Explanation', 'Review' and 'Argument' texts of Jinha's in order to find out his control of writing development with these particular genres. Although each text type has its characteristics and different purpose, the basic cognitive skills such as logical sequence (cause and effect) and critical thinking are necessarily required in all. In this respect, these three factual writing genres appear to have developed coincidentally in close co-relationship. While Explanation and Argument texts were more explicitly taught at school, in terms of the structure and language features, the Review texts were more practiced and influenced by the researcher at home. The explicit teaching of the genres and the regular practice sessions helped Jinha develop control over these text types in terms of their overall organization, use of technical words, expression of logical sequence in written language and ability to make appropriate choices within the Mood (choice of modal operators) and Transitivity (choice of Process and Participants) systems. Overall, Jinha's factual writing of Explanation, Review and Argument seems to have given him a great deal of confidence first in controlling the structures of each genre and later in developing more various points of the language features. The last text type that we shall explore is 'Procedure' which mostly was guided by Jinha's class teachers in Year 2 to Year 4 (age 7 to 9).

4.7. Procedure

Compared with other factual writing types, procedural texts have a very distinct schematic structure of a list of sequences of actions, or steps to be performed in order to do something. Since the procedural texts play an important part in our everyday life and are used in many contexts (inclusive of recipes, science experiment, machinery manuals), children get exposed to these texts from an early age. In Jinha's case, the class teachers gave several opportunities to him to internalize the necessary linguistic features of procedural writing in various contexts based on school curriculum (cooking recipe, instructions to play a game (how to play a game), a machine design (how to design a machine), science experiments (the most popular one)). The following are the instructions written by the teacher on the whiteboard and copied by Jinha into his workbook.

Table 4-25. Class Instruction on Procedure Text Writing

Procedure	
Title	Aim or what you are doing
Material	Quantities, ingredients, type of ingredients
Method	Steps, numbered points in order
	Gives you clear instructions
	Action verbs
	Present tense

Even though each text relates to a different context and may vary in framework headings, the language features are similar in the use of imperative mood choices in the beginning of each sentence, temporal sequencing of actions and timeless tense. For further linguistic Explanation, we shall examine Jinha's procedural texts selected for the purpose of tracing his developmental improvement in this particular text type. The first example text is as follows:

Table 4-26. Jinha's Procedure Text in Year 3

TEXT FP-2	<Title: Violet Crumble Recipe>
Equipment	- Wooden spoon
	- Square tin
	- Stove
	- Sauce pan
	- Mixing bowl
	- Teaspoon

241

	- Baking paper
Ingredients	- 1 cup sugar - 4 + bsp of golden syrup - 3 tsp bicarb soda - 1 block of melted chocolate
Method	Step 1: <u>Mix</u> golden syrup and sugar in a saucepan <u>simmer</u> on low heat for 7 mins. Step 2: <u>Remove</u> from heat and quickly <u>add</u> bicarb and mix in. Step 3: <u>Pour</u> into a tin lined with baking paper. <u>Leave</u> to set.

The above Procedure text was written in Year 3 at school just after a cooking class. This way Jinha had opportunities to develop an understanding of the content, through the hands-on experiences and the use of oral language. In this text, Jinha seems to have managed the overall schematic structure quite successfully. Also, the modeling of the genre provided by the teacher (using whiteboard or OHP) could have supported Jinha's learning to control some of its typical features. For instance, the task of beginning with the imperative mood of action verbs in each clause is successful. In this regard, it might be acceptable to point out that Jinha did not have much difficulty in controlling this distinctive feature of Procedure text from the beginning stage, probably because he had already been quite aware of the basic structure and language features of Procedure texts through oral experiences and the explicit teaching on the genre.

However, the following example demonstrates that the real challenge for Jinha in mastering the Procedure text seems to be writing more concrete and precise steps in detailed description in the method part, so that the reader can follow the instruction without any comprehensive difficulty.

Table 4-27. Jinha's Procedure Text in Year 5

TEXT FP-5	<Title: Evaporation>
Aim	To find out which cloth dries the quickest
Materials	- Bucket of water - Clothes - Something to hang the cloths on
Procedure Method	1.<u>Get</u> all your materials ready 2. <u>Dip</u> all the cloths into the water and <u>squeeze</u> all the water out. 3. <u>Hang</u> the cloth out in different places and in different positions. 4. <u>Write</u> down your results.

Results	The cloths that were scrunched up didn't dry. And it did meet the aim.

Text FP-5 was constructed as a post-activity of a science experiment under the Theme of 'water'. Each step was accompanied by a simplified drawing in order to elaborate the steps for the readers. The temporal sequencing of actions is explicitly signaled by the use of numbering. In the topical Theme position the imperative mood choices seem to be appropriate. The part of 'Result' was added as this text is based on a science experiment. Actually, each step in the Procedure method and the Results seem to require more detailed and concrete description but Jinha managed to construct his Procedure in a very simplified manner along with drawings. A more advanced writer would add more description and more step divisions. However, as a whole, this text shows Jinha's reasonable competence in writing a proper Procedure genre in a different context (such as science experiment). The field has changed from that of commonsense experiences (such as cooking) to constructing uncommonsense knowledge.

Table 4-28. Jinha's Procedure Text in Year 5 (A Better Developed Example)

TEXT FP-9	<Title: What material absorbs water?>
Aim	To find out what types of paper absorb the most water
Materials	- 5 long glass test tubes - 5 different papers - A bottle of water - 1 eyedropper - Sticky tape
Method	1. Fill all the test tubes (**up to the mark 50**). 2. Make it exact (**with the eyedropper**) 3. Fold the pieces (**in a strip thin enough to fit in the test tube**). 4. Put sticky tape (**on the top of all the strips of paper**). 5. Get some help and put all the pieces of paper in (**at the same time**) (**in to the same depth**). 6. Leave them all (**for five to ten minutes**). 7. Take them all (**out**) (**at once**). 8. Write (**down**) the results. The test tube with the least amount of water in it has absorbed the most water.
Results	The tissue absorbed the most water then it was the newspaper, colored paper, plain paper and magazine paper (**hardly**) absorbed any water (**at all**).

Text FP-9 is another Procedure text that Jinha constructed

after a science experiment at school. As can be seen, this text contains an increased number of steps in the Method element, compared with the earlier Text FP-5. In Text FP-9 Jinha seems to have attempted to give more detail and necessary information. This is realized with further elaboration constructed mainly in the 'circumstances' (refer to the bold typed words with bracket) and nominal groups constructing participants (refer to the boxed words). Even though Text FP-9 seems to be a better developed example of the Procedure text than Text FP-5, the material section should have indicated or named the five different papers for the readers' understanding. Also, each step in the method part still needs more clarification for the exact referencing.

However, as a whole, Text FP-9 reveals Jinha's awareness of the schematic structure of the Procedure text type and shows how he makes the linguistic choices appropriate for the genre. Mastering this particular genre also means that Jinha is learning the appropriate ways of constructing factual experience in the English-speaking culture. For the relatively short period, Jinha surely had been developing his writing on this particular genre in more varied contexts. This learning was supported by hands-on experiences and conversations accompanying these experiences both in the home and at school, as well as explicit modeling of the target text type.

4.8. Conclusion

In this chapter, Jinha's factual writing from Kindergarten to Year 5 has been examined in the context of both school and home. Among the various factual text types, the Report, Explanation, Review, Argument and Procedure were selected for more detailed text analysis in order to find out how Jinha had been developing his writing along with his development of awareness of different writing purposes, schematic structures and language features.

Compared with Jinha's Narrative writing (Chapter 3), this factual writing development seems to be more positively influenced by the explicit teaching of the Genre-based

Approach at school and in the home. In other words, the effectiveness of the model writing and joint construction as part of the process of writing the various factual texts can be shown throughout the selected factual writing examples. Jinha's example shows that factual writing such as Report, Argument, Explanation and Procedure can be effectively modeled by teachers when done explicitly, and even young children can learn appropriate schematic structures and language features when supported by modeled writing and joint construction of factual texts. Accordingly, the Genre-based Approach that had been conducted in Jinha's school from Year 2 seems to have been quite helpful and useful for Jinha as an ESL student to have learnt various factual writing texts that are closely related to further academic texts and social functions. Given that Jinha was exposed to mostly English oral language at school (whereas the communication at home largely occurred through the medium of Korean), it was particularly helpful to have this explicit teaching of English factual writing. The Genre-based Approach adopted by Jinha's school teachers, supplemented by the explicit way of teaching, enabled him to develop various factual texts to satisfy different purposes. Particularly the process of internalizing the schematic structures of various factual writings was successfully realized by the guide worksheet (framed sheet) and the repeated and regular explicit teaching.

Learning to control factual writing is also important in that it helps to develop awareness of the differences between the written and spoken modes of language. In the analysis of Jinha's factual texts, some aspects of written mode such as nominalization, abstract language use, lexical density, the use of relational processes (to establish classification or definition), tense, reference system and conjunction choices have been highlighted to illustrate this issue. With the aid of modeled writing and joint construction, Jinha accelerated his awareness and control of this kind of written language features. Particularly in Explanation and Report texts, the use of abstract language and the application of more complicated and varied nominalization were apparent reflecting the expectations of the text types (to clarify and elaborate the key word concept).

Chapter 5. Sunyoung's Factual Writing in English

5.0. Introduction

In the previous Chapter 4 we examined how Jinha developed his factual writing in various text types during his early and mid primary years (from Kindergarten through year 5) in both school and home context. Compared with Jinha's case, the analysis of Sunyoung's factual writing development covers a shorter period, focusing on her early-primary period from Kindergarten through Year 3.

5.1. The Contexts of Sunyoung's Factual Writing (School and Home)

Sunyoung started primary school in Australia, when the Genre-based Approach to teaching writing was beginning to find its way into the classrooms of the school she attended. Sunyoung seemed to settle into the school routines quite effortlessly and adapted well to the literacy programs operating in the school. She enjoyed literacy-related activities. And, the teachers considered her to be among the higher achieving students.

As a young student she seemed to be more interested in reading and writing Narrative texts than factual ones. During her first years in school, Sunyoung's personal Recounts, Narratives and journals (including diary, travel journal, letter and cards) far outnumbered her factual writings. She also seemed to be developing her Narrative skills very successfully. Her competent Narrative writing brought praise from her teachers and, as a result, she felt encouraged to continue doing this. Narrative writing at this time was the child's preferred type of writing. In an attempt to encourage the child to engage with factual reading and writing, for better balanced literacy development, the researcher organized factual reading and writing activities in the home. Even though Sunyoung did not seem to enjoy this type of literacy activity, in most cases she accepted the researcher's suggestions and took up reading and writing factual texts. A hard-worker, Sunyoung tried her best in doing her homework involving writing factual texts or doing related research work. While doing the homework, she had many good examples of the Genre-based Approach and scaffolding appropriate to her age and personality through shared reading, oral discussion and joint construction. In this chapter Sunyoung's factual texts are examined, the contexts of Sunyoung's factual writing development are articulated and parallels are made between her's and Jinha's factual writing development.

5.2. Overview on Sunyoung's Factual Writing

Sunyoung's factual writing development was almost the same as Jinha's in terms of time-sequence (until Year 3). As with Jinha, Sunyoung started Report writing in Kindergarten, mainly handling science Reports on subjects such as animals (dogs, dinosaurs, platypus, red pandas and polar bears). The Report writing developed continuously until Year 3 and she expanded her topics to some social studies. One remarkable difference between Jinha's Reports and Sunyoung's is the degree of personal elements included in the initial period. In Jinha's case, even his earlier texts show a strong attempt to move away from personal reference and from Reporting personal experience, but in Sunyoung's initial attempts of Report texts personal references remained interspersed throughout entire texts. In some cases the Report texts were written as Recount writing, in the sense that the writer did not attempt to take an impersonal stance. One reason for this that could be that, at the time, Sunyoung was very involved in Narrative writing and personal Recount writing where the expression of personal feelings and comment is expected. However, as time passed, Sunyoung showed some distinct development in her control of factual writing. Thus, she gradually developed control over the schematic structure and language features of a number of factual genres, and Report writing was the first showing this type of development.

Sunyoung wrote her first Argument texts in Year 2 (age 7) whereas her Explanation writing developed over Years 2 and 3. Particularly in the beginning the growth appears to be minimal. This could be attributed, at least partly, to the fact that Sunyoung's classroom teachers did not single out Explanation as a distinct text type, often failing to explicitly differentiate it from Report and Recount type texts. There was no Argument writing taught in Sunyoung's Year 2 classroom and she personally was not encouraged to write factual Arguments either. When she was in Year 2, however, the word was out that the state-wide testing (the NSW writing competition) would include an Argumentative text writing task. [48] Having discovered this, the researcher organized some 'home tutoring' for Sunyoung in an attempt to expose her to the genre, and help her master some of its typical features.

The texts that Sunyoung produced after being shown some examples of Argumentative writing resemble the model text very closely. Opponents of the Genre-based Approach to teaching writing claim that such an approach stifles the students' creativity, but mastering the basic schematic of the genre and some of its typical language features is an important step in children becoming effective writers. The Genre-based Approach to teaching writing also gives young writers confidence that they can approximate the conventional expectations of the text type. Sunyoung initially was not enthusiastic about writing factual texts at home. She knew she was good at Narrative writing but she was less confident about writing factual texts. However, after several opportunities to look at the model texts and then to construct her own factual texts, she appeared to enjoy argumentative writing more.

The first Procedure text was written by Sunyoung in Year 2, at school. All the Procedure texts were written in school in response to specific tasks set by the teacher. Sunyoung never initiated Procedure writing; however, she always followed the teachers' instructions and produced the expected text type within the designated time frame and met the teachers'

---

[48] More detailed explanation on this will be provided later in this chapter.

expectations regarding the quality of writing.

The following tables show the number of texts of the various factual types produced by Sunyoung (Report, Explanation, Procedure and Argument) (Table 5-1) and topic details (Table 5-2, 5-3, 5-4 and 5-5) with time sequence:

Table 5-1. Sunyoung's Factual Texts in English over the Four Years of Schooling

Years in school / Type of text	Kinder	Year 1	Year 2	Year 3	Total Over 4 years
Report	5	3	4	2	14
Explanation			4	1	5
Procedure			9	2	11
Argument			4	2	6

Table 5-2. Sunyoung's Report Texts

	Title	Year in School	Place	Text types + Comments
1	Platypus	Kinder	School	Science Report
2	Dinosaurs	Kinder	Home	Science Report
3	Friendship	Kinder	Home	Social Studies
4	Habitats	Kinder	Home	Science Report
5	Dogs	Kinder	Home	Science Report
6	Red Panda	Year 1	Home	Science Report
7	Polar Bears	Year 1	School	Science Report A good example of the class teacher's systemic writing process
8	A Wolf's Life	Year 1	School	Science Report
9	Insects	Year 2	School	Science Report
10	The Past Times of Australia	Year 2	School	Social Studies
11	Tsunamis	Year 2	School	Science Report
12	Winds, Storms and Cyclones	Year 2	School	Science Report
13	Days, Years and Seasons	Year 3	School	Science Report
14	Seasons	Year 3	School	Science Report

Table 5-3. Sunyoung's Explanation Texts

	Title	Year in School	Place	Comments
1	Tornadoes (How it works)	Year 2	School	Using Explanation Plan – based on Genre Approach

		Year 2	Home	
2	Fire (How Fire causes) and Bees (How they live)	Year 2	Home	
3	Can I get a drink of water?	Year 2	Home	How text -
4	What can old photographs tell us about the past?	Year 2	School	How text + Report
5	How does the moon change its shape?	Year 3	School	Using Report format

Table 5-4. Sunyoung's Argument Texts

	Title	Year in School	Place	Comments
1	Should zoos be destroyed?	Year 2	Home	in the preparation of NSW Writing Test
2	Faulty silver pen should be replaced..	Year 2	Home	Letter of Complaint
3	Should schools let children do homework everyday?	Year 2	Home	
4	Should bulling be punished strictly?	Year 2	Home	
5	Our class wants all schools to wear their school uniform.	Year 3	School	Exposition; taking one point of view (based on Genre Approach)
6	Writing a letter to Sheriff of Nottingham stating their opinion	Year 3	School	A letter stating her opinion (A good example of Class teacher's systematic planning)

Table 5-5. Sunyoung's Procedure Texts

	Title	Year in School	Place	Comments
1	3D Photo Frame	Year 2	Home	As homework (Art)
2	Rain Gauge	Year 2	Home	How to make a science tool
3	How it works	Year 2	Home	
4	Instructions for my design	Year 2	Home	Art
5	How to play Kongi (Traditional Korean Game)	Year 2	Home	
6	How to design a model shelter	Year 2	School	Theme related work
7	Planting a bulb	Year 2	School	Science experiment

8	Hot Air (to find out if hot air rises)	Year 2	School	With a guide sheet (structured frame)
9	Terrarium (To demonstrate the water cycle)	Year 2	School	Science Experiment
10	Plan of Solar System	Year 3	School	Theme related work
11	Procedure about Eggheads	Year 3	Home	Homework

5.3. Report Writing

As discussed in the previous chapter, "Reports are factual texts that present information clearly and succinctly" (Education Department of Western Australia, 1997: 85), and they require very different text organization and language features from what is required in Narrative writing. As was the case with Jinha, Reports were the earliest factual texts produced by Sunyoung, and they were first done in Kindergarten (age 5). There were four texts, described as 'science Reports' that dealt with animal related topics such as 'platypus', 'dinosaurs', 'dogs' and 'habitats'. Only one text can be classified as a social science Report, having the concept of 'friendship' as its Field. Only one of the Report texts (SFR-1) was produced in school. The remaining four texts were written at home. There was no explicit teaching of Report writing in the Kindergarten class although the students were shown some model Report texts by the teachers. In the meantime, at home, Sunyoung was provided some guidance on how to write Report texts by the researcher.

Sunyoung, however, tended to write in her own way when writing Report texts during this time, mostly maintaining some aspects of Recount writing. This is a notable point because it shows a big difference between Jinha's and Sunyoung's approaches toward factual writing. Compared with Jinha's Report texts in Kindergarten, Sunyoung's Reports are closer to the mixed form of Report and Recount.[49] At this early stage in her schooling, Sunyoung

---

[49] For another possible reasons of Sunyoung's mixed form (Recount + Report), this kind of text is quite common in books for young readers. Also, teachers sometimes encourage children to write about factual phenomena, presenting it

has probably not been exposed to clear examples of Report writing at least at school. Sunyoung's early interest in Narrative reading and writing and familiarity with it (which was cultivated by the school teachers) may have influenced the language choices she made in her early factual writing attempts.

The following texts (SFR-1, SFR-2 and SFR-3) demonstrate Sunyoung's initial Report texts' characteristics very clearly:

Table 5-6. Sunyoung's Report Texts in Kindergarten

Text SFR-1 (Kindergarten, age 5)	
Title: Platypus	Elements of schematic structure
1. I am a Platypus.	1) + 2): Sort of Classification - Identification
2. My name is Platy.	
3. I like mud.	3) + 4): Description – particular aspect of eating
4. So as yabbies.	
5. I live in the river.	5): Description - Location
6. I have a long beak.	6) + 7): Description - Appearance
7. A male platypus has claws.	
Text SFR-2 (Kindergarten, age 5)	
Title: Dinosaurs	Elements of schematic structure
1. Dinosaurs were long living animals.	1) Classification (definition) : dinosaurs
2. We weren't there before dinosaurs.	2) + 3) Description (about time)
3. But now dinosaurs are extinct.	
4. Meat eaters are called carnivores.	4) Meat eaters - Classification
5. After dinosaurs came, we came.	5) Description (about time)
6. In my class we learning about dinosaurs.	6) 7) 8) – Recount writing
7. Imagine you riding on a dinosaur.	Personal Comments
8. Well bye then see you tomorrow.	

through the Narrative genre. For example, they may ask children to write a story, pretending that they are a chicken hatching out of an egg, etc.

Text SFR-3 (Kindergarten, age 5)

Title: Friendship	Elements of schematic structure
1. Friendship is like being friends.	1) Definition of 'friendship'
2. Friends are very special.	2) Description : 'very special'
3. If you didn't have a friend, you will be lonely.	3) + 4) Description: 'not lonely'
4. and there will be no people to play with.	Elaboration of the concept
5. Being a friend is not hard.	5) Another description of friendship: 'not hard'
6. It is same as pets.	6),7), 8), 9): Exemplification
7. You can have friends as pets.	Comparison with pets
8. You don't only have to play with people.	
9. You can play with pets too.	

First, in Text SFR-1, the text content includes a sort of classification of platypus (identification), followed by five separate sentences of description on the topics of eating, location and appearance. In accordance with the conventions of the science Report, Sunyoung uses technical vocabulary such as platypus, yabbies, beak, claws and male platypus. She also includes features that are relevant description and the use of the relational processes and the timeless present tense. The final sentence (7) demonstrates a successful use of a generalized statement. However, it is particularly not able that the Themes of this text are the first pronoun 'I' (4 times), and not 'platypus' that is, generalized participants (a whole class of things). This makes the whole text sound like Narrative writing (imaginative) or Recount writing (story Recount). Whereas Jinha in his early Report texts demonstrates quite a successful control of generalized participants which helps achieve the impersonal Tenor in his factual texts, Sunyoung does not yet fully make this differentiation. As a result, her text combines features of both factual Report and fiction writing.

The next Text SFR-2 is also a typical example of mixed Report-like text and Recount features. From sentences 1 to 5, the text is more like a Report and includes the definition of dinosaurs and further descriptions related to the 'times' they belonged to. However, in the later parts, sentences 6, 7 and 8 there is a change in tone of the text to Recount writing along with personal comments. Her clustering of relevant information was not good, either. The descriptions about 'the times' were not put together logically (see sentences 2+3 and 5). In terms of language features, this text still uses personal or subjective language such as 'we', 'in my class' and 'well, bye then, see you tomorrow'. Even though it includes some difficult technical terms such as 'extinct' and 'carnivores', on the whole Sunyoung wrote a simple description with a few refined adjectives. There was no reference term, either. With specific regard to Transitivity, both relational processes (were, are called) and material processes (came, learn, ride) were employed, but the text does not demonstrate consistent use of tense (usually timeless present tense) but rather a mix of present and past tense. The range of Theme choices such as generalized participants (dinosaurs, Meat eaters), personal pronoun (we), linking words (but, after), adverbial phrase (in my class), and imperative verb form (imagine) also indicates that this text is a mixture of Report and Recount.[50]

The next Text SFR-3 was self-initiated at home (not following reading a relevant reference book but just her own idea). It is quite an important text in the sense that we can assume it demonstrates her ability with written language on a totally different topic namely 'social studies'. In terms of text organization, the text starts with the definition of 'friendship' as a sort of classification, which is similar to above two examples (Text SFR-1, SFR-2), but the elaboration of the concept includes the use of the more sophisticated logical methods of Exemplification and Comparison (with pets). In other words, she organizes her

---

[50] Another two texts SFR-4 and SFR-5 do not use the schematic structure of Report but these texts also demonstrate her initial attempts of factual writing in her own ways along with drawings. Particularly in Text SFR-5, she arranges several facts on dogs by the form of dotted memorandum, which cannot be evaluated as a proper Report text. However, as mentioned earlier, Sunyoung might have had her trial and error period in the kindergarten, not restricting her style of factual writing to any particular genre. This kind of Sunyoung's relatively free style of Report writing during the Kindergarten period becomes more structured and developed in her Year 1 with the help of the class teacher's use of modeled writing and joint construction.

ideas more cohesively, in logical order (successfully elaborates on and interprets important information). There was the first attempt at using a reference system 'it' (sentence 6: which refers to 'being a friend'). As for Transitivity, in order to identify the concept of 'friendship', Sunyoung successfully employs the relational processes (is, are, be, is – identifying, have - possessive) along with some material processes. Theme choices such as generalized participants (friendship-friends-Being a friend-it) also make the whole text focus on the main idea of 'friendship'. Most importantly, in this text, Sunyoung's usage of nominal groups, that can be a distinctive feature of written language, was presented as follows:

- Friendship is <u>like being friends</u>.
- There will be <u>no people to play with.</u>
- <u>Being a friend</u> is not hard.

Specifically, in 'being a friend' there is use of nominalization of an abstract notion realized in an abstract noun – 'friendship'. The use of nominalization and the use of the 'to infinitive' (post modifying phrase) as in 'no people to play with' make the text sound like the written mode and a Report-like text.

During the next period of Year 1, Sunyoung's Report writing developed toward a more structured format, with using sub-headings in use and most Themes of generalized participants dealt with in a consistent way. The personal elements of the former texts (in Kindergarten) had been removed remarkably. Most of the content which was referred to from the relevant factual book on the topic seems to have been either copied down or re-written (paraphrased) by her own words. Sunyoung's Year 1 class teacher provided a balanced writing approach mixed with the Whole Language Approach and the Genre-based Approach. The teacher's guided writing proved to be quite effective for the young children. Along with the structured guided writing with interesting activities Sunyoung (and most other children) immersed herself in the total process of factual writing and, as a result, she could construct much more developed Report writing at the end.[51] For a more detailed analysis, the following is a selected text excerpt from Text SFR-7:

Table 5-7. Sunyoung's Report Text in Year 1

Text SFR-7 (excerpt)*	Title: Polar Bear (What do Polar Bears look like?)
Sub-heading**	Content
1) Eyes (description)	They have inner eyelids because it protects the polar bear from the sun. They have very good eyesight to see things from far away.
2) Paws (description)	The polar bears have hair under their paws to keep them quiet to sneak up on seals. They also can sneak up on hunters. The paws are slightly webbed so it can help the polar bear swim.
3) Nose (description)	The polar bear covers its black nose so the seals can't see the black nose. It has a very good sense of smell to smell if any hunters are coming.
4) Coats (description)	It has a thick layer of fat to keep the polar bear warm. If people put on oil on their skin, it would just wash off but the fur of a polar bear would stop the oil to keep it warm. The polar bear has several layers of fur to keep the polar bear warm.

Note: *The book of Polar Bear (Text SFR-7) made by Sunyoung is composed of 14 sub-headings.

**The sub-headings in the left hand column were written originally by Sunyoung.

In this text the reference system was much more employed in thematic positions and this makes each passage sound more focused and cohesive. Even though there are some inconsistencies in the use of reference, as in 'they have inner eye lids because it protects the polar bear from the sun', the

---

[51] Particularly the whole process of Text SFR-7 is harmoniously coordinated showing both the Whole Language Approach and the Genre-based Approach in a systematic way. With various kinds of classroom worksheets, the pre-activities or post-activity of the Report writing were done so the children would be more motivated and practised for the real Report writing. Most specifically, the class teacher carefully performed 'brainstorming' (checking prior knowledge of the topic 'polar bear'), 'shared reading' and 'joint construction of a part of a Report as a model'. She demonstrated ways of overcoming the tendency to begin every sentence with the subject-noun (polar bears) with careful use of pronouns such as 'it' or 'they' and use of pointing words (e.g. these, this). Also, she showed how each new paragraph should begin with a topic sentence that introduces the information that follows. In doing this factual writing the children were supposed to organize their Report writing for the final product as 'Bear Book' which has several sub-headings. They did not have to write lengthy paragraphs on any one particular sub-heading. The purpose of Report writing meant the class teacher focused on limited teaching points such as use of pronouns, topic sentences and sub-headings.

whole text demonstrates that Sunyoung is quite successful in using more mature referencing than in the earlier texts (using personal and demonstrative anaphoric reference which keeps the cohesion of the text). The original copy of this text shows that the class teacher made corrective feedback that focused on the reference system rather than other points. Throughout her Report writing process, therefore, Sunyoung seems to have developed her awareness of the reference system appropriate to constructing a written Report. In terms of Transitivity, the possessive relational processes (have, has) are employed in many cases and, also, some modal operators as in 'would just wash off' and 'can stop' were used to express certainty more effectively. The use of technical terms such as 'good sense of smell', 'several layers', 'protects', 'eyesight' and 'slightly webbed' is reasonably good for her age. Finally, in specific regard to nominal groups, Sunyoung starts to use 'to-infinitive' in post-modifying a head noun as in 'a very good sense of smell (to smell if any hunters are coming)' and 'a thick layer of fat (to keep the polar bear warm)'. Compared with the former Report texts (in Kindergarten), as a whole she certainly developed her writing skills while working under the structured and systematic literacy programs in her school.

Sunyoung's Report writing in the next period, Year 2, reflects her engagement with 'uncommonsense' knowledge as well as her developing control of written language. During this period, she had more chances to write a range of science Reports such as Reports on 'insects', 'tsunamis' and 'winds, storms and cyclones' as well as a social studies Report regarding 'the past time in Australia'. It is significant in the Report texts that she attempts to employ more technical languages to deal with 'uncommonsense' knowledge. Also, even in terms of generic structure, her Report texts demonstrate, to some extent, logical sequence through paragraphing. The linguistic experience in Year 1 seems to be enhanced by the continued teaching of the Genre-based Approach. It would seem that Sunyoung's learning of the conventions of the genre was facilitated by the class teacher's enthusiastic application to the linguistic programs. An analysis of Sunyoung's best instance of her grade 2 natural science Report writing follows:

Table 5-8. Sunyoung's Report Text in Year 2

Text SFR-9	\<Title: Insects\>
Elements of the schematic structure	Sunyoung's Text
1) General Classification about 'Insect' species	Insects are some of the oldest creatures on Earth. Also there are more insects than any other species. There are still hundreds of insects left.
2) Description – Body structure (appearance)	A insect needs an abdomen, thorax, head, six legs and a exo-skeleton.
3) Description – the usage of insects (historical approach)	A long time ago Egyptians made a lot of thing with the body of scarab beetles, such as jewels, necklace, rings and gold.
4) Description – Bad habits (points)	Insects can also cause bad habits like they can make people itch and sometimes even death. Also they may spread diseases and destroy crops but watch out because they can spoil your picnics.
5) Description – Good habits (points)	Did you know that insects have good habits too? They control other pests and they could protect plants. Worms also create a wonderful compost heap. Bees and butterflies spend their time pollinating flowers and one more thing, bees make honey.
6) Description – General other facts – Concluding statements	Unfortunately other nasty insects can get their own meals with different insects too, but insects can camouflage, roll into balls, stick to plants and spit poison or acid. They can get shelter and warn other insects off by their bright colors.

The above Text SFR-9 was constructed in the school context, following a shared reading session on the topic of 'insects'. The reference book contained several sections of explanation on insects that was understandable to the grade 2 children. The technical terms were also explained by the class teacher using simpler words. The reference book was available to the children during their writing session. Even though the teacher did not elaborate the text organization by sub-headings, Sunyoung seems to have managed her Report writing reasonably logically in terms of selecting her description details. In Transitivity, the choice of the relational processes (are) is important for building classificatory information and the other action verbs (mainly material processes) also contribute to the formation of several descriptions on insects. In specific regard to

Theme, this text illustrates a varied range of choices including the use of conjunction words and adverbial phrases as a marked Theme. Without sub-headings, Sunyoung seems to have woven the whole Report text successively with the help of these marked Themes. Even though this Text SFR-9 does not construct abstract notions to a great extent, the text is, overall, a successful example of the Report, particularly in the area of the generic structure of the text type.

The next period, Year 3 can not be evaluated as a big growth in a continuum of Sunyoung's Report writing development, but along with the school curriculum of 'space', she attempted to conceptualize this rather difficult science topic in her writings as follows. Text SFR-13 shows development in the use of nominal groups and constructing participants.

Table 5-9. Sunyoung's Report Text in Year 3

Text SFR-13	<Title: Days, Years and Seasons>
Elements of schematic structure	Sunyoung's text
1) Classification or General Statement about 'Earth'	The Earth is the only known planet [[which people can survive on]]. It revolves around the Sun and creates the seasons. It takes one whole year for the Earth to revolve once.
2) Description Earth and Seasons: Why the Earth has four seasons? -- The Element of Explanation	The Earth has four seasons, Summer, Autumn, Winter and Spring. As the Earth rotates and this, the Sun stays in its position and shines brightly. So, because of this, the part [[that is not facing the Sun]] is dark, and the other part [[facing the Sun]] is light (day). There is an invisible line [[dividing the two hemispheres [[called the equator]]]]. It is also called an Axis. The two hemispheres are both symmetrical parts. One being the Northern Hemisphere, the other is the Southern Hemisphere.
3) Personal Comments – not quite necessary (the element of Recount)	Year3/4 observed an interesting activity [[based on this Report]] and learnt a couple of new facts.

As shown above (particularly the underlined phrases), this text includes several elaborate nominal groups which have embedded clauses as part of their structure in the Qualifier position. For example, the following clause includes a participant constructed in an elaborate nominal group which has two embedded clauses within its structure. One is embedded within the other embedded clause.

e.g.) an invisible line [[dividing the two hemispheres [[called the equator]]]]

The use of these nominal groups makes the whole text sound like the written mode. To express a challenging scientific topic, Sunyoung employs reasonably elaborate nominal groups. In terms of text organization, this seems to be mixed with the features of Explanation (the second part) and Recount text (the third part) which add her personal comments. The reference system using the pronoun 'it' (the earth – it, the equator – it) is appropriate and the choice of 'one – the other' phrases is also sensible. Also, this text uses many subject-specific terms which are critical in building the Field of seasons on earth: 'axis', 'equator', 'hemisphere', 'invisible line' and 'symmetrical parts'. To sum up, the main two aspects demonstrating the child's growth in control of factual writing in Text SFR-13 are 1) elaboration of the nominal group to pack in increased amounts of Field-related information and 2) use of subject-specific/ subject-related, technical terms constructing the participants. Both features are really important for children to learn to control when mastering factual writing.

So far we have examined Sunyoung's Report writing development by considering some selected example texts completed from Kindergarten to Year 3. To sum up the most important points that occurred through the time sequence, the following can be said. Sunyoung might have had her trial and error period in Kindergarten (the beginning period of her Report writing) when she attempted various kinds of Report-like writings but did not employ the conventional style of Report writing.[52]

---

[52] This is the difference between Sunyoung's texts and Jinha's Kindergarten texts that were quite successful in many aspects of Report writing. The different output between Jinha and Sunyoung during the beginning period can be explained in terms of their personal preferences for Narrative or Report writing (not from the different school context). As mentioned before, at this time in her development, Sunyoung was much more interested in reading and writing Narratives and, therefore, the personal element of the Narrative or story Recount writing might well have significantly influenced her Report writing. She also was encouraged to write Narratives by her teachers who openly praised her. In school there was

After the kindergarten period, Sunyoung gradually develops her Report writing by using more input from factual reading as well as a more systematic application of the Genre- based Approach that was taught in her classroom. During her Year 1 period, she develops her paraphrasing skills from the reference books and reference system by using proper pronouns. The Whole Language Approach was also integrated into the Genre-based literacy program so that the young children could keep their motivation and interest in writing activities. During the next period Year 2 and Year 3, Sunyoung's text organization skills show development, a development that accompanied her cognitive growth. Her logical thinking and awareness of text cohesiveness apparently helped her organize her Report texts in a more structured and sensible way. Paragraphing without sub- headings was attempted in this period, and through various thematic choices the whole texts achieved their cohesiveness. It is also true that some of her Report texts still show the elements of Explanation or Recount writing. Overall, however, there has been significant progress made on the way to controlling the Report text type during Sunyoung's first four years of primary school.

It is noteworthy that Sunyoung's Report writing obviously provided her with valuable opportunities to build up 'uncommonsense' knowledge and the ability to employ many technical terms and nominal groups to express more complex concepts. Specifically in regard to the nominal groups, she explores the potential of the nominal group and its capacity to expand and is able to pack in further experiential information. Sunyoung uses 'epithets' and, importantly, 'classifiers' to construct Field-specific participants. She has also increased her use of embedding in the qualifier position, which helps her make her later Reports lexically dense. Along with her development of text organization, increased control of reference system, various Theme choices and logical paragraphing, Sunyoung are seen

---

probably less expectation for Jinha to be a good Narrative writer. It could also be that story writing was perceived to be more of a thing that girls do, particularly in the society outside the classroom.

to be developing in her written mode and she appears to be writing with confidence (similar to Jinha's case).

5.4. Explanation

Sunyoung's first Explanation text was written in Year 2 with the guidance of teachers using the Genre-based Approach in her classroom. The teachers provided some support to students when introducing Explanation writing. The students had opportunities to write several Explanation texts during Years 2 and 3. There were some model texts shown to the children in Year 2, but there was no further explicit teaching beyond the first two lessons. At home, the many opportunities for oral interactions in her mother tongue (Korean) with her parents sometimes explicitly contributed to building up logical thinking about sequential order. In the home in oral interactions, the parents encouraged Sunyoung to explain how things happen. The parents (particularly the researcher) asked the child to talk through a sequence of events when explaining. This kind of conversation commonly occurred in Korean. Sunyoung was also encouraged by the researcher to read factual texts at home. The child, usually willingly, responded to the suggestion. The child and the researcher read the book together or, the child read silently to herself in the presence of the researcher. After the text was read, the child was encouraged to explain what it was about. During this process prompting questions of 'how' and 'why' were made by the researcher both in Korean and English. Sunyoung often wanted to clarify unknown concepts or subject-specific terms, so the researcher explained what the words meant using mainly Korean. Sunyoung appeared to listen very attentively. Her subsequent oral account of what a text was about showed that the researcher's explanation had helped her understand the text and learn some key vocabulary.

The class teachers (from Year 2) actively adopted the Genre-based Approach in teaching how to write Explanation texts. Even though there were only a few sequential Explanation texts constructed in Sunyoung's classroom, Sunyoung appeared to involve herself in this type of writing session in a positive manner. Since there were few chances for the young children to practise this kind of challenging text type, the text organization and language features of Sunyoung's overall Explanation texts seem to be somewhat incomplete compared to the conventional Explanation model. The following Text SFE-1 is representative of Sunyoung's early Explanation texts written in school.

Table 5-10. Sunyoung's Explanation Text in Year 2

Text SFE-1	<Title: Tornadoes>
Definition: What is it?	A tornado is a large whirlwind [[that spins around causing a lot of damage]].
Components/Parts Description of the parts	A tornado is started in thunderclouds. Then it forms in warm, damp air when winds hurl into each other from different directions. In that way it makes a funnel of clouds.
Operations How it works – cause and effect.	Air gets sucked into the funnel and spins very fast. When the tornado's end reaches the ground the tornado turns dark inside. This is because it takes the entire dirt, dust and other plants high into the sky.
How it works	Even though it sounds like a vacuum cleaner's hose, a tornado can be many meters high and can move along about 500km per hour.
How it works	They last from about 5 minutes to 5 hours. That is a lot for a tornado especially when you think about how far they would go and how much damage they would cause.
How it works	To make it stop, the tornado will probably get clogged up with dust and dirt and will get thinner and thinner until it disappears.
Interesting Comments Special Features Evaluation	It is a very rare and dangerous accident for people.

The above Text SFE-1 was constructed by referencing the information text sheet titled 'How are tornadoes formed?' which was in the format of a dialogue between two speakers. Along with the information text sheet about tornadoes, the class teacher handed out a structural guide sheet of an 'Explanation Plan' to the class. The 'Explanation Plan' (the same format was used in Jinha's Year 4-5 classes) consisted of the following elements: 'Definition (What is it?)', 'Components/Parts (Description of the parts)'. 'Operations (How it works – cause and effect)', 'Applications (When and where it works or is applied)' and 'Interesting Comments

(Special features, Evaluation)'. Firstly, Sunyoung was supposed to fill in each section of the Explanation plan in a simpler way of writing (not necessarily in complete sentences), by referencing the information sheet. Actually, she highlighted the relevant phrases and clauses in the process of selecting the relevant information. Then, she was required to write a complete text, using a word processor.

When her writing of the final copy (the real Explanation text SFE-1) is compared with the information sheet, it is evident that Sunyoung is able to combine the relevant information into a whole Explanation text by employing some connectives or necessary phrases and adding her evaluative comment in the last part. The underlined parts are those that Sunyoung paraphrased or added to the original information sheet. Even though there is an incorrect reference example (as in 'They last from...') and some grammatical errors, through this kind of systematic guided writing Sunyoung seems to have been able to develop her awareness of the sequential Explanation's generic structure and other language features (e.g. general participants, the consistent use of present tense and impersonal objective language). Again, it is significant that, while the given information sheet dealt with factual information on tornadoes was in the form of an interactive dialogue, Sunyoung converts this to the written mode of Explanation text by successfully omitting unnecessary parts and adding some cohesive phrases.

Unfortunately, Sunyoung's classes (Year 2, Year 3) did not offer frequent opportunities for using the systematic Genre Approach in constructing Explanation texts. Therefore, Sunyoung's further Explanation-like texts do not seem to reflect her remarkable development with this particular genre, but reveal the use of a mix of genres (for example, Report or Recount writing).

Table 5-11. Sunyoung's Explanation Text in Year 3

Text SFE-5	<Title: How the Moon changes shape>
Definition: what is it?	**The Moon** is a rocky, reflecting sphere [[that is seen in the sky]]. **It** is round and rocky.
Operations	**The Moon** looks **as if** it shines **but** it is only reflecting

How it works: cause and effect	the sunshine from the Sun. **When** the Moon is only a half Moon or a Crescent, **the Moon** has not faded away. **It** is just too dark to see the other part.
How it works: elaboration	**The Moon** can also appear in the late afternoon other than the night sky. **It** all depends on **how** the Sun is. **The Moon** has a cold atmosphere [[that no one or nothing can ever survive on]].
How it works: elaboration	**The Moon** orbits the Earth. **It** is much smaller than Earth. **In Earth**, you can see only one side of the Moon. **Today** the Moon is still orbiting around the third planet, Earth...

The above Text SFE-5 constructed in Year 3 is another good example of her development in writing Explanation texts. For this text construction, in line with her theme work ('space' for the concerned term), Sunyoung referred to a factual book used at school after shared reading. After that, she attempts to organize relevant facts in her own way without any structural guide sheet. More precisely, this text is mainly composed of two parts, namely 'Definition of the Moon- Phenomenon Identification' and 'Explanation Sequence- How it works'. Even though there had been no regular practice with writing Explanation texts, a type that seems quite difficult for young writers to write effectively, this sample text demonstrates her reasonable competence by showing cohesion through the reference made to the generalized non-human participant 'the moon'. Also, the text includes a range of subject-specific terms and some complicated nominal groups (as underlined above) as in 'a rocky, reflecting sphere that is seen in the sky' and 'a cold atmosphere that no one or nothing can survive on'. The bold typed words in Text SFE-5 also demonstrate that thematic cohesion has been achieved throughout the text.

As exemplified through above two texts, Sunyoung's emergent Explanation texts were attempted over the two years (Year 2 – Year 3) with or without the guidance of school context and parental scaffolding mainly through oral interaction. Even though her classes did not continue to use the framework of Explanation based on the Genre Approach (which triggered Sunyoung's initial awareness of the generic structure of Explanation in the case of SFE-1), she seems to have managed her Explanation writing and shows a development of an awareness of the impersonal mode of written language, at least with sequential Explanation. The role of the reading material with the Field building information seems to have been an important factor in helping the child construct her Explanation texts.

5.5. Argument

Sunyoung's first Argumentative texts were constructed in the family context in Year 2. The researcher, being aware of the state-wide writing tests[53] scheduled for later in the year, and that the Argument genre would be the text type tested, encouraged the child to practise argumentative writing in the home. In Year 3, at school, Sunyoung was supported to learn more about writing argumentative texts by the class teacher. The analysis of Sunyoung's texts below demonstrates her growing control of the Argument genre during Years 2 and 3.

Table 5-12. Sunyoung's Argument Text (A Letter of Complaint) in Year 2

Text SFA-2	<Title: Faulty silver pen – a letter of complaint>
Addressing to whom to read	Dear Sir / Madam,
About the topic	Re: Faulty silver pen
Explaining why she wrote this letter to you (providing adequate information as the background context)	I bought a pen at 'The Reject Shop', 23rd May, and I paid $5.95. I tried to write a letter with the pen the next day, but all it wrote was simply invisible message. I thought that the ink possibly couldn't have run out and checked but nothing was wrong. Also I checked thoroughly for other problems and so far nothing was wrong with the pen.
Stating her opinion: please replace the pen with a new one	That night all my proud feelings washed away and I felt very sad. I would like to replace it with a new one. I also have the receipt enclosed. I am

[53] The exact name of the state-wide writing test was Australian School Writing Competition which was sponsored by the University of New South Wales (Educational Testing Centre). The test target group in primary level was from Year 3 children to Year 6. The same grade children were supposed to compete with the writing task which was controlled by each grade's proficiency (difficulty) level. Sunyoung participated in the Competition as a Year 2 student (one year younger than other participants) for the purpose of experiencing the formal Competition. Next year, in Year 3, Sunyoung got Distinction in the writing task of 'a Tele-Review for a new TV show' in which she needed to add her opinion on the tele program (whether the tele program is worth watching or not).

	looking forward to your reply.
Ending words	**Yours faithfully** 12 Mackellar Cres. Cook, 2614 Phone: 62515691

Text SFA-2 was based on her real experience even though the letter of complaint was not sent to the concerned shop manager. Sunyoung appeared to be really motivated when she was encouraged by the researcher to write expository texts done for authentic reasons. Through the experience of addressing this kind of social issue in an authentic situation, she must have developed the important awareness that some kind of writing can be a powerful and useful medium by which to participate with the majority in society. It is also significant that she also might have practised effectively expressing or shaping her own opinion or view with proper manners (an important social function).

While borrowing the mode 'letter' within which various kinds of genres can be expressed, this expository text does not share the common language features of 'Argument texts' such as impersonal and objective language and generalized participants through nominalization and passive voice. Text SFA-2, however, demonstrates her reasonable competence in achieving the purpose of the particular genre (which is to express the statement of the issue - the faulty pen, the supporting Arguments, explaining the problem, and the concluding element, with a request to replace the pen). All the sections are constructed in an attempt to approximate the cultural conventions (see the underlined words) of this kind of writing.

Text SFA-3 that was constructed in Year 2 shows Sunyoung's initial attempt with conventional Argument text.

Table 5-13. Sunyoung's Argument Text in Year 2

Text SFA-3	<Title: Should schools let children do homework everyday?>
Opening Statement[54]	All schools are different in some way. When most children hear about homework, you can hear them moan and try to get the school teacher to stop

---

[54] In Text SFA-3, the part of Opening Statement seems too prolonged and out of focus.

	them from doing all this hard and inquisitive homework. Most children think homework is challenging if you work on it everyday. In my opinion, I think more advanced kids may like to have a go to put their pencil on a worksheet everyday, and start filling out the questions. [[Why I think that more advanced kids should try to work on homework everyday]] is explained below.
Supporting ideas (not good for ordinary students)	Firstly, if any kid tries to fill out questions and sums everyday, it might be very hard and challenging. Although it is always good to have a go, you need your head to have some rest. School children never know [[how hard the teacher summarizes homework]].
Supporting ideas (necessary only for advanced students)	Secondly, if no one has a go of working at homework everyday, then it is just a waste of time for the teacher summarizing homework. Also it doesn't help you to get the habit to learn more and become more clever.
Concluding Statement	Because of these reasons, I suppose that school teachers can send homework once a week, but I might study more on my opinion.

Text SFA-3 was also constructed at home in preparation for the nation-wide writing test and with the researcher's assistance through oral discussion. Before the production of this text, Sunyoung was taught about the generic structure of an Argument text (that is, 'thesis statement' followed by 'supporting ideas' with evidence and examples and finally 'concluding statement') and some language features such as cohesive connection words (firstly, secondly, by the reason of) and modal words (should, might). Also she had a brief oral discussion on this issue with the researcher. When the researcher suggested the topic, Sunyoung appeared very interested and keen to address it. During the oral discussion session she expressed her opinion quite reasonably that schools should not let children do homework everyday because most children would suffer from the policy. She added that only advanced students like herself would get benefit from doing homework everyday. However, in her real writing time (done as independent writing), she seems to have had some difficulty in maintaining her point of view clearly and logically. In terms of logical cohesion, she failed to address her opinion on the issue as in 'should schools let children do homework everyday?' by stating as follows: 'why I think that more advanced kids should try to work on homework everyday is explained below.' More reasonable thesis statement is likely to be: 'schools should not let children do homework everyday mainly because most children would suffer from the policy (1).' Thus, the logical focus does not look right even from the opening paragraph (in spite of her attempts at generalization when shaping the background context).

The supporting idea of the second paragraph seems to provide relevant evidence for the assertion of the above reasonable thesis statement (1), not her own statement. She also abruptly adds the teacher's suffering to check up all homework, which might confuse the reader about the writer's intention. The second supporting idea of the third paragraph counters the assertion, showing an abrupt change in her point of view. She states that if nobody does homework everyday, it would not be good for the teachers (because the teachers need reasonable working time by homework check up) and more advanced students (because they had better build up a good habit of everyday homework). Her concluding statements end up with the teacher's point of view as in 'school teachers can send homework once a week!'

Even though Sunyoung seems to have followed the conventional text organization successfully along with the use of textual structural Theme choices (e.g. firstly, secondly), this kind early expository sample does not satisfy the primary purpose of the Argument, which is to express clearly her opinion on the given issue. This might reflect her difficulty with converting the logical oral discussion to the written language. The two more expository texts that were constructed in the period of Year 3 are now examined for the developmental comparison.

Table 5-14. Sunyoung's Argument Text in Year 3

Text SFA-5	<Title: We should wear school uniform>
Opening Statement	Our class wants all schools to wear their school uniform.
Supporting Ideas – point	Firstly because school uniforms have their

269

1 (representing their school community)	personal logo [[which represents their schools, that includes the school color, which is important to us]] for we wear it to school to demonstrate that we are a part of the school community. Our school has the color blue to show the sea [[which 'Captain Cook' came by]].
Supporting Ideas – point 2 (easily identified in the case of school excursions and other occasions)	Secondly, our school uniform represents us on excursions and makes same that people can easily find us and we are easily identified as a part of a school group. School uniforms are helpful in this way because we don't become lost.
Supporting Ideas – point 3 (very easy to wear, you don't have to make choices what to wear every morning)	Additionally, school uniforms are very easy to wear with the soft material [[that makes them comfortable and practical]]. When you want to wear school uniform, you don't have to make choices of what to wear every morning. Also school uniforms are more affordable and you may wear it over and over which makes it more easier for you as well as your parents.
Concluding Statement – restating of opinion	So as demonstrated, there are many positive reasons [[to wear school uniform]]!

Text SFA-5 was constructed with the guidance of the Genre Approach used at school, along with the framework sheet of 'Argument Plan'. At first, Sunyoung's class had a teacher-led discussion on this issue and the class teacher wrote down the points for and against the statement on the whiteboard. Sunyoung chose to agree with the statement that 'we should wear school uniform.' After filling in the assertion points with statements of evidence on the framework sheet, she finally constructed her Argument text as independent writing. The Procedure of constructing this text was different from that used in constructing the former text SFA-3, in that she had another step for planning the Argument logically and selecting relevant evidence through the worksheet.

In the 'thesis' part, the student is supposed to write "an opening paragraph that consists of a thesis (or position) followed by a brief summary of the Arguments to follow" (The Education Department of Western Australia, 1997: 144). Considering this, the above Text SFA-5 does not have such an elaborate thesis part, but it has a brief statement. However, the parts of supporting ideas surely demonstrate that Sunyoung has presented each paragraph for the purpose of stating the points in support of the school uniform, successfully by including several generalized statements and using controlling words ('firstly', 'secondly', 'additionally' and 'so as demonstrated'). Whereas the child still has to learn to construct a fully developed paragraph, using a key sentence and elaborating sentences as a whole, in terms of logical cohesion, this text is much more developed as an Argument text than Text SFA-3.

Table 5-15. Sunyoung's Argument Text (A Letter of Request) in Year 3

Text SFA-6	<Title: Letter to the Sheriff of Nottingham>
Addressing to whom to read this letter	Dear Sheriff,
Opening Statement (purpose of this letter)	I am writing a letter to you to tell my opinion.
Stating her opinion with Supporting ideas (point 1: Robbin Hood is just trying to help the poor so he is not an outlaw)	As you know, the rich have lots of money and the poor are beggars and starve. So please don't chase Robin Hood for he is just trying to help. Please be merciful to him. And I ask you not to call him an outlaw for his is not. I am not saying that the rich are selfish but I am asking you to be kind to him.
Elaborating her opinion with supporting ideas (point 2: if you catch Robin Hood, his lots of noble friends would be deeply hurt.)	Lots of people are Robin Hood's great and noble friends and if you catch him, they would be deeply hurt. So please leave Robin, his friends and Sherwood Forest in peace, for it is a wonderful place. I know it is very easy for you to hold your anger, so please take my letter seriously.
Ending signature	Yours Faithfully Sunyoung Hwang.

Again, in construction of the letter of Request[55] which can be closely related to an authentic context in our real life (one of our social functions), Sunyoung demonstrates her ability to achieve the purpose of effectively expressing her opinion to the Sheriff (the evil character in the story of Robin Hood) giving consideration to the reader's position (Sheriff). In a similar way to that used in the former text example of SFA-2 (a letter of complaint), Text SFA-6 also includes a great

---

[55] 'Students were read the story of Robin Hood. They then decided whether Robin Hood was doing the right thing or the wrong thing by stealing from the rich and giving to the poor. They then discussed their opinion with a partner. After doing this they wrote a draft letter to the Sheriff of Nottingham stating their opinion. They then wrote a final copy into their books.' (from the lesson note written by Sunyoung's class teacher)

deal of spoken mode and lack of examples of nominalization or passive voice because of personal form of the letter. However, constructing this kind of authentic text must have helped Sunyoung build up her awareness that writing is an important medium that can be used to participate as a competent member of society in the English-speaking cultural world. She is able to construct her opinion while respecting the counterpart's position or emotional factor at the same time, which is a very important social skill in any real argumentative conversation or negotiation. Sunyoung's class teacher commented on this text writing thus: "You have stated your opinion beautifully!"

Overall, Sunyoung's construction of Argument texts helped her to explore the construction of her opinion and its justification in a varied range of authentic contexts as well as in relation to formal Arguments. As with Jinha, she seems to be developing her awareness that there are differences between written mode and spoken one throughout the expository text writing. Since her construction of expository texts almost always was preceded by oral discussion (both at home and at school), she became more aware of some language features and characteristics such as the cohesive device, the choice of Themes and the passive voice. Whereas Sunyoung's initial texts demonstrate her immaturity of logical cohesiveness, mainly because she started to write Argument texts at an earlier age than Jinha, her expository texts in Year 3 show a developed sense of expressing her point of view with far better control of making statements of opinion and providing supporting evidence. Her texts show her increased control over the construction of generalized statements, and over selectivity and elaboration of the statements of supporting evidence. More significantly, Sunyoung has had several opportunities to practise the construction of letters of complaint and request in authentic contexts and, as a result, she has been able to develop an awareness that writing can be an important tool to use to take part in an English speaking culture as a competent social member.

5.6. Procedure

As mentioned earlier (Section 4.5), procedural texts are built up around a sequence of events (Martin, 1985). In a development similar to Jinha's development pattern in Procedure writing, Sunyoung started to write this particular genre, which has the characteristics of material processes foregrounded in the Theme position as imperative mood, from Year 2 in school. During the period of Year 2, the class teacher gave several homework tasks involving writing Procedure texts to the children for the purpose of familiarizing them with the generic structure of Procedure as used in different fields such as art design, science experiment and game instruction. Followed the explicit teaching of Procedure writing using structured worksheets and model writings, Sunyoung did not seem to have much difficulty in constructing this particular genre even by herself at home. The researcher did not have any need to provide support by scaffolding while Sunyoung did her homework. This is similar to Jinha's highly independent Procedure writing experience. Both subjects were explicitly taught the generic structure and language features of Procedure writing at school and also they had several chances to practise their learning through homework or other follow-up class activities. As a result, from the time of its introduction in Year 2, both subjects' Procedure writing seems to be fairly satisfactory and meets the conventional linguistic features of the particular genre. Both children appear to have learnt to control the type of temporal sequencing that is expected in Procedure texts. During the next year (in Year 3), Sunyoung kept writing Procedure texts with increasing confidence. The following selected texts demonstrate Sunyoung's reasonable competence in writing a Procedure genre.

Table 5-16. Sunyoung's Procedure Texts in Year 2

Text SFP-1	Title: 3D Photo Frame (constructed at home)
Title	3D Photo Frame
Materials	The Material Used: 2 Tissue boxes. 2 Toilet paper rolls, Color papers, Scissors, Sticky tape, Photos, Photo slips, Glue, Texters
	1. Get your tissue boxes and cut the

		piece of plastic [[which are on the boxes]].
Method : How to Create	2.	Stick the colored paper *on your boxes with glue.*
	3.	Make a roof *with colored paper.*
	4.	Carefully put one of the toilet rolls *under your roof.*
	5.	Put a toilet roll *on top of the roof for your chimney.*
	6.	Put your photos *in a photo slip* and then put it in the boxes.
	7.	Sticky tape the boxes together.
	8.	Put designs on.
	9.	After that you do another layer of sticky tape.

Text SFP-7		Title: Planting a bulb (constructed at school)
Aim		To plant a bulb and to care for it until it flowers nicely
Materials		The Material Used: Soil, Bulb, Milk carton, Water, Paddle pop stick, Texter
Method: How to Create	1.	Cut a one liter milk cartoon *in half.*
	2.	Cut drainage holes *in base of carton.*
	3.	Put 2-3cm of soil *in carton.*
	4.	Place bulb painted side up onto soil.
	5.	Cover bulb with soil *until there is about 1-2cm soil above bulb.*
	6.	Label paddle pop stick *with name* and insert *into soil.*
	7.	Water bulb. (using soluble fertilizer if desired.)

The two texts shown above (Text SFP-1 and Text SFP-7) constructed at home and school respectively during the Year 2 period indicate that Sunyoung does not have any trouble presenting Procedure texts in each field. In terms of text organization, she states the title or aim correctly and for the part of material she shows an appropriate layout with a list of the material used. For the method part, she states instruction in the correct sequence and with adequate details. In Transitivity, the underlined material verbs meet the purpose of identifying each step to the reader. Except for the last step of Text SFP-1 as in 'After that you do another layer of sticky tape', she omits 'you' and starts sentences with a verb or adverb (as in 'carefully put'), using action verbs. She uses a generalized 'you', which refers to readers in a general way.

Also, both texts include several 'where', 'when' and 'how' circumstantial phrases and clauses in order to add precise details (see the italic word phrases and clause such as 'on top of the roof for your chimney' and 'until there is about 1 - 2cm soil above bulb'). It appears to be significant that the young writer is able to manage her precise expressions to guide readers accurately. Also, considering the matter of complex sentences, Text SFP-1 includes an embedded clause used in the qualifier position within the nominal group structure (as in 'the piece of plastic which are on the boxes'), whereas Text SFP-7 shows the non-finite dependent clause (see the boxed words) used to describe the manner in which the process in the main clause occurs. Considering that these two texts were constructed by herself either at home or school in Year 2, it can be said that she reveals an awareness of the schematic structure of the text type and makes the linguistic choices appropriate for the genre. The following Text SFP-10 is further evidence of her reasonable competency in constructing Procedure text.

Table 5-17. Sunyoung's Procedure Text in Year 3

Text SFP-10	<Title: Plan of Solar System>
Aim	To plan and make a model of our Solar System
Materials	The Material Used: Pipe cleaners, 16 Balls paint, Paint brush, Spray paint, Wooden stick, Cardboard star
Method: How to Create	1. Make a base by putting the balls with pipe cleaners. 2. Poke the wooden stick *in the top*. 3. Adjust the pipe cleaners *around the stick*. 4. Paint the biggest ball [[you have]] in either yellow, orange and red. If you want, spray paint it. 5. Now paint 9 balls. These are the planets. 6. Poke them *on the pipe cleaners*. 7. Put your design *on the cardboard star*.

Text SFP-10 written in the beginning of Year 3 reveals almost the same competence in writing the Procedure genre as the former two texts produced in Year 2. Compared with Jinha's Procedure texts that were produced in the period of his Year 2 and 3, the overall assessment of them would be similar. There is use of the non-finite dependent clause (see the boxed phrases – as in 'by putting the balls with pipe cleaners') and the use of embedding, a feature which makes the text more elaborate, and also many examples of circumstances (see the italic words). In addition, from an examination of all her Procedure texts from Year 2 to Year 3, it can be concluded that she understands a large range of contexts where written Procedures may be used to tell how to do or make something.

5.7. Conclusion

In this chapter, Sunyoung's factual writing from Kindergarten to Year 3 has been examined in the context of both school and home. Among the various factual text types, Report, Explanation, Argument and Procedure were selected for more detailed text analysis in order to explore Sunyoung's developing control over factual writing, a form of writing that is considerably different from Narrative writing. Compared with Jinha's case, Sunyoung's factual writing was limited to her early primary schooling (Kindergarten to Year 3) and the range of factual writing was somewhat narrower. In addition, while analyzing each of Sunyoung's factual genre and comparing with Jinha's, her personality (as a hard worker) and personal preference to Narrative writing were considered as the variable factors. Except for these differences, Sunyoung's factual writing contexts at school and home were similar to those of Jinha. With this in mind, the next two paragraphs sum up the analysis of each factual genre constructed by Sunyoung. If necessary, the comparative analysis between Jinha and Sunyoung will be referred to. After that, as concluding comments, the effectiveness of the Genre-based Approach and the significance of the developments in factual writing as well as some recommendations for the factual writing literacy program will be addressed.

In her Report writing done in Kindergarten, Sunyoung developed mostly science Reports first and then later on explored Report writing in the field of social studies at school and home. In both contexts there were discussions of the topic prior to writing, as well as demonstrations of successful examples of the genre. Compared with Jinha, however, Sunyoung's initial attempts in Report writing tended to include personal comments, which is a common feature in personal Recount writing. From Year 1, her Report writing became less personal and more objective.

The Explanation text that is quite challenging for young writers was attempted by Sunyoung in Year 2, being modeled by the teacher at school. However, since this text type does not clearly show the genre structure and language features (compared with Report writing or Recount), Sunyoung as a younger writer seems to have had some difficulty in adapting to the proper Genre expectations. At home the researcher needed to increase the support given to her so that she could understand the difficult topic related terminology and maintain more demanding logical sequence. Jinha also showed similar developmental patterns for Explanation texts in general, but he had many more chances to practise writing justification for his opinions in an Argument, as Argument is also included in Review texts. Whereas her Explanation texts still remain quite embryonic, they show some of the child's awareness of the elements of the generic structure. Whereas Sunyoung appears to have found it challenging to construct a fully developed Argument when she first began writing Argumentative texts in Year 2, the support which she got from the researcher in the home and school helped her develop control of the genre and produce significantly more competent Argument texts a year later.

Procedure texts were also showing development with the school's systematic teaching of the Genre-based Approach and follow-up homework and activities. Just as in Jinha's case, Sunyoung could construct reasonably good Procedure texts that demonstrate particular linguistic features for the genre. This reflects that both children, as young writers, developed control over the distinctive language features and text organization of the Procedure. The modeling of the genre both children had in school must have been helpful here. The children's relative success in mastering the genre features of Procedure could also be explained by the fact that this text type may be easier for young writers than other factual genres. At least partially, this relative ease can be attributed to the fact that Procedure texts are present in children's everyday life, and that they commonly construct commonsense knowledge and build on concrete experiences that are written in this genre.

More specifically regard in to the Genre-based Approach, during the initial period Sunyoung revealed some negative points: she was too obsessed to fit her writing to the stereotyped modeling. One possible solution might be to allow more flexibility to younger writers, at least as they start out. Jinha, with whom the Genre-based Approach had been applied from Year 2, did not undergo any stress in the process of constructing his factual writings, whereas Sunyoung sometimes complained that the text organization and language features in each genre (especially Explanation and Argument) were difficult for her. When time passed and more experience with text construction was accumulated, her writing of factual genres became better developed. However, it appears that with younger writers like Sunyoung, we have to accept that in their learning to control factual writing, they will take time learning the genre conventions with regard to the text organization and language features (such as, for example, the expectation of the impersonal stance, partly constructed through the choice of the third person in the person system, and the fact that the first person choice is not appropriate). Also, as shown in the Sunyoung's case, for particularly young graders (maybe from Kindergarten to Year 2), more motivated and stimulating activities done in connection with the text construction is recommended. The Genre-based orientation towards supporting the children's learning to write seems to have been very helpful, particularly in the area of learning to write factual genres. For ESL children like Jinha and Sunyoung, the model writing and joint construction of texts using the Genre-based Approach proved to be a particularly powerful assistant, helping them develop control over the genre features.

Compared with her development in Narrative writing, Sunyoung's factual writing provided the opportunity for her to explore another important feature of written language such as the use of 'general participants'. In Narrative writing, Sunyoung's development in the area of 'process' was remarkable. Not only a wide range of material processes but also mental and verbal processes were used in her Narrative writing, and also more complicated verbal groups were realized in many cases. Meanwhile, in her factual writing, the area of 'participant' appears to be elaborated through exploitation of the potential of the nominal group by expanding it in order to pack in experiential information. In addition to this, the factual writing triggered more use of the passive voice along with more choice of generalized participants as a Theme. Subject-specific terms should be elaborated in the factual genres such as Report or Explanation. In the process of doing this, more complicated nominal groups that include using relative pronouns and infinitives are practised. Also, in terms of the text organization in their factual writing, both Jinha and Sunyoung learn to construct such elements as 'generalization', 'definition', 'classification', 'comparison', 'justification' and 'time-sequential order' so that they can meet the schematic structure expectations of each of the genres. The children demonstrate increasing textual cohesiveness in their factual writing, particularly through their growing control of the reference system.

Lastly, considering nominalization, one of the characteristics of the most typical written mode, Sunyoung seems to reveal as less development than Jinha mainly due to her age factor. Halliday (1994) and Derewianka (1995) have found that nominalization occurs later in children's language, at age of about 9-10 in their writing. This is a feature of the written mode of language, and control over it is a sign of children's general development of control over writing. Given her young age over the period studied, relatively few examples of nominalization (than Jinha's) are found. This is similar to Aidman's (1999: 313) study in which the researcher noticed the emergence of nominalization in her daughter's writing in Year 3 (between age 8 and 9). In this regard, it is recommended that more explicit teaching take place in order to increase the word power in the noun category as one way of supporting young writers in this matter. Particularly the exercise of transforming verb or adjective words to the relevant nouns would be good for the young writers so as to develop their awareness of abstract nouns and the process of nominalization. Also, more sample writings should be shown to the young writers so that they can gain a sense of whole text features. The social functions and purposes should be taught in regard to each writing genre so that learners know why this writing is necessary and useful in real life. Even young writers tend to be more motivated in their writing sessions when they see the writing is used in the real world.

Chapter 6. Conclusion & Implications

6.1. Narrative Writing in English

Both children have demonstrated a significant growth in their control of Narrative writing in English. They have progressed from their early short texts to much lengthier Narratives. The growth in length is particularly significant in Sunyoung's case. Sunyoung has shown a much stronger motivation for writing Narrative in English than her brother, on many occasions initiating Narrative writing and choosing this activity in the home as well as in the classroom. Both children have demonstrated a significant growth in mastering the schematic structure of Narrative, moving from very incomplete texts that often lack either a distinct Complication or Resolution or both, to more comprehensive text construction that shows the major stages of the genre.

Table 6-1. Comparative Analysis of Jinha and Sunyoung's Narrative Texts (English)

	Jinha	Sunyoung
Contexts	- Year 2 – Year 5 (11 Narrative texts) - Mostly produced at school and as homework at home. - Maximum length: one page (short story style) - Genre Approach – worksheets, Guided reading - Relatively not too interested	- Kindergarten – Year 3 (18 Narratives) - Getting much lengthier up to 10 pages - Strong motivation – initiating Narrative writing at home - Genre Approach at school : stimulating activities along with structured explicit teaching
Control of Schematic Structure	- Orientation stage: much easier - Complication / Resolution: not distinctive in initial periods - Foreshadowing elements emerging (rather explicitly) - Evaluative elements – attributive relational process, existential process, mental process	- Similar development patterns - Evaluative elements: Sunyoung developed more various ways including mental process, 'it' or 'that' pronouns as thematic choice, monologue - In the middle period (Sunyoung: Year 2, Jinha:

281

		Year 4) – dialogic exchanges, attempts different style (Korean diary texts: same tendency)
Transitivity – Use of Process types	-Initial period: material processes + relational processes - Later period: adds a range of mental processes	- Use of behavioural and verbal processes: more symbolically than Jinha - Enhancing situational contexts - Overall, lexically a wide range of processes (wider than Jinha's)
Theme Choices	- The tendency of extending the range of thematic choices - Unmarked topical Theme + textual Themes (structural conjunctions: e.g. and, but) -Temporal circumstantial clauses, adverbial phrases -Interpersonal Themes (dialogic exchange) - Thematic equatives	- Development patterns similar to Jinha's - Unmarked subject Theme – more abstract nouns, impersonal things (e.g. a gust of wind, darkness, anger) symbolic meaning - Structural conjunction Theme – changes to 'dependent non-finite clauses'
Nominal Groups	- In the positions of 'participants' - Pre-modifier + post-modifier - Qualifier – definite relative clause - V-ing, P.P, to infinitive	- Developmental patterns overall similar to Jinha's, but more varied examples (from more texts)
Mood System	- Mostly in their dialogic sections of Narrative texts - Different mood clauses and modality system (modal auxiliaries, finite operators, modal adjuncts (not many)	- Developmental patterns overall similar to Jinha's - More lengthy dialogue style Narratives - Increased control over interpersonal meanings (including a range of choices of modalization and modulation)

As shown in Table 6-1, Sunyoung's development in the area of 'Process' is remarkably prominent. She uses a greater range of mental and behavioural processes than Jinha, which has allowed her Narrative texts to reveal the inner world of participants and situational contexts more successfully; this has often been linked to her strength of building up Evaluative elements. By using dialogic exchange in her Narratives, Sunyoung demonstrates an increased control of the interpersonal meanings. Even though there is a general pattern of development in Narrative writing such as expanding a range of Theme choices, process types and developing control over the schematic structure over time demonstrated in both children's Narrative texts, Sunyoung's texts show more mature linguistic features in every aspect along with quite advanced novel-like Narrative writing (Text BB-18; age 8:6). Jinha, who has also successfully advanced his control of Narrative writing (Text B-10; age 10:3) shows an ability to orchestrate many of the important features involved in writing English Narrative.

6.2. Factual Writing in English

In the area of factual writing, both children explored a range of texts this being expected because it was in the primary school curriculum (see Table 6-2). Over the period being studied both children demonstrate a significant growth in the control of several factual genres, in terms of their ability to use schematic structure and linguistic choices at sentence level. Both Jinha and Sunyoung show a development in their control of constructing such essential elements of factual genres as 'generalization', 'definition', 'classification', 'comparison', 'justification' and 'time-sequential order' and show they are able to meet the schematic structure expectation of each of the factual text types.

Table 6-2. Comparative Analysis of Jinha's and Sunyoung's Factual Writing (English)

	Jinha	Sunyoung

Context	- From Kindergarten to Year 5 (early and mid-primary period)
	    Kinder – Year 1: Whole Language Approach and Process Writing
	    Year 2 – Year 5: mostly Genre Approach
	- Wider range of factual texts
	- Shows strong motivation and
		- From Kindergarten to Year 3 (early primary period)
		    Whole period – Genre Approach at school
		    At home: scaffolding literacy using mother tongue along with Genre approach
		- Earlier start of Explanation and Argument

	interest	- Relatively not interested in factual reading and writing
Report	Start: Kindergarten - Science Report -> Social Studies (increasingly complex and challenging concepts) - Produced texts better approximating the conventional expectations (impersonal, objective) even in initial Period	Start: Kindergarten - Kindergarten: includes more personal comments and first person pronouns as thematic choice (in Personal Recount writing) - Develops control over the Report genre (less personal, more objective)
Procedure	Start : Year 2 - Reasonably competent Procedure texts from the initial period	Start: Year 2 - Developed control over the distinctive language features and text organization (Modeling by Teacher very helpful)
Explanation	Start: Year 3 - Comparatively smoother development than Sunyoung ; many opportunities to practise writing justification (Review texts) and oral discussion – in class and home	Start: Year 2 - Quite challenging to her in initial period (not have clear-cut in genre structure and language features) -> increase supporting level to explain topic-related terminology and logical sequence
Review	Year 2 – Year 5 (23 texts at home) - Books and Films review - Naturally integrated to the child's home activities such as reading books, watching TV or movie - Helpful to argumentative texts (Why – explanation	- Embryonic texts
Argument	Start: Year 4 - First – Schematic structure - Later – language features elaboration Explanation -> Review -> Argument - Need more preparation, cognitively critical thinking: discussion in mother tongue	Start: Year 2 - start two years earlier than Jinha at home – preparation of NSW Writing Test - Initially struggled due to lack of logical sequence in written mode (problematic - whole text cohesiveness) - Next year (Year 3): produced competent argument texts along with scaffolding literacy
	- Positively / effectively influenced by the explicit teaching, including model writing, joint construction, guided worksheets	

Overall Conclusion regarding Jinha's and Sunyoung' Factual Writing Developme nt (in English)	- Closely related to further academic texts and social functions
	- Positive effects of scaffolding literacy at home in mother tongue using the Genre Approach
	- Contributed to written language development / control of the following linguistic features:
	  ● nominalization
	  ● abstract language
	  ● use of general participants
	  ● lexical density
	  ● use of relational processes (in classification / definition)
	  ● conjunctions
	  ● referencing

In factual texts, both children show growth in control of such features of written language as abstraction, nominalization, increased lexical density, choice of conjunctions and use of reference.

Compared with their development with Narrative writing, the two children's factual writing in English (see Table 6-2) provided them with the opportunity to explore further important features of written language such as the use of 'general participants', as well as the use of relational processes for classification and definition. In factual writing Jinha has demonstrated more significant growth than Sunyoung in terms of employing nominal groups, maintaining the impersonal stance and logical sequence, particularly in Report and Explanation text types.

Throughout the period, Jinha has shown more interest in science related text types such as Report and Explanation texts. This has contributed to a significant growth in his mastering of written language (the use of abstract language and specific subject related terms with more elaborate nominal groups). Even though Sunyoung has not shown much interest in this area of writing, she, also, has developed control of the distinctive features of each text type, particularly in the later period (Years 2-3). It appears that such learning has been significantly enhanced due to the implementation of the balanced literacy pedagogy in the school where there was a focus on a Genre-based Approach to teaching writing.

6.3. Implications

6.3.1. Genre-based Approach as an Effective Tool for Biliteracy Development

This section addresses the research aim of 'examining the enhancing effects of Genre-based Approach in terms of the primary-aged ESL children's biliteracy development both at their school and in the home'.

In this case study the Genre-based Approach has proved to be an effective tool through which the ESL children have been able to develop their writing in a wide range of text types. The explicit teaching of the schematic structure and language features of different genres, through modeling and joint construction employed at their school, has possibly increased their control over writing in a wide range of text types. Particularly, as ESL children having a relatively limited exposure to the English-speaking environment compared to their native English-speaking counterparts, this structured approach that uses explicit teaching methods could have provided them with practical guidance as to how to construct the different text types. At home, while doing their writing assignments as homework, the researcher (as their mother) was able to help the children by explaining the schematic structure and language features of the target text types using the mother tongue, along with organizing guided reading of relevant texts. In Korean writing, modeling and joint construction were employed to support the children's literate practices of diary writing and personal writing (especially during the initial period).

Specifically in regard to controlling a range of genres in the primary schooling, Jinha and Sunyoung showed they developed control over Narrative, Recount, Report, Procedure, Explanation, Review (Jinha) and Argument in their English school curriculum whereas more personal writing, including diary, letters and E-mails, were developed in Korean, mostly in the home environment. There are overlapping text types such as Recount, Diary (Journal writing) which the children have written both in English and Korean. Overall, the children's writing across the two

286

languages has developed to meet a range of authentic social purposes. That is, most English genres were developed through the needs of academic schooling whereas the choice of Korean text types developed to achieve the social purposes of communicating with their relatives in Korea as well as expressing their thoughts. Considering that biliteracy development takes a lot of time and energy on the part of the bilingual children who are supposed to be simultaneously committed to many other areas of learning, it can be suggested that they should not be expected to develop control over the register choices concurrently in both languages, but rather that they choose the most suitable ones according to specific bilingual contexts (by consideration of their social functions). Over time, they should be able to extend their genre choices in further writing development.

Another important contribution of the Genre-based Approach to the children's biliteracy is that it has facilitated the children's awareness of the difference between spoken and written language and consequently, has helped develop control over various aspects of written language. For instance, through Narrative writing the children have developed control over the range of process types and the complex verbal system, along with circumstantial elements, whereas in Factual writing the development of nominal groups, including nominalization, has occurred more remarkably than with any other element. In addition, in E-mail writing of the Korean texts such category realizing interpersonal meanings as the Mood and Modality system shows that it has been significantly developed along with other aspects of written language. In this regard the primary school academic curriculum based on Genre Pedagogy can be recommended for the balanced development of young children's writing, particularly in ESL contexts.

This case study demonstrates an overall positive influence of the Genre-based Approach on the children's biliteracy development. It has been critical for the children's familiarization with a range of genres necessary to function in their socio-cultural contexts as they were growing up. This process of learning different text types along with a range of social functions can be linked to the process of preparation for the children growing up to become competent social members in both the English- and Korean-speaking contexts of Australia and Korea respectively. In addition, and more basically, the young ESL children's biliteracy development in this case study has shown that it is the whole process by which the young children become aware of the differences of spoken and written language and gain control over a range of written genres and further develop the awareness of linguistic differences and similarities across their two languages. This growing awareness and appreciation of the social value and power of biliteracy seems to have translated into the children's sense of pride in being bilingual as they have grown older.

6.3.2. Some Implications of the Study of Jinha's and Sunyoung's Genre Writing: Based on the Comparative Analysis

Since this case study has documented the biliteracy development of two Korean ESL children of different age and gender, we need to consider how these factors could possibly have influenced the children's writing development across the two languages. We will also consider the findings and issues related to the children's genre preference based on gender difference between the young writers.

Difference in Genre Preference Between Boys and Girls from a Socio-Linguistic Perspective

The tendency found in other research for there to be difference in genre preference between boys and girls has been found in this case study as well. Thus Jinha, the boy two years older than his sister, shows more interest in science and math from an early age (before starting primary school). Sunyoung, on the other hand, being a young girl, reveals enthusiasm for reading storybooks. When they started to be involved in the various literate practices during their primary schooling, their preference for different genres was noticeable in their reading and writing both at school and home. It is likely that, as a result, even though educated in the same school where Genre-based Approach had been adopted, Jinha has shown more strength in writing of such factual text types as Report, Explanation and Review whereas Sunyoung has demonstrated more mature texts in English Narrative and Personal writing and also in Korean (diary, E-mails) along with the display of a strong self-motivation to write these genres. In more detail, specifically in regard to their linguistic realization, Jinha shows a more impressive control over relational and existential processes, the impersonal stance and nominal groups (including control of nominalization) as prominent language features of factual writing. Compared with Jinha, Sunyoung shows far more advanced control over the use of mental, behavioural and verbal processes along with control over the Mood and Modality system in building up experiential and interpersonal meanings through use of dialogue in Narrative and personal texts.

In this case study, the children's personal preference for different genres can be partly attributed to the socio-cultural influences surrounding their school and home contexts. As mentioned earlier, their literacy development cannot be understood only in relation to the literate practices of reading and writing. It should be interpreted by extending the linguistic view to socio-cultural contexts which constantly and implicitly, and sometimes explicitly, shape their motivations, purposes and values along with contemporary literacy tendencies, including stereotyping or convention (e.g. encouraging gender difference in choosing a writing genre) in connection with the literacy education. It is possible that Jinha's interest in factual topics has been subtly encouraged by both the teacher's expectations in school (that boys should be more interested in factual writing rather than in writing 'stories'), as well as by the expectations of the larger English-speaking society where he was growing up. It has long been commonsense understanding that 'boys will be boys', and that reading and writing are generally 'sissy' activities, more suited to the girls. Whereas very few teachers express this opinion openly, it is an unstated understanding that 'nice' girls are supposed to be good at story writing, while being successful at Narrative writing has never been a sign of masculinity. Jinha also appears to have received more praise from his teachers and the researcher for successfully constructed factual texts rather than for Narratives. This seems to have worked in sustaining his interest in factual writing. It is also important to remember that Sunyoung's early fiction writing experiences were quite successful from the start, and she received much praise from her classroom teachers and her parents for the stories she produced. Thus, she might have developed a special kind of pride and sense of self as somebody who is particularly good at Narrative writing. Accordingly, the implicit and explicit enhancement by influential adults might have been, at least in part, the reason for the difference in their genre preference, followed by their different developmental patterns in genre writing. To sum up the issue of the possible socio-cultural influence of gender difference on the two Korean children's genre writing development, it is noteworthy that this case study provides further evidence of the social construction of literacy practices.

6.4. Concluding Comments

The longitudinal case study documented in this book traced two Korean children's biliteracy development in Australia (in an ESL context) over six years. It is argued here that the whole process of ESL children's biliteracy development can be identified as a case of 'empowering' additive bilingualism. Throughout their successful biliteracy development these children also showed significant academic growth and a building of their positive bicultural and bilingual identity.

Given this whole record of the Korean ESL children's biliterate development, the book entitled *Engaging Young Writers with Powerful Academic Texts* selectively presents their English text development using SFG (Systemic Functional Grammar) analysis. The other book will include further Korean text development and addresses both bilingual and biliterate issues to continue this story and complete the documentation of the full longitudinal case study.

This book provides readers with the successful case study of two ESL Korean children's English text development in an Australian school and home context. The included genre texts mainly are narrative and factual texts. i.e., report writing, explanation, review, argument, and procedure. This case study strongly claims that these minority ESL Korean children had the highest positive influence on their English text development when they had the chance to learn a range of powerful texts explicitly throughout an academic curriculum that stressed a genre-based approach and scaffolding of literacy at home. They were thus able to develop the different range of text genres that featured the various schematic structures and linguistic aspects, including "process", "nominal groups", "interpersonal modality system", "theme choices" and "cohesive devices".

Throughout their English text development, they became aware of the difference between the written mode and the spoken one and gradually became more confident in making linguistic choices appropriate for each written genre. That also means they could explore their choices while still developing control over factual writing, indeed, a far different form of writing than the narrative form. As a result, their English text development at school and home let these children increase their awareness that writing is an important medium to use as a competent member of society in the English-speaking world, and successfully linked that skill to the Korean text development for the most powerful biliterate development.

Appendices

Appendix 3-1

Jinha's Narrative Texts

Text B-0 (age 6)
<u>One day I was playing outside when I found the weirdest</u>
<u>egg.</u>
I ran towards it. It was a purple light corlured egg. So I
picked it up and brang it to his hase. It hatched in a fuw
weeks. When it hatched it looked like this. It had two long
legs. It could jump really high.
1. ending one
   I brang it and my dad was having super and suddly it
   jumped into my dads super
2. ending two
   It got airsik so I let it go and everyone was happy
3. ending three
   The strange creacher made a holl in the wall and jumped
   out of the house.
4. ending four
   The strange creacher was my friend and I told my dad
   it was firends.

Text B-1 (age 7:4)
Once upon a time there lived two children. One named Jack
and one named Jessy. One day Jessy and Jack went for a
walk. They sat on a bench and they were geting ready for
lunch. Jack had vegetable and he didn't like it. When he had
dinner he had a sandwhich. He though it was yum. Mum said
it has vegetable. From them on he liked vegetables.

Text B-2 (age 8:3)
Title: The Problem of the Flushing Toilet
It started at school. I saw a person go into the toilet. I
wonder why...... Just then I saw the toilet had moved out of
place ("like a G string"). But when I turned around I heard
something crack. When I turned around I saw that the toilet
had moved again! So I went in and flush! It swallowed me
up.

Text B-3 (age 8:4)

Title: A Scruffy Dog Called Ragbag

Once there lived a dog called Ragbag. Ragbag mad lots of mess. One day when I came in my room I saw a terrerble mess. Also in the corner of the room I saw ragbag chewing on my uncle's shoe! And there was my chip packet thrown on the floor. So my mum got very angry and she said that I had to clean all of it up. I tried to explain to mum but the words seem to be stuck. So I had to clean the mess up. And I sended my dog ragbag out of the house. But when I came 1 hour later, I say he was digging in the garden. What a naughty dog.

Text B-4 (age 8:5)

Title: The UFO

A million years ago before Christ me and Michael was walking the dark when we saw, it couldn't be, it has to be and it is a UFO! We was in planet X. The UFO was destroying the wildlife. The fight began. Well the UFO had great powers and so we could not escape the UFO and the UFO had set a bomb in the forest and soon the wildlife will be doomed! But when I was thinking the UFO had trapped us in a ring of fire. Just then Michael saw a red button. It said in clear black words "WARNING" so Michael got a stick and threw it at the button. It hit and boom! The lights turned off and the five elements shot out and hit the spaceship and the bomb amazingly disappeared. And at the end we saved the wildlife.

Text B-5 (age 8:6)

Title: Run Away Vegetabes!

One milion years ago there lived some vegetables. Surprisingly they were alive. One fine day they were resting in their patch when tug! Someone pulled carrot, potato and celery out of the ground. In addition they are all friends so they were used to each other. Oh Oh the human was making vegetable soup! Just as the knife went down the fruits ran away! The ran as fast as they could and just as they thought they were safe a dark shadowy figure in front of them. It was that human. Carrot couldn't stand it. In a blink of an eye he poked the human! The human ran off in pain and anger and never came back again.

Text B-6 (age 9:4)
Title: Fantasy Story

One dark stormy night, the people in the street including me stopped dead still in the middle of the road because we saw a quick flash and there, we would see just there hovering in the sky a balloony figure. It was not just an ordanary balloon, it had teeth. Some people though it was a UFO but others thought it was some sort of a alien from mars. Some people thought it was a friendly alien but not for long. In a blink of an eye it started launching missiles at us. We quickly hid in a safe place and some police started shooting at it with their guns. Luckylily the creature escaped and no people died. We heard on the news people in Africa and Asia have reported about the same creature. It had known to be called 'megasnap'. There was one major question. Was it evil......? The next day a plane saw the creature and that Megasnap bit that plane's wing off! Now this was getting deadly sierious. That same night the people switch on the spotlights to look for the Megasnap. We didn't know where it was but this meant one thing, war! The next day the genal of the army sent an interplanetry spy, to look and destroy the creature. Now it was pretty obious that this creature was evil. When the spy had found Megasnap. They fought and fought. At the end the trees were all ashes there was fire everywhere and the spy had died but the good news was that Megasnap had

Text B-7 (age 9:6)
Title: The Mystery of the Haunted House

I was at school talking to my friends, Tom and Michael. "Have you heard about the Haunted House? They say that people go in and never come out!" said Tom. "Cool! Let's go explore it!" exclaimed Michael. "Wouldn't our parents get worried?" I said. "I don't really care if they get worried or not." said Michael. "Okay then. We'll meet each other at the playground." Me and Tom say. The next day we met at the playground. "Okay, lets go to the haunted house." I sigh. We go over to the haunted house. I take a deep breath and knock on the door. "Knock! Knock! Knock!" The door swings open easily with a creaking noise. I could here the door slam shut behind us. "It's creepy in here." I said. "Hey Michael let's get out of here! Michael! Michael! Where are you?!" I shouted. I heard a bloodcurling scream from the cupboard. I ran to the cupboard. Locked!

Text B-8 (age 9:11)
Title: Blood Plague
Once upon a time there lived a heart, a red blood cell and a white blood cell. They were all friends except the white blood cell. Every day the red blood cell would bring oxygen to the heart and the white blood cell would watch television all day long. One disastrous day on December the 19th 1900, a virus got into the heart. "White blood cell, come on and help fight the disease!" pleaded the red blood cell. "Oh shut up will you! I'm trying to watch this cartoon!" shouted the white blood cell. Soon the white blood cell fell asleep on the couch and in his dream he heard a man say 'white blood cell, if you don't fight the disease and win the heart will die therefore you will die as well. It is your choice.' Just then the white blood cell woke up startled. "I have a mission to complete!" With that, the white blood cell raced over to the heart and mumbled a few words and all of a sudden "pop!" and he was inside the heart. He had a sword in his hand. He marched over to the disease fearlessly and shouted "Disease you shall die today!" "Ha! You can't destroy me! Prepare to Die!" "Clang! Clang! Smash! Arrrrrrrrrrrrrrrrrrrrrrrrr" The white blood cell with a lot of practice stabbed the disease in the chest. As if by magic the disease started to disappear. "Nooooooooooooooooooooo!" And the next thing the white blood cell knew was he was standing next to the heart. The red blood cell came over and said "Thanks! Without you we couldn't survive." So they became friends and they lived happily ever after.

Text B-10 (age 10:3)
Title: Remote Control
Hi. I'm called Michael and I'm 10years old. I love flicking the channels with our remote control. One day, I was watching TV and clicking from channel to channel ('cause there was nothing to watch). I was about to turn the tele off, my dad came in with a shoebox. Inside was a brand new remote control. Dad said that it could control not only our

TV but also everything else. Just then mum came in and started a lecture about how I watched too much television and how I didn't do any homework. For a little joke I pointed the remote at my mum and pressed the mute button. Magically and most surprisingly she started the lecture silently. So I pressed the mute button again and her voice returned.

At first I thought having a remote control that could control even humans was very fascinating and so I brought it along to school. That's when matters started to get out of hands. Firstly, I got it confiscated for fiddling with it in class. And then a boy made a smart remark about me having to bring a remote control in class and then everybody started cracking up. When I finally got it back I slipped to the canteen to get something to eat. I purposely froze the canteen manager and unfroze her again. Then just for fun I froze another kid and kicked off with his food. After class at lunchtime I decided to beat up the bullies in the whole school. They were all one year older than me and they had bashed me up tones of times and I am paying back. So I called them out to the soccer field. They came and I bravely said, "come on fight me!" and they charged at me as if they were mad bulls. In the blink of an eye I whipped out my remote and pressed the pause button at them. But it didn't work!! Just then I saw that the batteries had run out. Sweat was trickling down my face. Just as they were about to charge into me... "Wake up! Sleepy head" that's when I realized I had fallen asleep in the couch clutching our old remote control. 'Phew! It was just a dream." I just noticed what the TV was advertising. It was a remote control that could control everything. With this I put down the remote control and said to myself 'I don't need that anymore, I've got my hands that I can rely on' and turned off the TV with my own hands and gave a relieved smile.

Text B-11 (age 10:5)
Title: The Haunted Watch
I'm called Chris and I'm 11years old. It all started with our family going to the mall. It was a normal *boring* day at the mall. That's until I saw a brand new watch in a new watch shop. Well I have a thing about watches you see. Whenever

I see one that's really cool I just have to get it. So I started pleading mum if I could get that watch. I tried about a hundred damn excuses but all she said was *nope*. So I said "Mom, if you get me that watch you can stop giving me pocket money." Now that changed it. She glanced at me with those narrowed eyes that looks like needles and said "You sure? You won't regret?"

"Of course you know that." So I simply got the watch. I had to try it on at home cause I couldn't get the box holding the watch off. Well I put the alarm on at 7:30 and I got ready for school and started walking. I couldn't help wondering why it was so dark. I looked at my watch. 8:30, oh great! I'm going to be late. When I got to the school there was nobody there. There were cricket sounds all around me. I quickly peered through the school window and saw the school clock. It read 12:30. Huh! What's going on here! I finally found out. When I dad bought the watch I didn't set it to the right time. The next day was a very important day because it was my piano exam. So as usual I set my watch to 4:00pm. So it rang at 4:00 pm. So I was just about to go out when the lounge room clock caught my eye. It read 8:30pm. That's when I figured it out. My clock was haunted. It could change time by itself. I went to work straight away. I got the watch and ran outside to the hopper I threw it in just as it was being emptied. I felt so refreshed but not for long. I went inside into my room but there I stood, frozen in horror. There on my dist was the watch. I went over to it at stared at it. It was the same watch. So I ran over to the toolbox got out the screwdriver and unscrewed the back of the watch. I pulled out the batteries and stared with my mouth hanging open. The batteries were out but the watch was still going. I was wondering what to do when I saw a book. Its title was weird and wonderful mechanical things. I flipped open the pages and found what I was looking for. The tick. It said a watch that can't be destroyed by force It can only be destroyed by love. So I hugged it and said good things to it. Then very slowly the numbers on the watch dimmed until it went away. With a relief I went back to the family room.

Appendix 3-2

Sunyoung's Narrative Texts

Text BB-1 (age 5:3)

One day I was building a time michine. Because I wanted to take an adventure with the dinosaurs. When I was finished I hoped in it. Then I took off on my time michice. When I arrived I got off and saw a Brachiosaurus standing right next to me. I played with him then I left that place. When I got home I told my mum about it. Then we had a cup of tea and went to bed.

Text BB-2 (age 5:7)

One scary night I was sleeping. I heard scary nosies. I heard a gosht going woooooo. I ran to my dads and mum. Dad hleped me sleep. Nest night I heard the noises again. Mum and dad looked out the window. They saw a gosht. They said let go in my room. In my dads room and mums it was peseful.

Text BB-3 (age 5:9)

Once there were 1 cat and 1 dog. They always had a fight. In fact they lived together. Also they lived in a town which was same as a city, and lots of ghosts were hiding in the town. They came out in some nights. Near it was a beautiful sparkling lake. One day they were fighting because cat stole dog's hand-ball. Dog was pretty annoyed. A wise elephant who lived next door said not to fight or I'll tell your mum. The wise elephant had a deep heart same as the lake. He told their mum and she said "Dog can stay in our house but cat can't" So cat had gone. Dog was sad and felt lonely. So did cat. Cat called his mum that he was sad. So his mum let him back and they never ever fighted again and mum was happy too!

Text BB-4 (age 5:10)

Once upon a time I got a pressent from my mum. It was a broom. My mum said it was magic. But I didn't belive it. One day I was cleaning the floor with my broom and I didn't regonise the botton and I pressed it and I was flying. And I belived in my mum.

Text BB-5 (age 5;?)

Title: Thunder Mountain

One lonley restalas wich flew out an eerie night to roam.
She met two hairy cretures on the way home. Lets all have
a party on this full moon night will need for Thunder
Mountain to Howl with all our might. Three tall and skinny
gobilens also said to meet. Four growly cats pounsed on
their feet. Five bony skelletons ratted in among the others.
Now let begin the party so...... Lets raise the roof tonight!

Text BB-6 (age 6:2)

Title: My Family

(by Sun-young and her family)
For a girl called Sun-young who loved her family

Chapter 1

Once there was a playful girl who loved her family. Her
name was Sun-young. She had one big brother, her mum and
her dad. One day she was out playing in her backyard when
she saw a strange man. She didn't talk to him at all. She
knew not to talk with strangers. He was shouting at the old
Granny next door who was always kind to us. I said "Stop"
in a very loud voice. Suddenly he looked straight at me. His
eyes were big and round and fierce. I tired to run away but
her was too fast. I ran into my house and slammed the door.
I was home all alone. My heart was beating faster and faster.
I looked out of the window. The man's eyes were glooming
in the sun. So I was terrified. He was so arngry he decided
to dress up into a postman. He knocked on the door very
loud. It was like one elephant jumping in our house. He said
in the key hole "Plese take this parcel." She thought it was
a stranger so this is what she said "Put it on the steps and
I'll pick it up later."

Chapter 2

He was angry because he couldn't trick her. He had another
idea. He wanted to make a trap. The man was very sneaky
and very very bad. He made the trap were he put the parcel
and put dirt over it. Then he waited behind a rock. I saw the
man hiding behind a rock. I waited utill it was night and then
I picked up my parcel and took it home. My family came

back. When it was morning the man found himslef in prison. He hated being in prison.

Chapter3
We came to see him. We smilled. But the man was sad.

Chapter4
We went back home and live happly ever after. But what about the man? Will he still live as happy as Sun-Young's family?

The End

Text BB-7 (age 6:7)
Title: The Rainbow Polar Bear
Once upon a time there lived a jealous polar bear all white and clumsy wouln't wake her stop being jealous of being the queen. But there was a brown bear queen already. "Puff!" I know I've got an idea. I'll kill the queen at midnight. So that night the rainbow Polar bear went to kill the queen. But it was cold and creepy but the rainbow polar kept going. The polar bear didn't know it was raining and the polar bear wasn't rainbow it was just that the polar bear wanted to be beautiful to be the queen. So she painted herself. So the rain washed the paint off. "I can't go in this plain old white fur to be the queen." So she ran as fast as she could back to her home. It was hard painting herself again so she poured some paint on to her. All different colors washed about her like star falling down. It will not rain in the morning I'll go the kill the queen now. The sun shined bright and dryed the polar bear's paint. "This time I'm not going to fail." But she did fail the grds saw her agrily stomping with the knife and blocked the way. While the polar bear was stomping home she saw a man with a long beard and dragged clothes just standing still. "Hey big fellow want to come with me to Canada there is lots of Polar bears there." "OK" So they left to Canada and met the polar bears and lived happliy ever after.

Text BB-8 (age 6;9)

Title: The Mischef Dog

It goes like this, once upon a time there lived a boy. He had no friends expect for a dog. Nobody ever was proud of that dog nobody expect the silly old boy. They lived in a deep little and poor cottage. The boy was a athon all his parents were dead. All the people didn't like that dog. I'll tell you why, it's all because he always lands in mischef. So that's why they usally all called the dog mischef dog. Once he chased a girls cat up the chestnut tree and the cat never ever came down. So the boy lost all his pocket money. He had nothing left expect his clothes and his dog. Most dogs eat dog food but this one didn't. He went off stealing other people's best dinner. On thing it seemed that the boy was never giving the dog a punishment. Anyway, that was the boy's hobby. That dog I mean the mischef dog was always running off like bad children do but this dog was worse. He always ending up in mischef when he came back but all the boy would do is laugh. One dark night the boy was waiting for his dog to come back and wondering what mischef that he would be doing but the mischef dog didn't come back. He was so tired he fell asleep. When it was morning and the dog didn't come up the boy was very worried. The boy put up wanted signs and lost signs too and seven days later the dog appered and to his suprize all the people were hugging him. Soon the boy knew what was going on. Instead of mischef this dog had saved the day by chasing the robbers out of the town!! The moral of this story is that everything can change.

Text BB-9 (age 7:3)

Title: This Diary Belongs to the Beutiful Butterfly

<Morning> Hello, I am the most beutiful butterfly in the whole world! "Yawn!!" Sorry and excuse me. Anyway to get on with me I have brightly coloured wings and I have six legs. I have four wings and two antennanes. <5 minutes past sunrise> I better get up and get some necter for me to eat. I live in rainforests and flowers. I can live also in your own backyard. Also I may live in bushes. <10 minutes past sunrise> I spend most of my time just pollinating flowers and flying around. I collet necter too. I slept in today... I'm sometimes very lazy but please don't call me lazybones. I beg you! <15 minutes past sunrise> Luckliy I don't get

attacked most of the time because I warn those pesty insects away by my colours such as red, black, white and other colours. That tells other insects that I am not that tasty. Soon I will start my life cycle again. By the way my life cycle starts off like this... I lay eggs then when they hatch slowly they turn into lava and they munch the leaves and soon they turn into such ugly caterpillers and make a cocoon and they turn into me!!

Text BB-10 (age 7:4)
Title: Space Adventure
10,9,8,7,6 Here I am strapped into the seat of the swift about to blast off into outerspace to where, no one knows. To have adventures and meet creatures that are only dreamed about... 5,4,3,2,1 Blast off! I travel off with my friend(JamiLee) and I enjoy watching stars. I never know where this space rocket might take me. This is my first ever space jorney I ever had in my life.

Suddenly I crash into something. This is not very good... But on the other hand, it might just be a huge rock. I slowly shiver out of the space rocket with JamiLee. We are in luck because we have landed on the moon. Then, we sink down into a strange room. To slimy creatures slither up to me and I back away. The slimy creatures lead me and JamiLee to a kitchen. They eat goey slimy bugs. JamiLee is about to be sick. The beds are also slimy but very soft. We stay here for one night. As we say goodbye the next day they seem to look poor. We travel back to our real planet(Earth). Just then a comet shoots and we are the only ones to save earth. We push it another direction. Luckliy the comet was small. When we land on planet Earth, I suppose slimy stuff compared to dry stuff are very different indeed. I get out and the people gasp! I say "why" and I was covered in mud and slime. At home I should of have taken a bath but I didn't because... Mum had made oranges for us and I peeled one and throued it at mum and JamiLee! We will have a orange fight! The oranges sqeched and sqeezed as they splat on people's faces! It was very fun. I think that my specail adventure starts now!! So this is why I have wrote this narrative of me and JamiLee traveling around in outerspace. I asked mum thoughtly "mum, will I ever be able to see those slimy friends that I met in outerspace with JamiLee?" Then

my my answered "in your dreams you will always see them vividily in your head." That very night I dreamt of me and JamiLee having a fun party with the slimy creatures.
Slimy narrative by Sunyoung

Text BB-11 (age 7:5)
Title: The Mystery
Chapter 1 (Losing stuff)
"Oh, no!!" Sarah, a girl who was fairly smart, cried. I lost my school homework! The teacher will ground me forever. "Gosh, what am I going to do!" She searched all aroud the place even in the laundry basket. Just then the phone rang. Sarah picked it up sighing. It was Sarah's best friend Janet. She was a girl who didn't like school and who adroed animals. "Oh, it's you" cried Sarah with relif. Is my homework book there? I lost it. "Well, I lost my dog Scamper!" They both carfully thought for a while. Hey, you think we should have a meeting at 2:30? OK! said Janet.

Chapter 2 (The great meeting)
Sarah run over to Janet's place sharp two thirty. Janet was there waiting for her. "Why were you so late?" She frowed. Sarah was out of breath. She tried to speak but she was so tired of out of breath that no words came out as she opened her mouth. Janet pasted Sarah a cup of water. "Thanks" panted Sarah. Anyway, how did you exactly lose Scamper? said Sarah. Well, first of all I would like to say... Sarah shouted in her ears, "We are not doing a interview we a just going to say the words!!!" Well sorry. Her voice was now a whisper since she was so frighted so much. Suddenly Janet spoke up. She was angry now! "Oh your so perfect!!!" Sarah was now too angry. Well how about you!! You have dog hairs all over your nose. Now for hevens sake lets start the meeting. OK, how Scamper ran away on my lead. She was talking fast, porposly so Sarah couldn't hear. "What she said?" "Fine if you have no ears at all maybe your are death" said Janet. "Oh so Scamper might not like you any more." And with that Sarah slammed to door shut. Janet stuck her touge out at the door. Then her mum came in. Janet quickly slipped her touge back in her mouth. Sarah was stomping out. "Is there a problem with you two." "Nothing" she said.

Chapter 3 (school time)

Sarah was worried about her homework book. She walked slowly to school. She was early as usal. When Mrs Honey, the teacher was marking the marking the roll off Janet came in with her hair pointing strait upwards. She finished the roll in a minute. Sarah knew what was next. Seeing who has done homework. She shivered in fright. All the other kids axept for Janet and Sarah brung in their homework. "All right" said Mrs Honey. "Sarah and Janet grounded for 2 weeks!" Everyone giggeled. "It's not funny!" shouted Sarah at Sarah at lunch time. "It is to me" said Janet. It was hometime. Since Janet and Sarah's homes were in the same direction they had to walk together. Sarah ran over to Janet's place at 4:30 exactly. It was getting dark and very dim to see her way. Sarah tripped over a tree root that was shaped into a curve. She screamed and a old lady and two men came to see what was happening. "Oh" exclaimed the fat lady. "I think you've broken a bone or something." Then the two men one long one short like a dwaf grabbed the nearest telephone and called the ambulane. It was not a very long time for the ambulance came. At last Sarah opened her eyes. "Where am I?" "In the hospital dear!" answered a nurse near by. Sarah tried to sit up but it hurt so much that she howled with pain. Newspaper men came rushing in the room and started reporting that a young girl was hurt. The very next day (Saturday) Janet came jumping in. "For heavens sake here you are!" she shouted rather grumply. "I was searching for you all over!!" "Sorry" said Sarah. "Sorry! You think sorry is enough!" Janet was boiling with anger. "I had to run to your house, the police station and the hostibal and here you are saying sorry!" "Bye then!" she said. "As long as I know where you are I'm not worried." She stomped away muttering some dry unintelligent words to herself. Sarah had to pay $15 per surgery. One day the doctor came in and said, "You have to report this news to your mother and father." "I don't have one" she whimpered sadly. The doctor cried. "You mean you're a athan!" "Yes" Said Sarah. "My mum and dad died when I was two." Sarah saw Janet's mum waiting for Janet. Janet's mum saw Sarah's frown and quickly caught up to her. "Are you two fighting?" Sarah sighed and ansewed slowly, "yes" in a rather dull voice. She quickly dragged them over to the nearest seat and started to speak.

Chapter 4 (Becoming friends)
"You know" she said softly. "I heard that Sarah lost her homework book. And did you know what? Janet lost our poor dog scamper. I recon you really want to find them." "We do" they cried. "Now if you two work together I recon you could find them quicker." Suddenly hearing this both kid's face brightened. They soon shook hands in a manner to be friends again. "Let's start finding!!" "Ok, but first we will have to make a plan." Sarah and Janet both followed Janet's mum.

Chapter 5 (Making plans)
Janet's mum pointed to a ragged chair and asked to sit down. Sarah, Janet's mum and Janet drank milo they all started giving ideas. As you might of knowed Sarah was the first person to put her hand up. She shouted, "We could put up signs!" Janet's mum said, "Ok, should we find Scamper first?" "Well, ok. My homework book isn't more special then a live thing." Sighed Sarah.

Chapter 6 (The busy day)
That afternoon was a busy time for all the kids. Also, Janet's mum had to type down all and excally 30 signs each with a photo of Scamper on it.

Chapter 7 (Waiting for a while)
"OK, we'll rest here for a moment, and Sarah, I am so sorry that I didn't let you go home." "It's all right" Sarah grinned. "My mum is going on a trip to a bilding called honey bee hive. So I get to sleepover!" "Horray!" everybody cried!

Chapter 8 (Check the signs on)
That day everybody looked out of the window. "It's the start of winter! And it's snowing. Oh dear, how are we going to find Scamper and my homework book?" "Don't worry, let's just start tapeing the signs on." Everybody was wearing a warm snow coat. It was freezing out there.

Chapter 9 (The big search)
We searched for days and days but still there was no hope.

And Sarah and Janet became sadder and sadder. They were very worried too of how Scamper could survive in the snow. They called out "Scamper!" loudly but still there was not hope.

Chapter 10 (Finding Scamper)
"There's no hope!" cried Janet tears coming out of her eyes. Janet's mum and Sarah was cheering her up. Just the phone rang everybody went silent. Janet's mum picked up the phone and "Woof! WOOF!" It was Scamper then a angry voice said "Come right here at once. This dog is getting my meat. I am the bucther by the way!" And he slammed the phone down. The kids went racing to the buther shop. There was Scamper with Sarah homework in his mouth!! "Two in one" said Janet patting Scamper. "For once you are right!" said Sarah.
The End

Text BB-12 (age7:5)
<u>**Title: Narrative**</u>
In the past there where so many planets. Each one had animals and food for everyone. It was very hard travel to another planet as well. It was also very beuitiful to see the star forming around the universe. The smallest planet had is animals on it. In was one day, when all the animals on the smallest planet had ran out of food they started to stave. They cryed and searched for one scrap but none was to be seen The king of the land sent some brave animals to search for a planet which had plenty of food. For weeks no news was found. Until one day, one animal that the kind had sent had flew over to the staving animals. With the galaxie's help they all set off to a planet in search of food. When they came to the planet which had so much food all of the animals rushed over to eat. It was such a lovely sight. The food sqelched into the animal's mouth and they had a lovely time together.

Text BB-13 (age 7:6)
I finally got to the last step and I accdentily slamed my face. I got up and it was just like I was in opposite land. Birds were chirping and they all were staring at me as if I was a slimy worm. Then I thought about how small I was and I

quickly dug my way though the grass. "Gosh!" I was so scared. Just then I heard my mothers voice. I ran to the door. "Oh no!" The cat! It's glowing eyes shined. I backed away. I ran away. I sat sobbing. Ouch! A prick from the rosebush had pricked me. I looked back to flick it away. Then a huge rose bush was standing right behind me! It was about 27 twice as long as me! I climbed up the prickly tree. It took me one whole hour. Oh I wish I was a kid again. Soon I had reached the top of the rose bush. I saw the next door neirbors house. I jumped over the fence. I wandered around the place untill I found the next doors(Mr Poppy's houses) pool. It was so warm. I try to float but I just sank. I almost nearly drowned. Untill I grabbed on to a half eaten lily pad. It was so relaxing. I had a nice nap. I was doozing in the sun.

Text BB-14 (age 8:1)
Title: Hannah's Space Trip

Hannah was a little girl. She was only 7, and she loved trips. But she hated space. One sunny day, Hannah was reading, when the door rang. A big post man waited impatiently at the door. Hannah raced out where her parents were reading a message out loud. The headline said 'SPACE' in big block letters. Before Hannah could complain her mother said "Hanna, look it's a draw to have a trip to space!" Hannah half smiled and half frowned. "Everyone is to draw!" winked Hannah's mum. Hannah groaned and faced the wall. It took a long time for Hannah to decide if she was going to space or not. Unfortunately the draw ended up that Hannah's family was to go. Hannah had to go too. Hannah cried "Oh not space!" Her mum said "Don't worry Hannah, this is a good opportunity for you to know and like space."

Soon Hannah was in the rocket ready to leave to her worst nightmare. "3,2,1, BLAST OFF!" The rocket zoomed up out of sight in a minute. Darkness shaded over the rocket as it was up in space. Hannah complained "I don't want to be in here!" "Let me out!" She skreamed the sentences a couple of times and then stopped. She was suddenly interested in the dark, lost, world.

Text BB-15 (age 8:2)

Title: Gravity

Yesterday seemed like an ordinary morning at first. I climbed out of bed like I normally do, only to discover that there was no gravity. This was strange. I was floating high up in middir. In my bedroom! I pondered if it was a dream. But no, I was actually floating. It took me a few minutes to turn the doorknob leading to the corridor. I took a few flights to my parent's room and whispered "Mum, Dad." Then came a laughter and flew Mum and Dad! I asked what was happening a few times but they were just as surprised as I was. My old dog 'Woof' was floating too! It was as if I had wings. My family and I glided and swirled around our corridor and escaped through a cracked window. This was amazing!! Soon Mum and Dad said "Now lets get back down." I groaned and tried to fly back down. But no matter how hard I tried all of us couldn't budge. It was now a disaster. We tried everything. Woof even prayed! But nothing would work. Now it was cold. We thought there past by. Other people had flew out of their homes. There still was no gravity. Woof and the animals were flying high up in the air. I had been seperated from 'Woof' and I was chattering my teeth. 4 hours passed pasted. Nothing changed. As redness poured the sky, I knew that my mum was slowly aparting from us. Was she lost forever? Suddenly, a gust of wind blew by and the gravity came back. I winked and mum. Dad laughed by Mum frowned. Now all the fun is gone, Mum turned back to a Mum.

Text BB-16 (age 8:5)

Title: Fred

I listened to the rain drumming on my roof. 'Bang!' The silence was broken by a roar. I turned on the light and stared at the atmosphere around me. Sitting under my fireplace was a rather sooty crocodile. "Er, Hi!" I whispered under my breath. He stared at me with two glary eyes. "Are you a crocodile?" I asked taking an awfully big risk. He snarled and flapped his huge wings ferociously. 'Oh no. I had just met an angry dragon.' I wanted to scream. But only a whisper came out. 'Not a dragon. Especially at midnight!' I pinched myself hoping this would be a terrible dream. But still, I stayed where I was with this dragon... I ran to the kitchen and quickly fed some meat to it. That seemed to settle him down a bit... He waddled into the bathroom making stomps like earthquakes. Luckily Mum and Dad wears earmuffs. When I was day dreaming a sprinkle of water woke me up. 'Oh darn, Mum's going to kill me!' When I ran to the bathroom the door was locked. 'Gee' I thought that this dragon was clever... I pulled out my clip and unlocked the door. The dragon was having a bath with my sparkle shampoo! One minute, I'm totally scared of this beast the other minute I'm mad at his!! I punch in the air forcing the dragon to back off. But he doesn't budge! He just stalks, I mean stomps to my room! Then my worst nightmare comes. I hear a groan from my mum's room! I ran to my room and pushed the dragon in a huge closet. I can barely shove his fat body in! I turn off the light and tuck myself in bed. Mum comes in. She yawns and glares around my room with narrowed eyes that look like needles. Then she banged the door and went bake to sleep. I open my eyes and looked in the closet where a note hung. It said: My name is Fred and I'll come back soon. I splutter in disgust. I wonder when that mischiveous little dragon will return...

Text BB-17 (age 8:5)
Title: Cub

On a cathedral, a little gargoyle was watching the city below him. He used to be scared of heights but now his hobby was to hang on a wall, or even better – a better, high one. The gargoyle's name was called 'Cub.' I was a pity that people called him 'Cub' because it wasn't a scary name like 'Blood Thriller' or something along those lines. Cub hated his name. He would do anything to change it! Another thing, why didn't he have legs like humans? Cub got so bored thinking about his name, he fell asleep. Cub woke up soon enough. A few seconds later, three men came barging in the cathedral. They stared at Cub, so he gave them a waring glare and shouted, "Go away!" That almost worked. They were just about to faint! Perhaps they had never seen a talking gargoyle before. Then the three men tried to knock me down the wall! Cub turned into stone and they punched him. The gargoyle just stared at them full of wonder whilst the men were sucking their fists and howling with pain. Cub jumped down his wall and hopped – well he had to hop, to a small door. He butted the door with his head and the door slowly opened little by little. And inside, was a squirmming figure of the priest! Cub found the key on the ceiling. Cub hopped as high as he could but somehow the key just didn't seem to come into his hands. So he went out, jumped on the main roof of the room the priest was in and used his horns to cut a small circle and it fell on to the ground with an ear-bursting 'bang!' Cub ran back into the room and found the key under the priest's foot. Cub quickly picked the key up and turned the lock on the priest. The priest thanked the gargoyle and from then on the priest called Cub, 'Hero.'

Text BB-18 (age 8:6)
Title: Face to Face with a Santa Clause
Chapter 1
Chris was 8 years old and still believed in Santa Clause. Nothing could ever make Chris change his mind. Well, maybe. Chris's big brother Matthew teased Chris and said "Chris, be more adult type." Chris' dad was visiting France.

It was that day that made Chris suspicious. In the early morning when Chris was sleeping, his mother woke him with a cup of freezing water. "Mum you always............" and before he could say another word, she panicked and said, "Get changed! Matthew has already gone to swimming!" Chris rubbed his sleepy eyes and slowly got changed and ready to go. He went to his mother and said. "I'm all done." His mother just told him to eat some cereal.

Chris smiled and thought how the crunchy cornflakes would shimmer into his mouth and he rushed to the kitchen. The kitchen was very small but Chris didn't mind. He thought he had the most beautiful window because he had always seen a lovely swaying of the trees and flowers. This had always been a lovely memory for Chris that he would never forget. As he was eating, he stared out the window half asleep and he saw a red shape sitting on the washing line with a naughty, twisted smile. He dropped his spoon and stared at the red, blurry shape. He knew that he was completely alone in the kitchen with only a spoon to fight with. Chris tried to figure out what the red blurry shape was by staring even harder than before. 'No it couldn't be', Chris had seen a strange

Santa Clause staring at him face to face. Chris faced the other way and then turned and looked at the Santa Clause. He wasn't gone but unfortunately was closer than before...

Chapter 2
Chris didn't know what to do. First he rubbed his sleepy eyes and stared again. It was still there!! He wanted to scream but nothing came out of his dried mouth. His face went white. He ran to his mother as fast as he could. "Mum, mum there is a strange 'Santa Clause' on our washing line!!" But his mother just slammed the door on his face and murmured, " Go do something helpful like eating your cornflakes." Chris slowly tiptoed as if the Santa Clause might hear him. When he reached the kitchen, he took a glimpse of his food and snatched it away so he could eat somewhere else. When Chris had eaten his breakfast, he waited for his mother outside her door. Soon she came out and Chris was trying to tell her what had happened, but she didn't believe him and told him he was saying complete nonsense. As they got in the car, Chris stayed silent with anger. 'How could she not believe him?' The Swimming Pool came close by. His mother parked the car and Chris ran up to the entrance of the building and got changed into his swimmers.

He waited for his mother to come and then jumped into the freezing water. All he could think of was that nasty Santa Clause. Chris usually took his swimming lessons seriously but not today. He was caught from the swim club teacher for listening inappropriately. Chris's mother gave him a hard stare. Then Chris noticed something strange. A red blurry shape sitting on the lane ropes. Santa Clause had followed him! A shiver went up Chris's spine. Was this rotten old Santa going to follow him everywhere?

Swimming lessons had finished. Chris's mother was going to give him an unpleasant lecture!! Matthew was already waiting for Chris with his mother. It seemed as if Matthew was ready to tease the Santa lover. Chris explained to his mother in the car. "There really was a mean Santa Clause sitting on the washing line!" He shouted. His mother told him that he was daydreaming too much. Chris looked down to his feet. Then he looked towards Matthew. He was making a sour face trying hard not to laugh. So was his mum. Chris made up his mind. He wasn't going to put up with his families disgusting behavior. He was going to show them that rotten Santa Clause face to face. For once and for all!! Chris's car arrived at his house...

Chapter 3
Chris's mother and Mathew leaped out of the car and hurried off in to the house leaving Chris behind to hold the swimming bags. Chris slowly hoped out of the car and opened the trunk. But on the trunk was Santa Clause. Chris shivered and noticed the Santa's smile was gradually forming bigger and bigger. Chris desperately made a grab for the bags and ran up the walkway towards his house. Santa Clause stared at Chris for a moment as if he was saying "Don't leave" and then vanished.

As Chris turned the doorknob, he began to think how he could prove that there really was a Santa Clause. As he stepped into his house, he dumped the bags on the ground and sat down on one of the closest chairs. He thought of yelling at them over and over again but he wanted to make sure they knew. Chris thought and thought. Then a brainwave swooped into his mind. "That's it, I could catch that dirty Santa Clause!" Chris jumped out of the old, wooden chair and sprang off towards him room. He was about to make a plan but there, lying on his bed was Santa Clause. "It seems as if you was waiting for me," Chris stammered. The Santa Clause didn't reply. Chris tried to tackle the Santa from his arm but Santa Clause fled. A few seconds later, Santa Clause appeared again. This time Chris was furious. He grabbed the Santa Clause and tackled him until he had to stay still. Then Chris yelled out loud to Matthew and his mum. "Mum, Matthew, I told you I was right!!" They both came running. Chris showed Santa to them. Matthew showed a puzzled face and asked "where?" His mother repeated Matthew's question. Chris whimpered sadly thinking that they still didn't believe him. Matthew frowned and said, "We need to see him you know." Chris shook his head. "He must have escaped," cried his mother. She was pulling a sour face trying hard not to laugh.

Chris set off crying and ran outside. He sat down on the concrete and sobbed. Then a strange thing happened. Santa came down pulling a twisted, mean smile on his face. For the first time he made a noise. He laughed and pulled a face. Then as usual, he vanished into thin air.

Chapter 4

Chris was really mad now. He sat down on the concrete crying and thinking of a new plan he could work on. Chris thought and thought. Nothing would come into his mind. He said to himself 'Why isn't mum and Matthew believing me?' 'I showed them that rotten Santa Clause.' Chris didn't know what to do. All Chris wanted was that mean Santa Clause to disappear. Chris slowly got up and turned the doorknob again. He stomped through the corridor and walked into his own lonely room. He sat on his bed and thought. 'Maybe lying on comfy spots would help thinking of a plan' thought Chris. So he snuggled into his favorite place and thought. He hoped that a new thought would come into his head sometime or another. Meanwhile, Chris's mother was teaching Matthew his homework. Suddenly, a new idea came into his mind. He would talk to the nasty Santa Clause and ask him if he could leave him alone!! He never knew that a Santa Clause who usually brought him presents, could bother him so much!

In a second, the mysterious Santa was sitting right next to Chris as if he had known the plan Chris was plotting on. When Chris saw Santa Clause, he almost jumped at least a foot in the air!! "Why are you here?" Chris asked. The Santa made a rude face but didn't answer. So Chris said, "Look here Santa, I need to talk with you." The Santa nodded but again didn't say a single word. He must have thought that Chris was going to pounce on him again. So Chris lied "It's really nice of you to keep me company but please, I want you to leave me alone." The Santa Clause pulled an I-will-not' face. Just then, Chris's mother came in Chris's room and asked whom he was talking to. Chris just said "no one" trying hard not to shout at her. So she walked away like a fashion model on a stage. Chris looked beside him. There was no Santa. He groaned loudly and searched for Santa.

Nothing was to be seen. Well, almost. Except for old shelves and clothes. Chris sighed, "I guess I failed on that plan as well." Then he walked out of his room and on to the tiles of the corridor that leaded to the dusty floor of the old kitchen............

Chapter 5

It was Christmas!! To Chris it wasn't very pleasant. He marched into the kitchen. He could smell hot toast in the toaster. His mother was cooking a delicious meal for three. Chris frowned at her and went into the lounge and sat there for a few minutes thinking about another plan he could try. He thought, 'If mum and Matthew didn't see the Santa Clause, then the Santa must be invisible to everyone except me!!' Chris now knew why nobody could see Santa except him. 'So, all my other plans were no use! Well, I will teach that Santa how to treat people nice!' Chris frowned and stood up ready to eat his breakfast. His mother was putting things on the table when she noticed Chris. "Oh, Merry Christmas Chris!" Chris made an effort to pull a vast smile to cover his angry face. He sat down on the table and waited for his food to be delivered on the table. Soon Chris's mother came with his hot and tasty food. She handed it to Chris and gave him a big hug. Chris found a fork in the dishwasher and began to gobble up his food. Just then Matthew came in with a history book and sat down on his chair. He always brought a book with him to the table.

After everyone finished off their breakfast, Matthew and Chris clambered over to a green Christmas tree with lots of enjoyable toys and goodies inside. They both unwrapped their presents desperately. Soon they finished ripping and thought they had completed all of the presents when Matthew noticed a dark red package with a card. It said: Dear Chris. Merry Christmas!! From the washing line Santa. Luckily, Matthew didn't care and started playing with his new toys so he didn't have a chance to look inside Chris's mysterious present. Chris tiptoed off to his room and took off the wrapper of the bright red package and peeked inside. There, inside the package was a strange black model. It looked like a remote control but smaller. Chris fiddled around with the strange object and read the card over and over again. 'Why did this Santa give this strange thing to me?' 'He is my worst enemy!' When Chris was thinking, he thought he heard a faint whisper coming from the object. A kind, Santa's voice drifted inside the thing...

Chapter 6

Chris almost jumped a foot in the air. Had he really heard Santa's voice? Chris pondered if he was dreaming for a moment. So Chris asked in to the object, "Who are you?" The whisper came again. It sounded like he was saying, "You know." But Chris wasn't sure. Then Chris heard his mother's voice calling, "Chris!" Chris hid the strange object under his bed and ran into the lounge room. Matthew was still playing with his new toys and testing out other boyish stuff. Chris's mother was reading a Christmas recipe for pudding. Chris tried to look as if nothing happened. He stammered a bit and then sat down on the sofa and stared at his toys. None of them was as realistic as the toy that Santa had given him.

For the first time of his life, Chris thought that Santa was nice. But he still thought he had to be a lot more careful about Santa Clause. 'If only that Santa knew how better it is to be good, kind and trusting instead of naughty and mean.' Chris wanted to make Santa a nice friend of his. When Chris was daydreaming, Chris's mother awoke him with a push and stuffed a magazine into his face. "Look Chris, a Santa Clause is coming into the local shops!" Chris made a so-what face and frowned. Chris's mother just ran over to Matthew and started to tell him the news. Matthew just went on playing with his toys again not listening to his mother. Chris was talking to himself in his head. 'I don't like those Santa Clauses anymore.' Then he sat up and then went to his room. He grabbed his mystery present and whispered. "Santa Clause!" Then an answer replied. "Yes." Chris smiled and whispered back, "Thanks for this lovely present!" Santa stayed still.

Chris had now thanked the Santa Clause for a good dead. Perhaps the Santa was a nice person but just didn't show his attitude? Chris wondered. Then a voice came from the object that said, "Whenever you need me, just call for me through this phone!" Chris nodded and said, "So that's what this strange thing is. Now thanks to Santa Clause, I finally know..."

Chapter 7
Chris stayed still on his bed. He suddenly sat up and asked through the phone, "Santa, why are you following me around?" Then Santa whispered back, " Because I want to." Chris nodded and collapsed down on to his bed.

At first Chris thought that he was daydreaming in school. He sat up and looked at the place around him. He couldn't believe what he saw! He was sitting on his bed in a red house. Of course, his house wasn't red. Then someone tapped him on the back. Chris turned and looked. It was Santa Clause! "Welcome to my house." He said proudly. Chris stood up onto the hard, red ground and shook Santa's hands. Somehow, Chris didn't like this house. He thought the roof was going to fall onto his head in a million pieces. "Would you like to explore?" The Santa suggested. Chris nodded his head. The house's floor was damp and cold to step on but it seemed like Santa Clause didn't mind. Chris followed the Santa Clause all around the place in case that he got lost. Then Santa Clause stopped and said to Chris, "You must stay outside this door." Chris didn't know what to say. His mouth was dry. Then when he tried to look at Santa to answer, he had already stepped into the dusty door. Chris stopped a tear from coming down his cheek. 'What if Santa was planning to leave me here so I couldn't go home?" Chris sat down on the floor and waited for Santa Clause to come out of the door. Chris waited for hours and hours with a serious face expression. Chris was now mad at Santa for two things. One, he lied. And two he left without saying anything. Chris tried to phone Santa Clause but the phone didn't connect. Chris threw the phone on to the ground. He wanted to go back home. He closed his sleepy eyes and opened them again. Then, he noticed he was still collapsed on his bed dreaming. Chris thought. 'Had this all been a dream?' But it had all been true. Chris searched in his jacket for Santa Clauses old phone. He tipped everything out of his pockets. There was no phone. Chris snarled and ran into the living room...

Chapter 8

Chris stomped into the living room. He was very angry. His mother was decorating the room and Matthew was sleeping on the sofa. Chris tried to push down his angry thoughts. But somehow he just couldn't. 'How can I not be angry when someone lied to me!' Chris thought. He went back to his room and once again collapsed down on to the bed. Something was poking his back. Chris guessed it was Matthew and turned his head around to his back. Nothing was there. 'That's strange.' Pondered Chris. He thought his eyes were playing nasty tricks on him. He snarled again. Chris felt like he was going to pick his pillow up and throw it onto the roof in any minute. He was very mad. Chris faced the wall and then dozed off to sleep. He had a very peculiar dream about himself becoming friends with the nasty Santa Clause. When Chris awoke, he cocked his head from side to side and then stomped off to the kitchen to get a cup of nice, cold glass of water. When he arrived to the kitchen, everything was silent. The trees weren't swaying anymore. Then he noticed a scrunched up paper on the wall saying, "Chris, Matthew and I have gone to the markets to buy some fruits. We will be back in 45 minutes." And down below was a scribbled word saying, "Mum." Chris was scared. 'Why do I have to be at home alone!' Chris shivered and sat down on a chair. He gulped and then stared down at the floor. 'Perhaps if I go to my friend's house for a couple of minutes?' thought Chris. He gulped and nodded to himself...

As Chris ran down the hallway that was leading to the door, he could make up a red shape guarding it. "Oh no!" shouted Chris. "It's that rotten Santa Clause again!" Chris steadily approached the door and tried hard not to snarl to the Santa Clause. The Santa Clause was chuckling to himself. Anger was boiling inside Chris's mind. He thought of hitting Santa. But for some strange reason, Chris's head seemed to be saying, "Be Santa Clause's friend!" But Chris couldn't. No, he wouldn't! Not with a liar like him. Chris began to turn back to his room. He was half frightened and half mad. Chris made his way to his room snarling again.

Chapter 9

For a second, Chris wished that he were never born. He

stomped back to his room and fell on his bed closing his eyes. He dozed off to sleep as he usually did. This time Chris dreamt about himself playing happily with the tricky Santa Clause. When Chris woke up, he shook his blurry head and stared around in his room. He sat up straight and headed for the kitchen to help himself to a glass of freezing water. He stared at one of the kitchen stools where a red jacket had been hung. He rubbed his eyes and stared back. The Santa Clause was sitting there grinning. 'Can't I ever get some peace?' yelled out Chris in his head. Chris made a go-away-I-don't-like-you face and stuck out his red, pointy tongue. He poured some icy cold water into a cup as quick as he could and then ran back to his room. When he reached his door, he sat down on his chair and drank his water making slapping and sucking noises. He almost chocked on his drink once he saw Santa Clause sitting beside him sticking his tongue out as well.

Chris began to act very rude to Santa Clause. He just stared at Chris strangely. All of a sudden, Santa Clause disappeared and came back with a piece of paper and a pen. 'That's strange?' thought Chris. Santa Clause started to write down a peculiar sign with the pen. Chris had no idea what the sign was and what it meant. Santa Clause finally placed the pen down and moved aside for Chris to look at it. On the paper was a messy word saying 'sorry.' Chris stared at the word for a couple of minutes and then back at Santa Clause. Chris half believed Santa Clause. Santa Clause sighed and then suddenly started to murmur, "You see, Santa Clauses all have different personalities. Other Santas say that I am annoying and clumsy so I have no friends. I was tired of hearing those words so I tried to prove that I was nice and actually wanted a friend. And then I met you. But I just couldn't help myself from acting differently from my mind. It's just my undesirable habit. But at least you seemed to understand me, and so I have to say that I want to be friends with you." Chris was flabbergasted to hear Santa's confession. And then he began thinking of the way he had been feeling lonely and left out recently after Santa Clause came. So far Chris had not experienced such a difficult time with no friends and no people believing him. And in that way, Chris began to feel as if he was a strange person compared with all the other people around him. He then realized it was just the same for Santa Clause as well. "It's okay." Chris replied, "I think I understand your feelings. Thank you for letting me know how lonely you were." Chris smiled. "Next Christmas, I will promise to deliver you a nice present!" Santa said, "So far I have been so naughty that I couldn't get a job for delivering presents to little kids like you. But now, I am going to be nice and get that job!" "But please don't sit on the washing line again. Just come down the chimney! That's the traditional way." Chris joked. Expecting the nice present for next Christmas, he was grinning from ear to ear and so was Santa Clause. Looking out the window, incredible white snow was drifting down...

Reference

Aidman, M. A. (1999). *Biliteracy Development Through Early and Mid-Primary Years: A Longitudinal Case Study of Bilingual Writing.* Unpublished Ph.D. dissertation, University of Melbourne.

Badger, R., & White, G. (2000). A process genre approach to teaching writing. *ELT Journal,* 54(2), pp. 153-160.

Baker, C. (2006). *Foundations of Bilingual Education and Bilingualism.* Clevedon: Multilingual Matters Ltd.

Bissex, G. (1980). *Gnys at Wrk.* Massachussets: Harvard University Press.

Brown, H & Mathie, V. (1990). *Inside Whole Language.* NSW: Primary English Teaching Association.

Brown, J. D. (1995). *Understanding Research in Second Language Learning.* Cambridge: Cambridge University Press.

Bruner, J. (1986). *Actual Minds, Possible Worlds.* Cambridge: Harvard University Press.

Cambourne, B. (1988). *The Whole Story.* NSW: Ashton Scholastic.

Cameron, L. (2001). *Teaching Languages to Young Learners.* Cambridge: Cambridge University Press.

Carrell, P. L. (1985). Facilitating ESL reading by teaching text structure. *TESOL Quarterly,* 19, pp. 727-752.

Christie, F. (1985). Varieties of written discourse. *Children Writing: Study Guide.* Geelong: Deakin University Press, pp. 11-51.

_____ (1989). Genres in writing. *Writing in Schools: Study Guide.* Geelong: Deakin University Press, pp. 3-48.

_____ (1991). Genres as social processes. In *Working with Genre: Papers from 1989 LERN Conference.* Leichhardt, Australia: Common Ground, pp. 73-88.

_____ (1992). Preparation of teachers for teaching English literacy: What constitutes essential knowledge? In N. Bird & J. Harris (eds.), *Quilt and Quill: Achieving and Maintaining Quality in Language Teaching and Learning.* Hong Kong: Institute of Language Education, pp. 222-239.

_____ (2005). *Language Education in the Primary Years.*

Sydney: University of New South Wales Press Ltd.

Collerson, J. (1983). One child and one genre: Developments in letter writing. In B.M. Kroll & G. Wells. *Explorations in the Development of Writing*. J. Wiley & Sons, pp. 71-93.

Cope, B., & Kalantzis, M. (1993). Introduction: How a genre approach to literacy can transform the way writing is taught. In B. Cope & M. Kalantzis (eds.), *The Powers of Literacy: A Genre Approach to Teaching Writing*. Bristol, PA: Falmer Press, pp. 1-21.

Cummins, J. (1976). The influence of bilingualism on cognitive growth: A synthesis of research findings and explanatory hypotheses. *Working Papers on Bilingualism*, 9, pp. 1-43.

_____ (1978). Metalinguistic development of children in bilingual education programs: Data from Irish and Canadian Ukrainian-English Programs. In M. Paradis (ed.), *Aspects of Bilingualism*. Columbia: Hornbeam Press.

_____ (1986). Empowering minority students: A framework for intervention. *Harvard Academic Review*, 56(1), pp. 18-36.

Davis, J. N., Lange, D. L., & Samuels, S. J. (1988). Effects of text structure instruction on foreign language readers' recall of a scientific journal article. *Journal of Reading Behavior*, 20, pp. 203-214.

Derewianka, B. (1990). *Exploring How Texts Work*. Newtown, NSW: Primary English Teaching Association.

_____ (1995). *Language Development in the Transition from Childhood to Adolescence: The Role of Grammatical Metaphor*. Unpublished Ph.D. dissertation. Sydney: Macquarie University.

Eggins, S. (1996). *An Introduction to Systemic Functional Linguistics*. London: Pinter.

Enright, D.S. & McCloskey, M.L. (1988). *Integrating English: Developing English Language and Literacy in Multilingual Classrooms*. Reading, MA: Addison-Wesley.

Fahnestock, J. (1993). Genre and rhetorical craft. *Research in the Teaching of English*, 27, pp. 265-271.

Freedman, A. (1993). Show and tell? The role of explicit teaching in the learning of new genres. *Research in the*

Teaching of English, 27(3), pp. 222-248.

Goodman, K.S., Goodman, Y.M. & Hood, W.J. (eds.) (1989). *The Whole Language Evaluation Book*. NH: Heinemann Educational Books.

Graves, D.H. (1983). *Writing: Teachers & Children at Work*. NH: Heinemann Educational Books.

Halliday, M. A. K. (1975). *Learning How to Mean: Explorations in the Development of Language*. London: Arnold.

_____ (1978). *Language as Social Semiotic: The Social Interpretation of Language and Meaning*. London: Edward Arnold.

_____ (1985). *Spoken and Written Languages*. Oxford: Oxford University Press.

_____ (1994). *An Introduction to Functional Grammar*. London: Arnold.

_____ (1996). Literacy and linguistics: a functional perspective. In R. Hasan and G. Williarms (eds.) *Literacy in Society*. Harlow: Addison Wesley Longman Limited.

Halliday, M. A. K. & Martin, J. R. (1993). *Writing Science: Literacy and Discursive Power*. Pittsburgh: University of Pittsburgh Press.

Halliday, M. A. K. & Matthiessen, C. M. I. M. (2004). *An Introduction to Functional Grammar*. London: Hodder Arnold.

Hammond, J. (1987). An overview of genre-based approach to the teaching of writing in Australia. *Australian Review of Applied Linguistics*, 10(2), pp. 163-181.

Hammond, J., Burns, A., Joyce, H., Brosnan, D., and Gerot, L. (1992). *English for Social Purposes: A Handbook for Teachers of Adult Literacy*. Sydney: National Centre for English Language Teaching and Research, Macquarie University.

Hammond, J. & Macken-Horarik, M. (1999). Critical literacy: Challenges and questions for ESL classrooms. *TESOL Quarterly*, 33(3).

Hasan, R. (1996). Literacy, everyday talk and society. In Hasan, R. & Williams, G. (eds.), *Literacy in Society*. Harlow, UK and New York: Addison Wesley Longman, pp. 377-424.

Hudelson, S. (1989). *Write on Children Writing in ESL*. New

Jersey: Prentice Hall Regents.

Hyland, K. (2004). *Genre and Second Language Writing.* Michigan: The University of Michigan Press.

Hyon, S. (1996). Genre in three traditions: Implications for ESL. *TESOL Quarterly,* 30(4), pp. 693-716.

Johns, A. M (1997). *Text, Role, and Context: Developing Academic Literacies.* Cambridge: Cambridge University Press.

Kamler, B. (1990). *Gender and Genre: A Case Study of a Girl and a Boy Learning to Writing.* Unpublished Ph.D. dissertation. Geelong: Deakin University.

Knapp, P. & Watkins, M. (2005). *Genre, Text, Grammar: Technologies for Teaching and Assessing Writing.* Sydney: University of New South Wales Press.

Krashen, S. D. (1981). *Second Language Acquisition and Second Language Learning.* Oxford: Pergamon.

_____ (1991). The input hypothesis: An update. Paper presented at the Georgetown University Round Table on Language and Linguistics, Washington, D.C.

Kress, G. (1993). Genre as a social process. In B. Cope & M. Kalantzis (eds.), *The Powers of Literacy: A Genre Approach to Teaching Writing,* Bristol, PA: Falmer Press, pp. 22-37.

Kroll, B. M. (1981). Developmental relationships between speaking and writing. In Kroll & Vann (eds.), *Exploring Speaking-Writing Relationships: Connections and Contrasts.* Urbana, Illinois: National Council of Teachers of English, pp. 32-54.

Lee, A. (1997). Questioning the critical: Linguistics, literacy and pedagogy. In Muspratt, S., Luke, A. & Freebody, P. (eds.), *Constructing Critical Literacies: Teaching and Learning Textual Practice.* Cresskill, NJ: Hampton Press, pp. 409-432.

Leopold, W. F. (1939-1949). *Speech Development of a Bilingual Child. A Linguists' Record (4 volumes).* Evanston, IL: Northwestern University Press.

Lingard, B. (2006). Pedagogies of indifference. Paper presented to AARE Conference in Adelaide, 26-30 November.

Luke, A. (1993). The social construction of literacy in the primary school. In Unsworth, L. (ed.), *Literacy Learning and Teaching: Language as Social Practice in the Primary School.* Melbourne, Australia: Macmillan.

_____ (1996). Genres of power? Literacy education and the production of capital. In Hasan, R. & Williams, G. (eds.), *Literacy in Society.* New York: Longman, pp. 308-338.

Macken-Horarik, M. (2002). "Something to shoot for": A systemic functional approach to teaching genre in secondary school science. In Johns, A. M. (ed.), *Genre in the Classroom: Multiple Perspectives,* Erlbaum, Mahwah, NJ, pp. 17-42.

_____ (2005). Tools for promoting literacy development in TESOL classrooms: Insights from systemic functional linguistics. *TESOL in Context,* 15(2). pp. 15-23.

Martin, J. R. (1985). *Factual Writing: Exploring and Challenging Social Reality.* Geelong: Deakin University Press.

_____ (1986). Systemic Functional Linguistics and an understanding of written text. In *Writing Project-Report 1986, Working Papers in Linguistics 4.* Department of Linguistics: University of Sydney.

_____ (1987). *Writing Project Report No. 5.* Department of Linguistics: University of Sydney.

_____ (1992). *English Text: System and Structure.* Philadelphia: John Benjamin.

_____ (1999). Mentoring semogenesis: "Genre-based" literacy pedagogy. In F. Christie (ed.), *Pedagogy and the Shaping of Consciousness: Linguistic and Social Processes.* London and New York: Continuum, pp.123-155.

Martin, J. R. & Rothery, J. (1984). Types of writing in infants and primary school. In L. Unsworth (ed.), *Reading, Writing and Spelling: Proceedings of the 5th Macarthur Reading /Language Symposium,* Sydney: Macarthur Institute of Higher Education.

Martin, J. R., Christie, F., & Rothery, J. (1987). Social processes in education: A reply to Sawyer and Watson (and others). In I. Reid (ed.), *The Place of Genre in Learning: Current debates.* Geelong, Australia: Deakin University Press, pp. 46-57.

Nunan, D. (1992). *Research Methods in Language Education.* Cambridge: Cambridge University Press.

Oldenburg, J. (1987). *From Child Tongue to Mother Tongue: A Case Study of Language Development in the First Two-and-a-Half Years.* Unpublished Ph.D. Dissertation, University of Sydney.

Painter, C. (1984). *Into the Mother Tongue.* London: Pinter.

_____ (1993). *Learning through Language: A Case Study in the Development of Language as a Resource for Learning from 2 1/2 to 5 Years.* Unpublished Ph.D. dissertation, University of Sydney.

Paltridge, B. (2001). *Genre and the Language Learning Classroom.* Michigan: The University of Michigan Press.

Peregoy, S. F. & Boyle, O. F. (1993). *Reading, Writing & Learning in ESL.* London: Longman Group.

Perera, K. (1984) *Children's Writing and Reading: Analysing Classroom Language.* Oxford: Basil Blackwell.

Perl, S. (1979). The composing processes of unskilled college writers. *Research in the Teaching of English*, 25, pp. 419-468.

Ronjat, J. (1913). *Le developpement du langage observe chez un enfant bilingue.* Paris: Champion.

Rothery, J. (1986). Teaching genre in the primary school: A genre-based approach to the development of writing abilities. *Writing Project Report – Working Papers in Linguistics 4*, Department of Linguistics: University of Sydney, pp. 3-62.

_____ (1989). Exploring the written mode and the range of factual genres. *Writing in Schools: Study Guide.* Geelong: Deaking University Press, pp. 49-90.

_____ (1990). *Story Writing in Primary School: Assessing Narrative Type Genres.* Unpublished Ph.D. Dissertation. Sydney: University of Sydney.

_____ (1996). Making changes: Developing an educational linguistics. In R. Hasan & G. Williams (eds.) *Literacy in Society.* London: Addison-Wesley Longman, pp. 86-123.

Rothery, J. & Christie, F. (1995). The craft of writing narrative. *Interpretations*, 28(3), Special edition: Linguistics and English. English Teachers' Association of Western Australia, pp. 77-96.

Saunders, G. (1988). *Bilingual Children: From Birth to Teens.* Clevedon: Multilingual Matters.

Swales, J. M. (1990). *Genre Analysis: English in Academic and Research Settings*. Cambridge: Cambridge University Press.

Talmy, L. (1988). Force dynamics in language and cognition. *Cognitive Science,* 12(1), pp. 49-100.

The Education Department of Western Australia (1997). *Writing Resource Book*. Victoria: Rigby Heinemann.

Toolan, M. (1988). *Narrative: A Critical Linguistic Introduction*. London: Routledge.

Van Maanen, J., Dabbs, J. M. & Faulkner, R. R. (1982). *Varieties of Qualitative Research*. Beverly Hills, CA: Sage.

Veel, R. (1997). Learning how to mean – scientifically speaking: apprenticeship into scientific discourse in the secondary school. In F. Christie & J. R. Martin (eds.), *Apprenticeship into Scientific Discourse*. Cassell: London, pp. 161-165.

Vygotsky, L. S. (1978). *Mind in Society: The Development of Higher Psychological Processes*. Cambridge, MA: Harvard University Press.

Walshe, R. D. (1981). *Every Child Can Write*. NSW: Bridge Printery.

Williams, J. M. & Colomb, G. G. (1993). The case for explicit teaching: Why what you don't know won't help you. *Research in the Teaching of English*, 27, pp. 252-264.

Wing Jan, L. (2001). *Write Ways: Modeling Writing Forms*. Melbourne: Oxford University Press.

Yerrill, K. A. J. (1977). *A Consideration of the Later Development of Children's Syntax in Speech and Writing: A Study of Parenthetical, Appositional and Related Items*. Unpublished Ph.D. dissertation. University of Newcastle upon Tyne.

Yin, R. K. (1984). *Case Study Research – Design and Methods*. London: Sage Publication.